Studying Literature 1

Christian Liberty Press

"Christian literature should illuminate the issues of life with the light of Biblical truth. It should dwell on themes of useful work, God's creation, the Holy Scriptures, and the experiences of those who are striving to lead a consecrated life. In a manner similar to the Law of God, good literature should be like a schoolmaster which leads us to Christ."

Michael J. McHugh

Copyright © 1993 Christian Liberty Press
Second Edition 2003

All rights reserved. No part of this book may be reproduced in any form or by any means, except for brief quotations for the purpose of review, comment, or scholarship, without written permission from the publisher, Christian Liberty Press, 502 West Euclid Avenue, Arlington Heights, Illinois 60004.

TABLE OF CONTENTS

Title	Author	Page
Preface		v
Introduction		vii
What Constitutes Value	S.R. Whately	1
Light Out of Darkness	William Cowper	5
Dawn	Edward Everett	6
Death of Little Nell	Charles Dickens	9
Speech of Paul on Mars Hill	Bible	12
God Is Everywhere	Joseph Hutton	13
The Baptism	John Wilson	15
God's Goodness to Such as Fear Him	Bible	20
Character of Columbus	Washington Irving	22
The Puritan Fathers of New England	F.W. Greenwood	25
Rip Van Winkle	Washington Irving	28
Teaching Children the Royal Law	Jacob Abbott	32
Patriotism Begins at Home	Michael J. McHugh	48
The Good Fight of Faith	J. Gresham Machen	51
God's Purposes for Emotion	Michael J. McHugh	61
The Reputation of George Whitefield	Michael J. McHugh	65
Praise for Creation and Providence	Isaac Watts	69
Beethoven and the Blind Girl	John Todd	71
The Path of Peace	Carol Lee Renne	75
Paul Revere's Ride	H.W. Longfellow	76
The Story of Alonzo	Jacob Abbott	81
Concord Hymn	R.W. Emerson	115
The American Experiment	Daniel Webster	116
Christ Has Risen	Carol Lee Renne	119
The Life of John Bunyan	William J. Long	120
The Assurance of Salvation	Paul D. Lindstrom	129
The Puritan Age	William J. Long	130
Choice Quotes from Shakespeare	Shakespeare	135
Washington's Farewell Address	G. Washington	136
The Bold Sound of the Trumpet	Wayne C. Sedlak	138
Mr. Kleinhorst's Auction	Sheryl Kramer	142
The New Year	A. L. Tennyson	145
America's Closet Christians	Rus Walton	147

The All-Seeing God	*Isaac Watts*	153
No Other Gods	*Sheryl Kramer*	154
The Priority of Education	*Laura Ingalls Wilder*	156
Memories of Home	*Laura Ingalls Wilder*	159
The Law of Sowing and Reaping	*Laura Ingalls Wilder*	161
The Good Shepherd	*C.H. Spurgeon*	163
Queen Isabella's Resolve	*John Todd*	165
The King of Love	*C.H. Spurgeon*	169
Christians Can Change the World	*Peter Hammond*	170
The Case of the Missing Keys	*Ruth E. McDaniel*	174
How to Be Happy	*Jacob Abbott*	179
The Good Samaritan	*Ruth E. McDaniel*	186
Until Death Do Us Part	*Ruth E. McDaniel*	191
Whoa, Car!!!	*Ruth E. McDaniel*	195
Perseverance of the Saints	*Michael J. McHugh*	198
The Importance of Family Worship	*James W. Alexander*	201
The Influence of Family Worship on Civil Government	*James W. Alexander*	209
The King's Quest	*Ruth E. McDaniel*	215
A Story of An Eccentric Woman	*C.H. Spurgeon*	242
The Word and the Image	*Gene E. Veith, Jr.*	249
George Washington Carver	*James S. Childers*	259

PREFACE

The study of literature is an important part of every young person's educational experience.

In good literature, one can meet and experience life by entering the lives of others for a time. The stories, poems, and biographies in this text will help the student realize that he is not alone in the challenges and wonders of life.

True Christian literature is preoccupied with glorifying Almighty God and strengthening the lives of all those who are sincerely seeking to worship and serve the Lord Jesus Christ. Young people in America today, especially Christian teenagers, desperately need to be exposed to reading material that will help them develop a Christ-centered worldview.

Not all of life is pleasant; not all problems are simple. Therefore, this literature text will present the students not only with delights but also with decisions; life does that too. Christ, the Master Teacher, told stories to help others gain insights and make decisions in a godly manner. Reading stories is still one of the best ways to develop a proper understanding of how to apply Biblical truth to everyday life.

We sincerely hope that this reading material will be used by God to strengthen the Christian home and school.

Michael J. McHugh
Arlington Heights, Illinois
1993

ACKNOWLEDGMENTS

The publisher would like to thank the following individuals for granting permission to use their copyrighted stories:

Sheryl Kramer

    Mr. Kleinhorst's Auction © 1993
    No Other Gods © 1993

Ruth E. McDaniel

    The Case of the Missing Keys © 1993
    The Good Samaritan © 1993
    Until Death Do Us Part © 1993
    Whoa, Car!!! © 1993
    The King's Quest © 1994

Wayne C. Sedlak

    The Bold Sound of the Trumpet © 1992

Rus Walton

    America's Closet Christians © 1992

Gene Edward Veith, Jr.

    The Word and the Image © 1990

INTRODUCTION

Many of the reading selections contained in this text are short stories. A short story is a fictional narrative of prose, usually under 10,000 words, that provides the reader with entertainment and insight.

A good short story will have well-developed characters that are involved with real-life believable situations. To properly understand any story, it is helpful to know the basic elements of structure that make up a well-written story. Well-educated readers will be concerned with what happens in the story—*the main plot*, who makes it happen—*the characters*, and the message that the author intended to impart—*the theme*. In addition, other elements should be routinely considered, such as *setting* (the time, location, and general circumstances) and *the mood* (the particular emotional tempo that the author presents with regard to his subject or audience), as well as the overall *unity* or *flow* of the story. A good work of prose will have each of these literary components working together in a sensible whole.

For the Christian, it is also important to analyze each story in light of Biblical principles to determine whether the "message" contained in the work harmonizes with Holy Scripture. Virtually all writers have a purpose to convey or some principles to impart through their writings. It is the responsibility of each child of God to determine whether the message contained in a particular story has a positive or negative life application. Too many Christian young people, and adults, have been duped into believing that ideas and principles can be neutral. The fact is, every single idea promoted by man has ultimate consequences for good or evil. A person's character is molded by his thoughts and actions: "For as he thinketh in his heart, so is he." (Proverbs 23:7)

It is very important that students learn how to accurately identify the key components of each reading selection. As a starting point, students should routinely attempt to identify any or all of the following components: a) *the main plot* b) *the key characters* c) *the primary theme* d) *the setting* e) *the mood or emotional style* f) *the appropriate life application or moral*.

Students who take the effort to carefully analyze the key parts of each story will be better equipped to comprehend the motives of the writer and, hopefully, use these skills to improve their own writing. Helpful comprehension questions have been provided in the text for selected writings. These questions can and should be used as a starting point for healthy discussion with others. They can also be used to analyze the key points of the story or poem. It should be understood that the questions in the text are not designed to be totally comprehensive and perfectly adequate. They are merely a starting point and basic guide for students to follow.

Obviously, the above information will need to be modified when students begin to analyze the poetry selections in their text. Nevertheless, students may still use some of the previously mentioned techniques to critique poetry while they also focus on new considerations such as a poem's meter and rhyme.

Finally, readers may also wish to utilize the following questions as they seek to properly analyze their reading selections. Some of these questions will not apply to each and every story in the text.

1. What is the main idea or thrust of the author's writing?
2. Who was the leading character(s) in the story?
3. Who are the secondary characters in the story?
4. Is there a key paragraph in the author's writings?
5. Do you agree with the message of the author?
6. Do you think that the writing style that the author used was effective? Would another style have been better?
7. Was the main message of the author consistent with Biblical Christianity?
8. Describe the mood of the story, as well as your own emotional response to it.
9. What purpose do you think the author was trying to accomplish with his story or poem?

May the Lord grant you wisdom as you study this text and wrestle with the issues of life.

What Constitutes Value

Gold and silver are the most convenient metals to use as money, because they take up but little room in proportion to their value. This is why they are called the *precious metals*. But why should gold and silver be of so much more value than iron? They are not nearly so useful. We would be very bad off without knives, scissors, shovels, and hammers; and these could not be made from anything better than iron; silver and gold would make very bad tools indeed.

To understand this, you must remember that it is not the most *useful* things that are the most valuable. Nothing is more useful than air and water, without which we could not live; yet these are, in most places, of no value, in the proper sense of the word; that is, no one will give anything in exchange for them, because he can have them without cost.

In some places, indeed, water is scarce; and then people are glad to buy it. You may read in Scripture of many quarrels that arose about wells of water; because in some of the Eastern countries water is so scarce that a well is a very important possession. But water is not more useful in those places where people are glad to buy it than it is in America, where, by the bounty of Almighty God, it is plentiful. It is the *scarcity* that gives it value.

Iron, where it is scarce, is also of great value; but in most countries this most useful of all metals, is also, through the goodness of Providence, the most plentiful. Still it is of some value; because it must be dug from the mines, and smelted in furnaces, and formed into tools, before we can make use of it. If knives and nails were produced by nature ready made, and could be picked up everywhere like pebbles, they would be of no value, because everyone might get them for nothing; but they would be just as useful as they are now.

Scarcity alone, however, would not make a thing valuable, if there were no reason why anyone would want to possess it. There are some kinds of stones which are scarce, but of no value, because they have neither use nor beauty. You would not give anything in exchange for such a stone; not because you cannot easily get it, but because you have no wish to own it.

But a stone which is scarce and very beautiful may be of great value, though it is of no use but to make an ornament for the person. Such are diamonds, and rubies, and many others. Many people will work hard to earn money enough to buy not only food and necessary clothing, but also laces, and jewels, and other luxuries; and they desire these things the more, because, besides being beautiful to the eye, they are regarded as a sign of wealth in the person who wears them.

Whatever is of value, then, must not only be *desirable* for its use or beauty, or for some pleasure it affords, but it must also be *scarce*; that is, so limited in supply that it cannot be had for nothing; and of all things which are desirable, those are the most valuable which are the most limited in supply – that is, hardest to obtain. This is the reason that silver and gold are of more value than iron. If they had been of no use or beauty at all, no one would have ever desired them; but being desirable, they are of greater value than iron, because they are so much scarcer and harder to obtain.

But besides being *desirable* and *scarce*, there is one more quality required for a thing to have value; or, in other words, to be such that something else may be had in exchange for it. It must be *transferable* – that is, you must be able to give it to another person. For instance, *health* is very desirable, yet it is something that everyone cannot obtain, and therefore we sometimes speak of health as being of value; but this is not the strict use of the word "value," for no one can give his health to another in exchange for something else.

The following questions will illustrate these elementary principles: *Why is air not an article of value?* Because, though it be very useful, it is to be *had for nothing. Why is some scarce kind of stone, that is of no use or beauty, not an article of value?* Because, though it is not a thing that everyone can get, no one *desires* to get it. *Why is a healthy body not an article of value?* Because, though it be very desirable, it is something that everyone cannot get, therefore it is not *transferable*.

Why is a shovel an article of value? Because it is, first, desirable, as being of use; secondly, limited in supply – that is, it is not what every one can have for nothing; and, thirdly, transferable – that is, one person can trade it to another. *Why is a silver spoon of more value than a shovel?* Because, though it be no more useful, it is more limited in supply, or harder to obtain, on account of the difficulty of working the mines of silver.

When anything that is desirable is to be had by labor, and cannot be obtained without labor, of course we find men laboring to procure it; and things that are of very great value will usually be obtained only after extensive labor. This had led some persons to suppose that it is the labor which has been bestowed on anything that gives it value; but this is quite a mistake.

It is not the cost of labor that causes a product to sell for a higher price; but, on the contrary, it is its selling for a higher price that causes men to labor in order to procure it. For instance, fishermen go out to sea, and toil hard in the wet cold to catch fish, because they can get a good price for them; but if a fisherman should work hard all night and catch but one small fish, while another had, perhaps, caught a thousand, the first would not be able to sell his one fish for the same price as the other could obtain for his thousand, though it would have cost him the same labor. And if a man, in eating an oyster, should chance to meet with a fine pearl, it would not sell for less than if he had been diving for it all day.

It is not, therefore, labor that makes things valuable, but their being valuable that makes them worth laboring for. And God, having judged in His wisdom that it is not good for man to be idle, has so appointed things by His providence, that few of the things that are most desirable can be obtained without labor. It is ordained that a man should eat bread by toil and sweat; and

STUDYING CHRISTIAN LITERATURE

almost all the necessities, comforts, and luxuries of life are obtained only by labor.

Comprehension Questions

1. Why are gold and silver precious and valuable?
2. Explain why useful things are not always valuable.
3. Does labor guarantee that an item will have value?
4. Is air considered an article of value?

Light Out of Darkness

God moves in mysterious ways
   His wonders to perform;
He plants His footsteps in the sea,
   And rides upon the storm.

Deep in unfathomable mines
   Of never-failing skill,
He treasures up His bright designs,
   And works His sovereign will.

Ye fearful saints, fresh courage take!
   The clouds ye so much dread,
Are big with mercy, and shall break
   In blessings on your head.

Judge not the Lord by feeble sense,
   But trust Him for His grace;
Behind a frowning providence
   He hides a smiling face.

His purposes will ripen fast,
   Unfolding every hour;
The bud may have a bitter taste,
   But sweet will be the flower.

Blind unbelief is sure to err,
   And scan His work in vain;
God is His own interpreter,
   And He will make it plain.

Dawn

Edward Everett, 1794-1865. He was born at Dorchester, Mass., now a part of Boston, and graduated from Harvard College with the highest honors of his class, at the age of seventeen. While yet in college, he had quite a reputation as a brilliant writer. Before he was twenty years of age, he was settled as a pastor over the Brattle Street Church, in Boston, and at once became famous as an eloquent preacher. In 1814, he was elected Professor of Greek Literature in his *Alma Mater*; and, in order to prepare himself for the duties of his office, he entered on an extended course of travel in Europe. He edited the "North American Review," in addition to the labors of his professorship, after he returned to America.

In 1825, Mr. Everett was elected to Congress, and held his seat in the House for ten years. He was Governor of his native state from 1835 to 1839. In 1841, he was appointed Minister to England. On his return, in 1846, he was chosen President of Harvard University, and held the office for three years. In 1852, he was appointed Secretary of State. February 22, 1856, he delivered, in Boston, his celebrated lecture on Washington. This lecture was afterwards delivered in most of the principal cities and towns in the United States. The proceeds were devoted to the purchase of Mt. Vernon. In 1860, he was a candidate for the Vice Presidency of the United States. He is celebrated as an elegant and forcible writer, and a chaste orator.

This extract, a wonderful piece of word painting, is a portion of an address on the "Uses of Astronomy," delivered at the inauguration of the Dudley Observatory, at Albany, New York. Note the careful use of words and the strong figures in the third and fourth paragraphs.

I had occasion, a few weeks ago, to take the early train from the city of Providence to Boston; and for this purpose rose at two o'clock in the morning. Everything around was wrapped in darkness and hushed in silence, broken only by what seemed at that hour the unearthly clank and rush of the train. It was a mild, serene, midsummer's night; the sky was without a cloud, the winds were gentle. The moon, then in the last quarter, had just risen, and the stars shone with a spectral luster but little affected by her presence.

Jupiter, two hours high, was the herald of the day; the Pleiades, just above the horizon, shed their sweet influence in the east; Lyra sparkled near the zenith; Andromeda veiled her newly-discovered glories from the naked eye in the south; the steady Pointers, far beneath the pole, looked meekly up from the depths of the north to their sovereign.

Such was the glorious spectacle as I entered the train. As we proceeded, the timid approach of twilight became more perceptible; the intense blue of the sky began to soften; the smaller stars, like little children, went first to rest; the sister beams of the Pleiades soon melted together; but the bright constellations of the west and north remained unchanged. Steadily the wondrous transfiguration went on. Hands of angels, hidden from mortal eyes, shifted the scenery of the heavens; the glories of night dissolved into the glories of dawn.

The blue sky now turned more softly gray; the great watch stars shut up their holy eyes; the east began to kindle. Faint streaks of purple soon blushed along the sky; the whole celestial concave was filled with the inflowing tides of the morning light, which came pouring down from above in one great ocean of radiance; till at length, as we reached the Blue Hills, a flash of purple fire blazed out from above the horizon, and turned the dewy teardrops of flower and leaf into rubies and diamonds. In a few seconds, the everlasting gates of the morning were thrown wide open, and the lord of day, arrayed in glories too severe for the gaze of man, began his reign.

I do not wonder at the superstition of the ancient Magians, who, in the morning of the world, went up to the hilltops of Central Asia, and ignorant of the true God, adored the most glorious work of his hand. But I am filled with amazement, when

STUDYING CHRISTIAN LITERATURE

I am told, that, in this enlightened age and in the heart of the Christian world, there are persons who can witness this daily manifestation of the power and wisdom of the Creator, and yet say in their hearts, "There is no God."

Death of Little Nell

She was dead. No sleep could be so beautiful and calm, so free from trace of pain, so fair to look upon. She seemed a creature fresh from the hand of God, and waiting for the breath of life; not one who had lived, and suffered death. Her couch was dressed with here and there some winter berries and green leaves, gathered in a spot she had been known to favor. "When I die, put near me something that has loved the light, and had the sky above it always." These were her words.

She was dead. Dear, gentle, patient, noble Nell was dead. Her little bird, a poor, slight thing the pressure of a finger would have crushed, was stirring nimbly in its cage, and the strong heart of its child mistress was mute and motionless forever! Where were the traces of her early cares, her sufferings, and fatigues? All gone. Sorrow was dead, indeed, in her; but peace and perfect happiness were born, imaged in her tranquil beauty and profound repose.

And still her former self lay there, unaltered in this change. Many times, the old fireside had smiled upon that same sweet face; it had passed, like a dream, through haunts of misery and care; at the door of the poor schoolmaster on the summer evening, before the little fire upon the cold wet night, there had been the same mild and lovely look. So shall we know the angels, in their majesty, after death.

The old man who was by the bedside held one of the girl's languid arms in his, and had the small hand tight folded to his breast for warmth. It was the hand she had stretched out to him with her last smile; the hand that had led him on through all their wanderings. Ever and anon he pressed it to his lips; then hugged it to his breast again, murmuring that it was warmer now, and as he said it, he looked in agony to those who stood around, as if imploring them to help her.

She was dead, and past all help, or need of help. The ancient rooms she had seemed to fill with life, even while her own was waning fast. The garden she had tended, the eyes she had gladdened, the noiseless haunts of many a thoughtful hour, the paths she had trodden, as it were, but yesterday, could know her no more.

"It is not," said the schoolmaster, as he bent down to kiss her on the cheek, and gave his tears free vent, "it is not in *this* world that heaven's justice ends. Think what earth is, compared with the world to which her young spirit has winged its early flight. If God allowed that one deliberate wish, expressed in solemn tones above this bed, could call her back to life, which of us would utter it?"

She had been dead two days. They were all about her at the time, knowing that the end was drawing on. She died soon after daybreak. They had read and talked to her in the earlier portion of the night; but, as the hours crept on, she sank to sleep. They could tell by what she faintly uttered in her dreams, that they were of her journeyings with the old man; they were of no painful scenes, but of people who had helped them, and used them kindly; for she often said "God bless you!" with great fervor.

Waking, she never wandered in her mind but once, and that was at beautiful music, which, she said, was in the air. God knows. It may have been. Opening her eyes, at last, from a very quiet sleep, she begged that they would kiss her once again. That done, she turned to the old man, with a lovely smile upon her face, such they said, as they had never seen, and could never forget, and clung, with both her arms, around his neck. She had never murmured or complained; but, with a quiet mind, and manner quite unaltered, save that she every day became more earnest and more grateful to them, faded like the light upon the summer's evening.

The child who had been her little friend, came there, almost as soon as it was day, with an offering of dried flowers, which he begged them to lay upon her breast. He told them of his dream again, and that it was of her being restored to them, just as she used to be. He begged hard to see her: saying, that he would be very quiet, and that they need not fear his being scared, for he had sat alone by his young brother all day long, when he was dead, and had felt glad to be so near him. They let him have his wish; and, indeed, he kept his word, and was, in his childish way, a lesson to them all.

Up to that time, the old man had not spoken once, except to her, or stirred from the bedside. But, when he saw the little boy, he was moved as they had not seen him yet, and made as though he would have him come nearer. Then, pointing to the bed, he burst into tears for the first time, and they who stood by, knowing that the sight of this child had done him good, left them alone together.

And, when the time came, on which they must remove her, in her earthly shape, from earthly eyes forever, he led him away, that he might not know when she was taken from him. They were to gather fresh leaves and berries for her bed.

And now the bell, the bell she had so often heard by night and day, and listened to with solemn pleasure, almost as a living voice, rung its remorseless toll for her, so young, so beautiful, so good. Decrepit age, and vigorous life, and blooming youth, and helpless infancy, on crutches, in the pride of health and strength, in the full blush of promise, in the mere dawn of life, gathered round her. Old men were there, whose eyes were dim and senses failing, grandmothers, who might have died ten years ago, and still been old, the deaf, the blind, the lame, the living dead, in many forms, came to see the closing of that early grave.

Along the crowded path they bore her now, pure as the newly fallen snow that covered it, whose day on earth had been as fleeting. They brought her to a peaceful spot near the old church that she used to frequent, and it received her in its quiet shade.

The day of one's death is appointed by God alone. It is an appointment that all people will keep, whether they be old or young, rich or poor. Precious in the sight of the Lord is the death of his saints.

Speech of Paul on Mars Hill

Then Paul stood in the midst of Mars Hill, and said, Ye men of Athens! I perceive that in all things ye are too superstitious. For as I passed by, and beheld your devotions, I found an altar with this inscription, TO THE UNKNOWN GOD. Whom therefore ye ignorantly worship, him declare I unto you. God that made the world and all things therein (seeing that he is Lord of heaven and earth) dwelleth not in temples made with hands; neither is worshiped with men's hands as though he needed anything, seeing he giveth to all life, and breath, and all things; and hath made of one blood all nations of men for to dwell on all the face of the earth, and hath determined the times before appointed, and the bounds of their habitation; that they should seek the Lord, if haply they might feel after him, and find him, though he be not far from every one of us: for in him we live, and move, and have our being; as certain also of your own poets have said, For we are also his offspring. Forasmuch then as we are the offspring of God, we ought not to think that the Godhead is like unto gold, or silver, or stone, graven by art and man's device. And the times of this ignorance God winked at; but now commandeth all men everywhere to repent: because he hath appointed a day, in the which he will judge the world in righteousness by that Man whom he hath ordained; whereof he hath given assurance unto all men, in that he hath raised him from the dead. And when they heard of the resurrection of the dead, some mocked: and others said, We will hear thee again of this matter. So Paul departed from among them. Howbeit certain men clave unto him, and believed; among the which was Dionysius the Areopagite, and a woman named Damaris, and others with them.

Acts 17:22-34

God Is Everywhere

Oh! show me where is He,
The high and holy One,
To whom thou bend'st the knee,
And prayest, "Thy will be done!"
I hear thy song of praise,
And lo! no form is near:
Thine eyes I see thee raise,
But where doth God appear?
Oh! teach me who is God, and where his glories shine,
That I may kneel and pray, and call thy Father mine.

"Gaze on that arch above:
The glittering vault admire.
Who taught those orbs to move?
Who lit their ceaseless fire?
Who guides the moon to run
In silence through the skies?
Who bids that dawning sun
In strength and beauty rise?
There view immensity! behold! my God is there:
The sun, the moon, the stars, his majesty declare.

"See where the mountains rise;
Where thundering torrents foam;
Where, veiled in towering skies,
The eagle makes his home:
Where savage nature dwells,
My God is present, too:
Through all her wildest dells
His footsteps I pursue:
He reared those giant cliffs, supplies that dashing stream,
Provides the daily food which stills the wild bird's scream.

"Look on that world of waves,
Where little creatures glide;
Within whose deep, dark caves
The ocean monsters hide:
His power is sovereign there,
To raise, to quell the storm;
The depths his bounty share,
Where scaly creatures swarm:
The master speaks His voice, when we are yielded and still."
His message brings us comfort in ages old and new, Peace, Be still!

The Baptism

John Wilson, 1785-1854, a distinguished Scottish author, was born at Paisley. When fifteen years of age, he entered the University of Glasgow; but, three years later, he became a member of Magdalen College, Oxford. Here he attained eminence both as a student and as an athlete. Soon after graduating, he purchased an estate near Lake Windermere, and became a magazine writer and editor. In 1820, he succeeded Dr. Thomas Brown as Professor of Moral Philosophy in the University of Edinburgh; this position he held for thirty years. His *Lights and Shadows of Scottish Life* was published in 1822. This is a collection of pathetic and beautiful tales of domestic life in Scotland. Professor Wilson was a man of great physical power and of striking appearance. In character, he was vehement and impulsive; but his writings show that he possessed feelings of deep tenderness.

The rite of baptism had not been performed for several months in the church of Lanark. It was now the hottest time of persecution; and the inhabitants of that parish found other places in which to worship God, and celebrate the ordinances of religion. It was now the Sabbath day, and a small congregation of about a hundred souls had met for divine service, in a place more magnificent than any temple that human hands had ever built to Deity. The congregation had not assembled to the toll of the bell, but each heart knew the hour and observed it; for there are a hundred sundials among the hills, woods, moors and fields; and the shepherd and the peasant see the hours passing by them in sunshine and shadow.

The church in which they were assembled, was hewn by God's hand out of the eternal rock. A river rolled its way through a mighty chasm of cliffs, several hundred feet high, of which the one side presented enormous masses, and the other corresponding recesses, as if the great stone girdle had been rent by a convulsion. The channel was overspread with prodigious fragments of rocks or large loose stones, some of them smooth and bare, others containing soil in their rents and fissures, and here and there crowned with shrubs and trees. The eye could at once command a long-stretching vista, seemingly closed and shut up at both extremities by the overhanging cliff. This majestic reach of river contained pools, streams, and waterfalls innumerable; and when the water was low – which was now the case, in the common drought – it was easy to walk up this scene with the calm, blue sky overhead, in utter and sublime solitude.

On looking up, the soul was bowed down by the feeling of that prodigious height of unscalable, and often over-hanging cliff. Between the channel and the summit of the far extended precipices, were perpetually flying rooks and wood pigeons, and now and then a hawk, filling the profound abyss with their wild cawing, deep murmur, or shrilly shriek. Sometimes a heron would stand erect and still, on some little stone island, or rise up like a white cloud along the black walls of the chasm, and disappear. Winged creatures alone could inhabit this region. The fox and wild cat chose more accessible haunts. Yet, here came the persecuted Christians to worship God. It was as if God's hand hung over their head those magnificent pillars and arches, scooped out those galleries from the solid rock, and laid at their feet the calm water, in its transparent beauty, in which they could see themselves sitting, in reflected groups, with their Bibles in their hands.

Here, upon a semicircular ledge of rocks, over a narrow chasm, sat about a hundred persons, all devoutly listening to their minister, who stood before them on what might be called a small, natural pulpit of living stone. Up to it there led a short flight of steps, and over it waved the canopy of a tall, graceful birch tree. The pulpit stood in the middle of the channel, directly facing the congregation, and separated from them by the clear, deep, sparkling pool, into which the scarce-heard water poured over the blackened rock. The water, as it left the pool, separated into two streams, and flowed on each side of that altar, thus placing it in an island, whose large, mossy stones were richly embroidered with a ring of golden blossoms.

THE BAPTISM

At the close of the divine service, a row of maidens, all clothed in purest white, came gliding off from the congregation, and, crossing the murmuring stream on stepping stones, arranged themselves at the foot of the pulpit with those who were about to be baptized. Their devout fathers, just as though they had been in their own church, had been sitting there during worship and now stood up before the minister. The baptismal water, taken from that pellucid pool, was lying, consecrated, in an appropriate receptacle, formed by the upright stones that composed one side of the pulpit, and the holy rite proceeded.

Some of the younger ones in that semicircle kept gazing down into the pool, in which the whole scene was reflected; and now and then, in spite of the grave looks and admonishing whispers of their elders, let fall a pebble into the water, that they might judge of its depth. The rite was over, and the religious service of the day closed with a psalm. The mighty rocks hemmed in the holy sound, and sent it in a more compact volume, clear, sweet, and strong, up to heaven. When the psalm ceased, an echo, like a spirit's voice, was heard dying away, high up among the magnificent architecture of the cliffs; and once more might be noticed in the silence, the reviving voice of the waterfall.

Just then, a large stone fell from the top of the cliff into the pool, a loud voice was heard, and a flag was hung over on the point of the shepherd's staff. Their wakeful sentinel had seen danger, and this was his warning. Forthwith, the congregation rose. There were paths, dangerous to unpracticed feet, along the ledges of the rocks, leading up to several caves and places of concealment. The more active and young assisted the elder, more especially the old pastor, and the women with the infants; and many minutes had not elapsed, till not a living creature was visible in the channel of the stream, but all of them were hidden, or nearly so, in the clefts and caverns.

The shepherd who had given the alarm, had lain down again instantly in his place on the summit of these precipices. A party of soldiers was immediately upon him, and demanded to know what signals he had been making, and to whom; when one of them, looking over the edge of the cliff, exclaimed, "See, See!

Humphrey, we have caught the whole tabernacle of the Lord in a net at last. There they are, praising God among the stones of the river Mouse. A noble cathedral!" "Fling the lying sentinel over the cliffs. It is just like a dirty Covenanter to deceive honest soldiers on the very Sabbath day. Over with him, over with him; over the edge into the pit." But the shepherd had vanished like a shadow, and, mixing with the tall green bushes, was making his unseen way toward a wood. "Satan has saved his servant; but come, my lads, follow me. I know the way down into the bed of the stream, and the steps up to Wallace's Cave. They are called rebel Covenanters. We'll all serve our King well today if we succeed in hunting down these traitors and see to their execution. Forward! my boys, halloo!"

The soldiers dashed down a less precipitous part of the wooded banks, a little below the "craigs," and hurried up the channel. But when they reached the altar where the old, gray-haired minister had been seen standing, all was silent and solitary; not a creature to be seen. "Here is a Bible, dropped by one of them," cried a soldier, and, with his foot, he spun it away into the pool. "A bonnet," cried another; "now for the pretty, sanctified face, that rolled its demure eyes below it." But after a few jokes and rude comments, the soldiers stood still, eying with a kind of mysterious dread the black and silent walls of the rocks that hemmed them in, and hearing only the small voice of the stream that sent a profounder stillness through the heart of that majestic solitude. "What if these cowardly Covenanters should tumble down upon our heads pieces of rock from their hiding places! Advance, or retreat?"

There was no reply; for a slight fear was upon every man. Musket or bayonet could be of little use to men obliged to clamber up rocks, along slender paths, leading they know not where. And they were aware that armed men nowadays worshiped God; men of iron hearts, who feared not the glitter of the soldier's arms, neither barrel nor bayonet; men of long stride, firm step, and broad breast, who, on the open field, would have overthrown the marshaled line, and gone first and foremost, if a city had to be taken by storm.

As the soldiers were standing together irresolute, a noise came upon their ears like distant thunder, but even more appalling; and a slight current of air, as if propelled by it, passed whispering along the sweetbriers, and the broom, and the tresses of the birch trees. It came deepening, and rolling, and roaring on; and the very Cartland Craigs shook to their foundation, as if in an earthquake. "The Lord have mercy upon us! What is this?" And down fell many of the miserable wretches on their knees, and some on their faces, upon the sharp-pointed rocks. Now, it was like the sound of a myriad of chariots rolling on their iron axles down the strong channel of the torrent. The old, gray-haired minister stepped from the mouth of Wallace's Caves, and said, in a loud voice, "The Lord God omnipotent reigneth!"

A waterspout had burst up among the moorlands, and the river, in its power, was at hand. There it came, tumbling along into that long reach of cliffs, and, in a moment, filled it with one mass of waves. Huge, agitated clouds of foam rode on the surface of a blood-red torrent. An army must have been swept off by that flood. The soldiers perished in a moment; but high up in the cliffs, above the sweep of destruction, were the Covenanters, men, women, and children, uttering prayers to God, unheard by themselves, in the raging thunder.

The message of this story is simple – the Lord answers prayer and protects His people.

God's Goodness to Such as Fear Him

Fret not thyself because of evil doers,
Neither be thou envious against the workers of iniquity;
For they shall soon be cut down like the grass,
And wither as the green herb.
Trust in the Lord, and do good;
So shalt thou dwell in the land, and verily thou shalt be fed.
Delight thyself also in the Lord,
And he shall give thee the desires of thine heart.
Commit thy way unto the Lord;
Trust also in him, and he shall bring it to pass.
And he shall bring forth thy righteousness as the light,
And thy judgment as the noonday.
Rest in the Lord, and wait patiently for him.

Fret not thyself because of him who prospereth in his way,
Because of the man who bringeth wicked devices to pass.
Cease from anger, and forsake wrath:
Fret not thyself in any wise to do evil,
For evil doers shall be cut off:
But those that wait upon the Lord, they shall inherit the earth.
For yet a little while, and the wicked shall not be;
Yea, thou shalt diligently consider his place, and it shall not be.
But the meek shall inherit the earth,
And shall delight themselves in the abundance of peace.

A little that a righteous man hath
Is better than the riches of many wicked;
For the arms of the wicked shall be broken,
But the Lord upholdeth the righteous.
The Lord knoweth the days of the upright,
And their inheritance shall be forever;
They shall not be ashamed in the evil time,
And in the days of famine they shall be satisfied.

But the wicked shall perish,

GOD'S GOODNESS TO SUCH AS FEAR HIM

And the enemies of the Lord shall be as the fat of lambs;
They shall consume; into smoke shall they consume away.
The wicked borroweth, and payeth not again;
But the righteous sheweth mercy and giveth.
For such as be blessed of him shall inherit the earth.
The steps of a good man are ordered by the Lord,
And he delighteth in his way;
Though he fall, he shall not be utterly cast down;
For the Lord upholdeth him with his hand.

I have been young, and now am old,
Yet have I not seen the righteous forsaken,
Nor his seed begging bread.
He is ever merciful, and lendeth,
And his seed is blessed.

Depart from evil, and do good,
And dwell for evermore;
For the Lord loveth judgment,
And forsaketh not his saints:
They are preserved forever:
But the seed of the wicked shall be cut off.
The righteous shall inherit the land,
And dwell therein forever:
The mouth of the righteous speaketh wisdom,
And his tongue talketh of judgment;
The law of his God is in his heart;
None of his steps shall slide.
The wicked watcheth the righteous,
And seeketh to slay him.
The Lord will not leave him in his hand,
Nor condemn him when he is judged.

Wait on the Lord, and keep his way,
And he shall exalt thee to inherit the land;
When the wicked are cut off, thou shalt see it.
I have seen the wicked in great power,
And spreading himself like a green bay tree;
Yet he passed away, and, lo, he was not;
Yea, I sought him, but he could not be found.

–Bible

Character of Columbus

Washington Irving, 1783-1859. Among those whose works have enriched American literature, and have given it a place in the estimation of foreigners, no name stands higher than that of Washington Irving. He was born in the city of New York; his father was a native of Scotland, and his mother was English. He had an ordinary school education, and at the age of sixteen began the study of law. Two of his older brothers were interested in literary pursuits; and in his youth he studied the old English authors. He was also passionately fond of books of travel. At the age of nineteen, he began his literary career by writing for a paper published by his brother. In 1804 he made a voyage to the south of Europe. On his return he completed his studies in law, but never practiced his profession. During his career he formed the acquaintance of the most eminent literary men of his time, and wrote several of his works; among them were: *The Sketch Book, Bracebridge Hall, Tales of a Traveler, Life and Voyages of Columbus,* and the *Conquest of Granada.* From 1842 to 1846 he was Minister to Spain. On his return to America he established his residence at "Sunnyside," near Tarrytown, on the Hudson, where he passed the last years of his life. A young lady to whom he was attached having died in early life, Mr. Irving never married.

His works are marked by humor, just sentiment, elegance, and correctness of expression. They were popular both at home and abroad from the first, and their sale brought him a handsome fortune. The *Life of Washington,* his last work, was completed in the same year in which he died.

Columbus was a man of great and inventive genius. The operations of his mind were energetic, but irregular; bursting forth, at times, with that irresistible force which characterizes intellect of such an order. His ambition was lofty and noble, inspiring himself by great achievements. He aimed at dignity and wealth in the same elevated spirit with which he sought renown; they were to rise from the territories he should discover, and be commensurate in importance.

His conduct was characterized by the grandeur of his views and the magnanimity of his spirit. Instead of ravaging the newly-found countries, like many of his contemporary discoverers, who were intent only on immediate gain, he regarded them with the eyes of a legislator; he sought to colonize and cultivate them, to civilize the natives, to build cities, introduce the useful arts, subject everything to the control of law and religion, and thus to found regular and prosperous empires. That he failed in this was the fault of the dissolute rabble in which it was his misfortune to command, with whom all law was tyranny and all order oppression.

He was naturally impetuous, and keenly sensible to injury and injustice; yet the quickness of his temper was counteracted by the generosity and benevolence of his heart. The magnanimity of his nature shone forth through all the troubles of his stormy career. Though continually offended and cheated, foiled in his plans, and endangered in his person by the seditions of turbulent and worthless men, yet he restrained his valiant and indignant spirit, and brought himself to forbear, and reason, and even to supplicate. Nor can the reader of the story of his eventful life fail to notice how free he was from all feeling of revenge, how ready to forgive and forget on the least sign of repentance and atonement. He has been exalted for his skill in controlling others, but far greater praise is due to him for the firmness he displayed in governing himself.

His piety was genuine and fervent. Religion mingled with the whole course of his thoughts and actions, and shone forth in his most private and unstudied writings. Whenever he made any great discovery he devoutly returned thanks to God. The voice of prayer and the melody of praise rose from his ships on discovering the new world, and his first action on landing was to prostrate himself upon the earth and offer up thanksgiving. All his great enterprises were undertaken in the name of the Holy Trinity, and he partook of the holy sacrament previous to embarkation. He observed the festivals of the church in the wildest situations. The Sabbath was to him a day of sacred rest, on which he would never sail from a port unless in case of extreme necessity. The faith thus deeply seated in his soul diffused a sober dignity and a benign composure over his whole deportment; his very language was pure and guarded, and free from all gross or irreverent expressions.

A peculiar trait in his rich and varied character remains to be noted; namely, that enthusiastic imagination which threw a magnificence over his whole course of thought. A poetical temperament is discernible throughout all his writings and in all his actions. We see it in all his descriptions of the beauties of the wild land he was discovering, in the enthusiasm with which he extolled the blandness of the temperature, the purity of the atmosphere, the fragrance of the air, "full of dew and sweetness," the verdure of the forests, the grandeur of the mountains, and the crystal purity of the running streams. It spread a glorious and golden world around him, and tinged everything with its own gorgeous colors.

With all the visionary fervor of his imagination, its fondest dreams fell short of the reality. He died in ignorance of the real grandeur of his discovery. Until his last breath, he entertained the idea that he had merely opened a new way to the old resorts of trade and commerce, and had discovered some of the wild regions of the East. What visions of glory would have broken upon his mind could he have known that he had indeed discovered a new continent equal to the old world in magnitude, and separated by two vast oceans from all the earth hitherto known by civilized man! How would his magnanimous spirit have been consoled amid the afflictions of age and the cares of poverty, the neglect of a fickle public and the injustice of an ungrateful king, could he have anticipated the splendid empires which would arise in the beautiful world he had discovered, and the nations, and tongues, and languages which were to fill its land with his renown, and to revere and bless his name for generations to come!

The Puritan Fathers of New England

One of the most prominent features which distinguished our forefathers, was their determined resistance to oppression. They seemed born and brought up for the high and special purpose of showing to the world that the civil and religious rights of man – the rights of self-government, of conscience, and independent thought – are not merely things to be talked of and woven into theories, but to be adopted with the whole strength and ardor of the mind. Their laws and covenants recognized the liberty of the individual under God's law. True liberty was not the power to live as one pleased but the freedom to live as God required.

Liberty, with them, was an object of too serious desire and stern resolve to be personified, allegorized, and enshrined. They made no goddess of it, as the ancients did; they had no time nor inclination for such trifling; they felt that liberty was the simple birthright of every human creature; they called it so; they claimed it as such; they reverenced and held it fast as the unalienable gift of the Creator, which was not to be surrendered to power, nor sold for wages.

It was theirs, as men; without it, they did not esteem themselves men; more than any other privilege or possession, it was essential to their happiness, for it was essential to their original nature; and therefore they preferred it above wealth and ease and country; and, that they might enjoy and exercise it fully, they forsook houses, and lands, and kindred, their homes, their native soil, and their fathers' graves.

They left all these; they left England, which, whatever it might have been called, was not to them a land of freedom; they launched forth on the pathless ocean, the wide, fathomless ocean, soiled not by the earth beneath, and bounded, all round and above, only by heaven; and it seemed to them like that better and sublimer freedom, which their country knew not, but of which they had the conception and image in their hearts; and, after a toilsome and painful voyage, they came to a hard wintry coast, unfruitful and desolate, but unguarded and boundless; its calm silence interrupted not the ascent of their prayers; it had no eyes to watch, nor ears to hearken, no tongues to report them; here, again there was an answer to their soul's desire, and they were satisfied, and gave thanks; they saw that they were free, and their souls smiled.

I am telling an old tale; but it is one which must be told when we speak of our forefathers. It is to be added, that they transmitted their principles to their children, and that, trained by such a race, our country was always free. So long as its inhabitants were unmolested by the mother country in the exercise of their important rights, they submitted to the form of English government; but when those rights were invaded, they spurned even the form away. For them, rebellion against tyrants, was obedience to God.

It should be understood that the principles of the American Revolution were not the suddenly acquired property of a few bosoms: they were abroad in the land in the ages before; they had always been taught, like the truths of the Bible; they had descended from father to son, down from those primitive days, when the Pilgrim, established in his simple dwelling, and seated at his blazing fire, piled high from the forest which shaded his door, repeated to his listening children the story of past persecutions and his resistance. These children learned that they had nothing to fear from ungodly men's oppression.

Here are the beginnings of the Revolution. Every settler's hearth was a school of independence; the scholars were apt, and the lessons sunk deeply; and thus it came that our country was always free; it could not be other than free.

As deeply seated as was the principle of liberty and resistance to arbitrary power in the breasts of the Puritans, it was not more so than their piety and sense of religious obligation. They were emphatically a people whose God was the Lord. Their form of government was as strictly theocratical, if direct communication be excepted, as was that of the Jews; insomuch that it would be difficult to say that there was any civil authority among them entirely distinct from ecclesiastical jurisdiction.

Whenever a few of them settled a town, they immediately gathered themselves into a church; and their elders were magistrates, and their code of laws was the Pentateuch. These were forms, it is true, but forms which faithfully indicated principles and feeling; for no people could have adopted such forms, who were not thoroughly imbued with the spirit, and bent on the practice of biblical Christianity.

God was their King; and they regarded him as truly and literally so, as if he had dwelt in a visible palace in the midst of their state. They were his devoted, resolute, humble subjects; they undertook nothing which they did not beg of him to prosper; they accomplished nothing without rendering to him the praise; they suffered nothing without carrying their sorrow to his throne; they ate nothing which they did not implore him to bless.

Their piety was not merely external; it was sincere; it had the proof of the good tree in bearing good fruit; it produced and sustained a strict morality. Their tenacious purity of manners and speech obtained for them, in the mother country their name of Puritans, which though given in derision, was as honorable a title as was ever bestowed by man on man.

That there were hypocrites among them, is not to be doubted; but they were rare. The men who voluntarily exiled themselves to an unknown coast, and endured there every toil and hardship for conscience' sake, and that they might serve God as the Bible commands, were not likely to set conscience at defiance, and make the service of God a mockery; they were not likely to be, neither were they, hypocrites. I do not know that it would be too exaggerated for us to say, that, on the extended surface of the globe, there was not a single community of men to be compared with them, in the respects of deep religious impressions and an exact performance of moral duty.

Rip Van Winkle

This story, written by Washington Irving, is set in the late 1700's and describes the strange experiences of a colonial hunter and woodsman who falls into a mysterious sleep that lasts for twenty years. The opening scene finds the disoriented woodsman on a road heading back to his home town. He thinks that he has only been asleep for a solitary night; but he is about to get the surprise of his life.

There was, as usual, a crowd of folks about the door of the inn, but none that Rip recollected. The very character of the people seemed changed. He looked in vain for his friend Nicholas Vedder, with his broad face, double chin, and baggy pants. In place of the usual sights stood a sea of strange sounds and faces that bewildered Van Winkle.

The appearance of Rip, with his long, grizzled beard, his rusty shotgun, his uncouth dress, and an army of women and children at his heels, soon attracted the attention of the tavern politicians. They crowded around him, eying him from head to foot with great curiosity. The orator bustled up to him, and, drawing him partly aside inquired on which side he voted. Rip stared in vacant stupidity. Another short but busy little fellow pulled him by the arm, and rising on tiptoe, inquired in his ear "whether he was Federal or Democrat."

Rip was equally at a loss to comprehend the question; when a knowing, self-important old gentleman, in a sharp cocked hat, made his way through the crowd, putting them to the right and left with his elbows as he passed, and planting himself before Van Winkle, with one arm cocked, the other resting on his cane. His keen eyes penetrated, as if into his very soul, and he demanded, in an austere tone, what brought Rip to the election with a gun on his shoulder, and a mob at his heels, and whether he meant to breed a riot in the village.

"Alas! gentlemen," cried Rip, somewhat dismayed, "I am a poor, quiet man, a native of the place, and a loyal subject of the king, God bless him!" Then a general shout burst from the bystanders. -- "A tory! a tory! a spy! a refugee! hustle him! away with him!" It was with great difficulty that the self-important man in the cocked hat restored order; and, having a tenfold austerity of brow, demanded again of the unknown culprit, what he came there for, and whom he was seeking. The poor man humbly assured him that he meant no harm, but merely came there in search of some of his neighbors, who used to live around the tavern. "Well, who are they? name them."

Rip hesitated a moment, and then inquired, "Where's Nicholas Vedder? There was a silence for a little while, when an old man replied, in a thin piping voice, "Nicholas Vedder! why he has been dead and gone for eighteen years! There was a wooden tombstone in the churchyard that used to tell all about him, but that's rotten and gone too." "Where's Brom Dutcher?" "Oh, he went off to the army in the beginning of the war. Some say he was killed at the storming of Stony Point; others say he was drowned in a squall at the foot of Anthony's Nose. I don't know; he never came back again."

"Where's Van Bummel, the schoolmaster?" "He went off to the wars, too; was a great militia general, and is now in Congress." Rip's heart died away at hearing of these sad changes in his home and friends, and finding himself thus alone in the world. Every answer puzzled him, too, because of the enormous lapses of time, and of matters which he could not understand --what was Congress, and Stony Point. He had no courage to ask about any more old friends, but cried out in despair, "Does nobody here know Rip Van Winkle?"

"Oh, Rip Van Winkle!" exclaimed two or three. "Oh, to be sure! That's Rip Van Winkle yonder, leaning against the tree." Rip looked, and beheld a precise counterpart of himself as he went up the mountain; apparently as lazy, and certainly as ragged. The poor fellow was now completely confounded; he doubted his own identity, and whether he was himself or another man. In the midst of his bewilderment, the man in the cocked hat demanded who he was, and what was his name.

"God knows!" exclaimed he, at his wit's end. "I'm not myself; I'm somebody else got into my shoes. I was myself last night; but I fell asleep on the mountain, and they've changed my gun, and everything's changed, and I'm changed, and I can't tell what's my name or who I am!"

The bystanders began now to look at each other, nod, wink significantly, and tap their fingers against their foreheads. There was a whisper, also, about securing the gun, and keeping the old fellow from doing mischief, at the very suggestion of which the self-important man in the cocked hat retired with some precipitation. At this critical moment, a young, attractive woman pressed through the throng to get a peep at the gray-bearded man. She had a chubby child in her arms, which, frightened at his looks, began to cry. "Hush, Rip!" she cried, "hush, you little fool! the old man won't hurt you."

The name of the child, the air of the mother, the tone of her voice, all awakened a train of recollections in his mind. "What is your name, my good woman?" he asked. "Judith Gardenier." "And your father's name?" "Ah, poor man! Rip Van Winkle was his name; but it's twenty years since he went away from home with his gun, and never has been heard of since; his dog came home without him; but whether he shot himself, or was carried away by the Indians, nobody can tell. I was then but a little girl."

Rip had but one question more to ask; but he stated it with a faltering voice: "Where's your mother?" "Oh, she, too, died but a short time since; she broke a blood vessel in a fit of passion at a New England peddler." There was a drop of comfort, at least, in this intelligence. The honest man could contain himself no longer. He caught his daughter and her child in his arms. "I am your father!" he cried. "Young Rip Van Winkle once, old Rip Van Winkle now! Does nobody know poor Rip Van Winkle?"

All stood amazed, until an old woman, tottering out from among the crowd, put her hand to her brow, and, peering under it in his face for a moment, exclaimed, "Sure enough! it is Rip Van

Winkle! it is himself! Welcome home again, old neighbor! Why, where have you been these twenty long years?" Rip's story was soon told for the whole twenty years had been to him like one night.

To make a long story short, the company broke up and returned to the more important concerns of the election. Rip's daughter took him home to live with her. She had a snug, well-furnished house, and a stout, cheery farmer for a husband, whom Rip recollected as one of the urchins that used to climb upon his back. Rip now resumed his old walks and habits. He soon found many of his former cronies, though all rather the worse for the wear and tear of time, and preferred making friends among the rising generation, with whom he soon grew into great favor.

Teaching Children the Royal Law

One word that virtually all young people will hear numerous times during their childhood years is the word love. Although the word love is one of the most frequently used words in the English language, its meaning is often misunderstood or perverted.

It is a mistake to assume that children understand the significance of the word love, simply because they hear it spoken on a regular basis. Parents today must teach their youngsters what it means to walk in love.

As we begin to consider the topic of Christian charity, it is important to stress the fact that love is pre-eminently something we do, not merely something we feel. It was Jesus who said, "If you love me, you will keep my commandments."

This view of the doctrine of love is well summarized by Christian author, George Grant, in his book entitled *Bringing In the Sheaves*. On pages 45-48, Mr. Grant writes:

The Good Samaritan is the unnamed lead character in one of Christ's best-loved parables (Luke 10:25-37). When all others, including supposed men of righteousness, had skirted the responsibility of charity, the Samaritan took up its mantle. Christ concluded the narrative, saying, "Go and do thou likewise" (Luke 10:37)...

...God desires all of us to display the Good Samaritan faith... The testimony of Scripture is clear: All of us who are called by His name must walk in love (Ephesians 5:2). We must exercise compassion (2 Corinthians 1:3-4). We must struggle for justice and secure mercy [as well as provide comfort] and liberty for men, women, and children everywhere (Zechariah 7:8-10).

In Matthew 22, when Jesus was asked to summarize briefly the Law of God, the standard against which all spirituality is to be measured, He responded, "You shall love the Lord your God with all your heart, and with all your soul, and with all your mind. This is the great and foremost commandment. And the second is like it; you shall love your neighbor as yourself. On these two commandments depend the Law and the Prophets."

Jesus has reduced the whole of the Law, and thus, the whole of faith, to love. Love toward God, and then, love toward man. But, at the same time, Jesus has defined love in terms of Law. In one bold, deft stroke, He freed the Christian faith from subjectivity. By so linking love and Law, Christ has unclouded our purblind vision of both. Love suddenly takes on responsible objectivity while Law takes on passionate applicability.

This sheds a whole new light on what is meant for us to "walk in love." If our love is real, then it must be expressed; it <u>will</u> be expressed. If our love is real, then action will result because love is something you do, not merely something you feel. Love is the "Royal Law" (James 2:8).

The Principle of Biblical Charity

This chapter is intended to persuade the reader that the impulse which should lead Christians to the performance of charitable works in this world, is not a hope of fitting ourselves by meritorious performances for God's service in heaven; but a spontaneous love for God and man, urging us forward in such a course while our hope of forgiveness for sin rests on other grounds altogether. (The only remedy for sinful man is to trust in the substitutionary work of Christ on Calvary.) Some other considerations in respect to the motives which should influence us as we seek to love others shall be presented in this chapter as well.

By engaging in the work of Christian charity, we do not by any means sacrifice our own happiness. Indeed, we often give up some ordinary means of enjoyment, but we do not sacrifice the end. Rather, we secure our own richest, purest enjoyment, though in a new and better way.

We also change the character of our happiness, for the pleasure which results from carrying happiness to the hearts of others is very different in its nature from that which we secure by aiming directly at our own. Now the reader should consider these things, and understand distinctly at the outset whether he is in such a state of mind and heart that he wishes to pursue the happiness of others, or whether he means to confine his efforts to the promotion of his own.

On some cold winter evening, perhaps, you return from the business of the day to your home, where I will suppose that you have the comforts of life all around you. You draw up your richly stuffed elbow chair by the side of a glowing fireplace, which beams and brightens upon the scene of elegance which your livingroom exhibits. A new and entertaining book is in your hand, and fruits and refreshments are by your side on a table. Here you may sit hour after hour, enjoying these means of comfort and happiness, carried away by the magic of the pen to distant and different scenes, from which you return now and then to listen a moment to the roaring of the wintry wind or the beating of the snow upon your windows. If you have a quiet conscience, you may find much happiness in such a scene – especially if gratitude to God as the giver of such comforts, and as your kind Protector and Friend, warms your heart and quickens your sensibilities. Here you may sit hour after hour, until Orion has made his steady way through the clouds and storms of the sky, high into the heavens.

But, though this might be enjoyable, there is another way of spending an hour of the evening which would also afford enjoyment, though of a different kind. You lay aside your book, trundle back your cushioned chair, pack your fruit and refreshments in a small basket, and take down from your bookcase a little favorite volume of hymns. Then, muffling yourself as warmly as possible in cap and coat, you venture forth in the midst of the stormy night.

The brick sidewalk is half hidden by the drifts of the snow, among which you make your slippery way until you turn onto a narrow sidewalk, guiding your steps to one of its humble houses. You enter by a low door. It is not, however, the abode of poverty. There is comfort and plenty under this roof; though on a different scale from that which you have left at home, it is not inferior in respect to the actual enjoyment they afford.

The mother who welcomes you is a widow, and the daily labor of her hands procures for her all that is necessary for her needs, and much besides, which she enjoys as luxuries. She enjoys them more highly than you do the costly splendors you have left. Her bright, brass lamps, which she toiled several days to earn, and the plain rocking chair in the corner, are to her as much, and far more, than your fancy chandelier with its cut glass crystals, or your splendid ottoman.

In a word, all the needs of this family are well supplied, so that I will not introduce the reader to a scene of abject poverty, as you may have supposed. You must bring something more valuable than money here if you wish to do good. You have something more valuable than money – Christian charity. This I will assume you have brought.

On one side of the fire is a cradle which the mother has been rocking. You take your seat in a low chair by its side, and leaning over it you look upon the pale face of a little sufferer who has been for many months languishing there. His disease has curved his back, brought his head over towards his breast, and contracted his lungs; he lies there in bonds which death only can sunder. Something like a smile lights up his features to see that his friend came again to see him, even through the storm. That smile and its meaning will repay you for the cold blasts which you encountered on your way to the sick room. After a few minutes conversation with the boy, you ask if he would like to have you walk with him a little. He reaches up his arms to you, clearly pleased with the proposal, and you lift him from his pillow – and you enjoy yourself more, than even he does. The relief he experiences in extending his limbs, cramped by the narrow dimensions of his cradle, begins his happiness.

You raise your arms. He is not heavy. Disease has diminished his weight, and you walk back and forth across the room with a gentle step, his head reclining upon your shoulder. The uneasy, restless expression which was upon his face is gradually changed for one of peaceful repose; until, at length, lulled by the gentle sound of your voice, he drops into a quiet slumber. You may walk with him frequently across the floor, before fatigue will counterbalance the pleasure you will receive in watching his placid and happy look reflected in the glass behind you when you turn.

Eventually he wakes, and you gently lay him down into his cradle again. You read him a hymn expressive of resignation to God and confidence in His kind protection. Kneeling down by his cradle and holding his hand in yours, you offer a simple prayer in his behalf. And when at length you rise to go away, you see his countenance and feel the spontaneous pressure of his little hand, telling you that his heart is full of happiness and gratitude. In witnessing it, and in recalling the scene to your mind in your cold and stormy walk home, you will experience an enjoyment which I cannot describe, but all who have experienced it will understand. This enjoyment is very different in its nature from the solitary happiness you would have felt at your own fireside. Which kind, now, do you prefer?

True, the case I have described is an experiment on a very small scale. The good done was very little; it was only a half hour's partial relief for a sick child, and another half hour's happiness for him afterwards, as he lies in silence and solitude in his cradle thinking about the kindness of his visitor. This is truly doing good on a small scale, but then it is made by just a small effort. It illustrates well, because of its being so simple a case, the point to be illustrated: that you may take two totally different modes to make a winter evening pass pleasantly, and it is not merely a difference of means when the end is the same, but a difference in the very end and object itself.

"But is not the end sought in both cases our own happiness?" you ask.

"No, it is not." And this leads me to a distinction, an important spiritual distinction which everyone who wishes to perform charity on the basis of right principles should understand. The distinction is contained summarily in the following propositions. I hope my reader will pause and reflect upon them, until their meaning is distinctly understood. Then, he will be ready to enter into the spirit of the remarks which follow. The propositions are elementary, for they lie at the very foundation of Christian love.

- One may do good for the sake of the credit or the advantage of it, in which case it is a matter of policy.

- He may do good for the sake of the pleasure of it. Here it is a matter of feeling.

- He may do good simply for the sake of obeying God and from the desire to have the good done. In this case, it is a matter of principle.

One may do good for the sake of the credit or the advantage of it.

This choice is the secret of a far greater proportion of the apparently benevolent effort which is made in the world, than is generally supposed. I do not by any means say that it is wrong for a person to desire the good opinion of others, and especially to wish to be known as a person of kind feeling for the needs and sufferings of others. This is probably right. The degree, the extent, to which this operates upon us as a stimulus to godly duty is the main point we need to consider.

There are various ways in which this principle may operate. You may go and visit the sick, carry comforts to the poor, and be very active in your efforts to gather Sunday school scholars, or you may distribute tracts or collect contributions for charitable purposes. Doing these things, you pass along from month to month, imagining that your motives and feelings are all right. Still, if you were ever to pause and reflect, and call your heart thoroughly to account, you would find that your real stimulus is the wish to be esteemed by all your Christian acquaintances as an ardent and a devoted Christian, or as an active, efficient, successful member or manager of a charitable society. Or, you may contribute money – alas! How much is so contributed because you know it will be expected of you. The box or the paper comes around and you cannot easily escape it. You do the good, not for the sake of having the good done, but to save your own reputation. Or, to take another case still, on a larger scale, one more gross in its nature, you may (if you are a man of business and wealth), take a large share in some costly, charitable enterprise, with the design of enlarging your influence or extending your business by the effect which your share in the transaction will produce upon the minds of others. It is true that this feeling would not be unmixed. You would look, and try to look, as much as possible at the benevolent object to be completed; and a deceitful and desperately wicked heart would try to persuade you that this is your sole, or at least your principal desire. If, however, you were suddenly laid up with a fatal illness, and could look upon these transactions in the bright spiritual light which the vicinity of another world throws upon all human actions and pursuits, you would see that in these cases you are doing good, not for the sake of pleasing God by doing His will, but to promote in various ways your own private ends.

Let it be understood that we do not say that this would be wrong, nor do we say it would be right. We say nothing about it. How far, and into what fields, a just and proper policy will lead a person in the transaction of his worldly affairs is not now our business to inquire. The subject we are considering is not policy but benevolence, and the only point which we wish here to carry is to persuade the Christian, who is commencing his course of godly action, to discriminate; to understand distinctly what is benevolence and what is not, and to have his mental and moral powers so disciplined that when he really is doing good for the sake of the credit of it, he may distinctly know it.

He may do good for the sake of the pleasure of it.

Doing good from the impulse of sentimental feeling is regarded among men as of a higher moral rank than doing good from policy (though it might be a little difficult to assign a substantial reason for the distinction). One of the lowest examples of doing good from mere feeling, is where we make effort to relieve pain because we cannot bear to see it. A wretched looking child, with bare feet and half naked bosom, comes to our door in a cold inclement season of the year. He comes, it may be, to beg for food or clothing. We might never have thought of making any search in our neighborhood for suffering people, but when such an individual intrudes himself upon us, we cannot bear to send him away with a denial. We give him food or clothing, or perhaps money; but our chief incentive for doing it is to relieve a feeling of uneasiness in our own minds. We do not say that this is wrong. All we say is that it is not acting from principle. It may be considered a moral excellence that the mind is so constituted in respect to its powers and sympathy with others that it cannot be happy itself while an object of misery is near, and the happiness of knowing that all around us are happy may be a type of enjoyment which it is very proper for us to seek. But still, this is doing good from feeling, not from principle.

Feeling will often prompt a charitable man to make efforts to promote positive enjoyment, and to relieve mere suffering which forces itself upon his notice. You "get interested," as the phrase goes, in some poor, unhappy widow and her children. The circumstances of her case are such, perhaps, as at first to make a strong appeal to your feelings; and after beginning to act in her behalf, you are led on from step to step by the pleasure of doing good until you have found her regular employment, relieved all her needs, and provided for the comfort and proper education of her children. All this may be right, but it may be simply feeling which has prompted it. There might have been no steady principle of benevolence through the whole case.

He may do good simply for the sake of obeying God and from the desire to have the good done.

There is a far wider difference between the benevolence of principle and the benevolence of feeling than Christians may realize. Principle looks first to God and His law Word. She sees Him engaged in the work of promoting universal holiness and happiness. Not universal holiness, merely as a means of happiness, but holiness and happiness; for moral excellence is in itself a good, independent of any enjoyment which may result from it. Thus, principle has two distinct and independent, though closely connected objects, while feeling has but one. Principle deliberately decides to take hold as a cooperator with God in promoting the prosperity of His kingdom. She does not rush heedlessly into the field and seize hold of the first little object which comes in her way. Instead, she acts upon a plan, and surveys the field. She considers what means and resources she now has, and what she may, by proper effort, bring within her reach. Principle aims at acting in such a manner as shall in the end promote, in the highest and best way, the designs of God. She feels, too, that in these labors she is not alone. She is endeavoring to execute the plans of a superior, and she endeavors to act, not as her own impulses might prompt, but as the laws and principles of the Bible dictate.

Doing good from motives of policy, the first of the inducements we have considered, is unlikely to find much favor with human hearts if it can be simply deprived of its disguise. But, the distinction between feeling and principle demands more careful attention. The two may sometimes cooperate. They do very well together, but feeling alone cannot be trusted with the work of Christian charity. She can aid and inspire principle, and enable her to do her work better, but she cannot be trusted alone.

We can more clearly show the distinction between the benevolence of principle and of feeling by an allegorical illustration. Let us suppose that one evening, Feeling and Principle were walking on a road, along the outskirts of a country town. They were returning from an evening service in a schoolhouse, a mile from their homes. It was a cold winter evening, and as they passed by the door of a small cabin with boarded windows and broken roof, they saw a child sitting at the door crying bitterly.

Feeling looked anxious and concerned.

"What is the matter, my little fellow?" asked Principle, with a pleasant countenance.

The boy sobbed on.

"What a house," said Feeling, "for human beings to live in. But I do not think anything serious is the matter. Let us continue."

"What is the matter, my boy?" asked Principle again, kindly. "Can you tell us what is the matter?"

"My father is sick," replied the boy, "and I don't know what is the matter with him."

"Listen," said Feeling.

They listened and heard the sounds of moaning and muttering within the house.

"Let us continue," said Feeling, pulling upon Principle's arm, "and we will send somebody to see what is the matter."

"We should go and see ourselves," said Principle to her companion.

Feeling shrunk back from the proposal, while Principle, with female timidity, paused a moment, from an undefined sense of danger.

"There can be no real danger," thought she. "Besides, if there is, my Savior exposed himself to danger in doing good. Why should not I? Savior," she whispered, "aid and guide me."

"Where is your mother, my boy?" she asked.

"She is in there," said the boy, "trying to take care of him."

"Oh, come," said Feeling, "let us go. Here, my boy, here is some money for you to take to your mother." Saying this, she tossed down some change by his side.

The boy was wiping his eyes and did not notice it. He looked up anxiously into Principle's face and said, "I wish you would go and see my mother."

Principle advanced towards the door, and Feeling, afraid to stay out or to go home alone, followed.

They walked in. Lying upon a tiny bed covered with dirty and tattered blankets was a sick man, moaning and muttering and snatching at the blankets with his fingers. He was evidently struggling with a high fever.

His wife was sitting on the end of a bench by the chimney corner, with her elbows on her knees and her face upon her hands. As her visitors entered, she looked up at them. She was the picture of wretchedness and despair. Principle looked glad, but Feeling was sorry they came.

Feeling began to talk to some small children who were shivering over the wood-burning furnace, and Principle approached the mother. They both soon learned the true state of the case. It was a case of common misery, resulting from the common cause of unemployment. Feeling was overwhelmed with painful emotion at witnessing such suffering. Principle began to think what could be done to relieve it, and to prevent its return.

"Let us give her some money so she can buy some wood and some bread," whispered Feeling, "and go away. I cannot bear to stay."

"She wants kind words and sympathy, more than food and fuel, for present relief," said Principle. "Let us sit with her for a little while."

The poor sufferer was cheered and encouraged by their presence. A little hope broke in. Her strength revived under the influence of heart-felt concern, which is more powerful than any medicated beverage; and when, after half an hour, they went away promising future relief, the spirits and strength of the wretched wife and mother had been a little restored. She had smoothed her husband's horrible cough and quieted her crying children. She had shut her doors, and was preparing to enjoy the relief when it should come. In a word, she had been revived from the brink of despair. As they walked away, Feeling said it was a most heart-rending scene, and that she would not forget it as long as she lived. Principle said nothing, but guided their way to a house where they found one whom they could use to carry food and fuel to the cabin, and take care of the sick man while the wife and her children sleep. They then returned home. Feeling retired to rest, shuddering lest the terrible scene should haunt her in her dreams, and saying that she would not witness such a scene again for all the world. Principle kneeled down at her bedside with a mind at peace. She commended the sufferers to God's care, and prayed that her Savior would give her some such work to do for Him everyday.

Although a very simple case, this is the difference between feeling and principle. The one obeys her own impulses, and relieves misery because she cannot bear to see it; the other obeys God. Because of this difference in the very nature of their benevolence, many results follow in respect to the character of their efforts.

First of all, feeling is unsteady. Acting merely from impulse, it is plain that she will not act unless circumstances occur to awaken the impulse. She, therefore, cannot be depended upon. Her stimulus is from without. It arises from external objects acting upon her, and so her benevolence rises and falls as external circumstances vary. The stimulus of principle, on the other hand, is from within. Hers is a heart reconciled to God as Lord, consistently united to Him with the desire to carry forward His plans. Consequently, when there is no work before her, she goes forth of her own accord and seeks work. She is, therefore, steady.

Second, feeling will not persevere. When she sees suffering she feels uneasy, and to remove this uneasiness, she makes gracious effort. However, there are two ways that she can choose to deal with suffering. She will cease to feel uneasiness not only when the need is relieved, but also when she becomes accustomed to witnessing it. She feeds a starving child, not because she wishes the child to be happy, but because she cannot bear to see him wretched. Now, when she becomes accustomed to seeing wretchedness, she can bear it easily enough; therefore, she cannot continue with any extended benevolent effort. Before long she becomes accustomed to the suffering and it ceases to affect her; thus, her whole impulse, which is her whole motive, is gone.

Feeling is also inconsiderate. What she wishes is not to do good, but to relieve her own wounded sensibilities. She will give a needy person money at the door, though she might know that he uses the money chiefly as the means of getting that which is the chief cause of his wretchedness. That is, however, of no consequence to her, for the particular misery she encountered will be out of her sight; her purpose is answered equally well, whether the misery is relieved, or only removed from view. Therefore, she is inconsiderate. She is acting with gracious intentions, but often increasing the evil she intended to remedy.

Fourth, feeling aims only at relieving visible wretchedness. Indeed, if she were wise, she might aim at promoting general happiness on an enlarged plan, for her own enjoyment would be most highly promoted by this. But she is generally not very wise, and while principle forms plans and makes systematic efforts to promote the general enjoyment, feeling continues in a state of moral inaction with respect to the work of doing good, unless there is some specific and obvious suffering to be relieved.

Lastly, feeling does not aim at promoting holiness or diminishing sin, on their own account. Principle considers sin an evil, and holiness or moral excellence, a good. She considers them on their own account, independent of their connection with enjoyment or suffering. She would rather have all men grateful, obedient to God, and united to one another, even if they were to gain nothing by it in respect to happiness. Feeling does not take this view of the subject. Nothing affects her but the sight or the tale of woe. If you can show her that sin is the cause of some suffering which she is endeavoring to relieve, she will perhaps take an interest in endeavoring to remove it as a means of accomplishing an end. But in respect to the universal reign of love to God and love to man, because of the intrinsic excellence of love, she feels no interest. She does not perceive this moral excellence. She may be herself entirely destitute of this love and blind to the true duty that God has for each of His children.

In these respects, and in many more connected to them, principle is very different from feeling.

The reader will, I hope, clearly understand the distinction between policy, feeling, and principle, as the chief motives in doing good. The question will naturally arise, at least it should arise: What is the character of our own benevolent effort? We shall all find that these motives are mixed in our hearts, and by a careful self-examination, we shall probably perceive that policy has more influence than either of the others. By policy I do not mean a deliberate intention to pretend to be generous to accomplish a sinister design; I mean doing good, with some real interest in it, but where the paramount inducement, after all, is the light in which the affair will be viewed by others. This may not be always wrong, as we have before remarked. A man ought not to be indifferent entirely to his own reputation. The favorable regard of the wise and good, everyone should desire, and it is right to take pleasure in the sense of its possession. But there are probably very few who would not be surprised, if they were to see their good deeds honestly analyzed. Such people would often see that a large part of their inducement during charitable activities was to be seen by men.

To discriminate between the benevolence of feeling and that of principle requires still greater care. The distinction is not exactly one between right and wrong, for to be influenced in our efforts by feeling is surely not wrong. We should feel deep compassion for the sufferings of others, and a great personal pleasure in the work of alleviating them. But principle should be the great basis of all our efforts at doing good. It is the only stable basis, and it is the only one which in any degree enables us to fulfill our obligations as the children of God. Doing good on principle is the only type of benevolence which is pleasing to Him.

If we wish to know which of these motives control us, we

must pause when we intend to make some effort to do good. We must allow our thoughts to go freely forward and see what the object is on which they will rest, as the end to be secured. When, for example, you are making efforts to prepare yourself for your duties as a Sunday school teacher, in what is it that your heart rests upon as the object you are pursuing? Let your imagination go forward, beyond your present preparation; follow her and see where she goes – what picture does she form? Does she exhibit to your eye the beautiful appearance of a full and an attentive class, to be noticed by the other teachers, the superintendent, or by some individual friend whose good opinion you particularly want? Does she whisper to you the praises of your fidelity and your success, or does she warn you of the reproof or the censure, secret or open, which you must expect if you are unfaithful? Or, does she lead you to the hearts of the children, and show you renewed, sanctified affections there? Does she picture to you their future lives, purified from sin, and lead you to expect through them the extension of the Redeemer's kingdom?

So when a friend calls upon you, to ask your subscription to a charity for example, and you sit listening to the story, determining whether to add your name to the list, what is it that your imagination reposes upon at the instant of decision? Is it the satisfaction of the applicant at finding you ready to aid, the sight of your name by those to whom the paper is to be circulated, or relief from the pain awakened by the sad details of the story? Or, is it the pleasure of obeying God and aiding in doing His work? What is it in such cases that your mind rests upon at the moment of decision? Recall a few such cases to mind, give the reins to your heart, and see where it will go. If you take off all restraint and let it move freely, it would run to its own end, and there repose itself upon the object it is really seeking.

Ultimately, the Christian who wishes to love others the way God intended must act upon principle. He must come and give himself up to his Maker's service and aim at carrying out all His plans. He must first strive to bring men back to their allegiance to God, since without this every other plan for promoting human happiness must fail. Then he must do all he can to promote the present enjoyment of all God's creatures, in

TEACHING CHILDREN THE ROYAL LAW

every way in his power. He must love happiness on a small scale, and on a large scale. He must wish that those all around him should enjoy themselves now, and a thousand years hence; and a thousand years hence as well as now. This benevolence must reign so constantly in the heart, as to give a habitual character to the feelings, an expression to the countenance, and tone to the voice. The cooperator with God must also speak in the same language to all around him, especially to those in his own family.

This, then my reader, is the work which you must do, if you wish to cooperate with God. These are the objects you must aim at, not merely now and then, when some details of suffering intrude themselves upon your mind and awaken a temporary feeling, but steadily and constantly, as the great business of life. Your own happiness will be much promoted; however, your aim in pursuing these objects must not be your own happiness, but rather the accomplishment of the objects themselves – extending the reign of holiness, and fulfilling your duty as a grateful and obedient child of God.

Until Christ comes, let us be given to love and hospitality. Our fiery devotion to spread Christian charity will light the way for our children and inspire them to dare great exploits for King Jesus.

My little children, let us not love in word, neither in tongue; but in deed and in truth. I John 3:18

Patriotism Begins at Home

The seed of the best patriotism is in the love that a man has for the home he inhabits, for the soil he tills, for the trees that give him shade, and for the hills that stand in his pathway. The love of home is rooted by God in the human soul.

This love has the power to blur the eyes of the dying soldier with the vision of an old homestead amid a green field and clustering trees. The memory of home follows the busy man through the clamoring world, and at last draws his tired feet from the highway and leads him through shady lanes and familiar pathways until he is once again at home – safe and secure. Citizens who have a safe place of warmth and rest, a place they can call their own, are the backbone of our Republic. Such people will endure great hardships and still insist upon defending their cherished place of rest and joy.

We often consider the barracks of our standing army with their rolling drums and their fluttering flags as points of strength and protection. But the citizen standing in the doorway of his home, contented on his threshold, his family gathered about his hearthstone while the evening of a well-spent day closes – he shall save the Republic when the drum tap is futile, and the barracks are empty. The true strength of the United States lies in the fact that many households are armed and ready to defend their families, homes, and freedoms. The cry of each American must always be, "long live the citizen army - long live the Militia!"

This principle of patriotism is not without Scriptural support as well. Nehemiah, the great servant of God, encouraged the children of Israel to rebuild Jerusalem and restore their nation after they returned from captivity. Nehemiah had the wisdom to organize the people by families and tribes because he realized that as the Jews began to rebuild their city, they would surely have to endure threats and persecution. The book of Nehemiah, chapter four, records the inspiring words of this great and godly leader as he admonished the people to "...Be not ye afraid of them: remember the Lord, which is great and terrible, and fight for your brethren, your sons, and your daughters, your wives, and your houses."

All Americans must realize that their home is their castle, and that their freedoms and political sovereignty come from no human agency. We must inspire our fellow citizens to be vigilant, self-governed under God's Law, and responsible. In practical terms, this means that we must encourage people to lean on the state for nothing that their own arm can do, and on the federal government for nothing that his state can do. Lead your neighbor to cultivate a dependence upon God and the Bible to the point of sacrifice, and learn that humble things with unbartered liberty are better then splendors bought with its price. Encourage no one to surrender his individuality to government nor merge it with the mob.

True patriotism will never endure in our beloved land without the courageous testimony of upright and fearless households, for the home is the birthplace of real patriotism. Let each citizen then, endeavor to labor by the sweat of his brow and by God's grace to build a strong household. Such a place will ever be the bedrock and temple of America's liberty.

Comprehension Questions

1. What did the author believe was the "seed" of the best patriotism?
2. Do you think this author considers the ability to own private property as an important and valuable right? If so, why?
3. Did this author believe that America's true strength came from standing armies? Explain your answer.
4. List two of the principles that this author believed were important for each citizen to understand regarding the role of government.

The Good Fight of Faith

The following address was given by Dr. J. Gresham Machen at Princeton Seminary in the late 1920's to an assembly of seminary students. His stern and compassionate plea for the students to resist growing liberalism and compromise was ultimately rejected by the leadership of Princeton. However, evangelical Christians today still have the same duty to challenge false teachings, wherever they are found, in the church, the seminary, or in the world.

The Apostle Paul was a great fighter. His fighting was partly against external enemies – against hardships of all kinds. Five times he was scourged by the Jews, three times by the Romans; he suffered shipwreck four times; and was in perils of waters, in perils of robbers, in perils by his own countrymen, in perils by the heathen, in perils in the city, in perils in the wilderness, in perils in the sea, in perils among false brethren. And finally he came to the logical end of such a life, by the headsman's axe. It was hardly a peaceful life, but was rather a life of wild adventure. Lindbergh, I suppose, got a thrill when he lifted off for Paris, and people are in search of thrills today; but if they wanted a really unbroken succession of thrills, I think they could hardly do better than to try knocking around the Roman Empire during the first century with the Apostle Paul, engaged in the unpopular business of turning the world upside down.

But these physical hardships were not the chief battle in which Paul was engaged. Far more trying was the battle that he fought against the enemies in his own camp. Everywhere his rear was threatened by an all-engulfing paganism or by a perverted Judaism that had missed the real purpose of the Old Testament law. Read the Epistles with care, and you see Paul always in conflict. At one time he fights paganism in life, the notion that all kinds of conduct are lawful to the Christian man, a philosophy that makes Christian liberty a mere aid to pagan license. At another time, he fights paganism in thought, the sublimation of the Christian doctrine of the resurrection of the body into the pagan doctrine of the immortality of the body.

At still another time, he fights the effort of human pride to substitute man's merit as the means of salvation for Divine grace; he fights the subtle propaganda of the Judaizers with its misleading appeal to the Word of God. Everywhere we see the great apostle in conflict for the preservation of the church. It is as though a mighty flood were seeking to engulf the church's life; dam the break at one point in the levee, and another break appears somewhere else. Everywhere paganism was sweeping through. Paul seldom had a moment's peace. He was continually called upon to fight.

Fortunately, he was a true fighter; and by God's grace he not only fought, but he won. At first sight indeed he might have seemed to have lost. The lofty doctrine of Divine grace, the center and core of the Gospel that Paul preached, did not always dominate the mind and heart of the subsequent church. The Christianity of the Apostolic Fathers, of the Apologists, of Irenaeus, is very different from the Christianity of Paul. The church meant to be faithful to the apostle; but the pure doctrine of the Cross runs counter to the natural man, and not always, even in the church, was it fully understood. Read the Epistle to the Romans first, and then read Irenaeus, and you are conscious of a mighty decline. No longer does the Gospel stand out sharp and clear; there is a large admixture of human error; and it might seem as though Christian freedom, after all, were to be entangled in the meshes of a new law.

The human instruments which God uses in great triumphs of faith are no pacifists, but great fighters like Paul himself. Little affinity for the great apostle has the whole tribe of compromisers ancient and modern. The real companions of Paul are the great heroes of the faith. But who are those heroes? Are they not true fighters, one and all? Tertullian fought a mighty battle against Marcion; Athanasius fought against the Arians; Augustine fought against Pelagius; and as for Luther, he fought a brave battle

THE GOOD FIGHT OF FAITH

against kings and princes and popes for the liberty of the people of God. Luther was a great fighter; and we love him for it. So was Calvin; so were John Knox and all the rest. It is impossible to be a true soldier of Jesus Christ and not fight.

God grant that you – students in this seminary – may be fighters, too! Probably you have your battles even now; you have to contend against sins gross or sins refined; you have to contend against the sin of slothfulness and inertia; you have, many of you, I know very well, a mighty battle on your hands against doubt and despair. Do not think it strange if you fall thus into divers temptations. The Christian life is a warfare after all. John Bunyan rightly set it forth under the allegory of a Holy War; and when he set it forth, in his greater book, under the figure of a pilgrimage, the pilgrimage too, was full of battles.

There are indeed, places of refreshment on the Christian way; the House Beautiful was provided by the King at the top of the Hill Difficulty, for the entertainment of pilgrims, and from the Delectable Mountains could sometimes be discerned the shining towers of the City of God. But just after the descent from the House Beautiful, there was the battle with Appollyon and the Valley of Humiliation, and later came the Valley of the Shadow of Death. Yes, the Christian faces a mighty conflict in this world. Pray God that in that conflict you may be true men; good soldiers of Jesus Christ, not willing to compromise with your great enemy, not easily cast down, and seeking ever the renewing of your strength in the Word and ordinances and prayer!

If you decide to stand for Christ, you will not have an easy life in the ministry. Of course, you may try to evade the conflict. All men will speak well of you if, after preaching no matter how unpopular a Gospel on Sunday, you will only vote against that Gospel in the councils of the church the next day; you will graciously be permitted to believe in supernatural Christianity all you please if you will only act as though you did not believe in it, if you will only make common cause with its opponents. Such is the program that will win the favor of the worldly church. A man may believe what he pleases, provided he does not believe anything strongly enough to risk his life on it and fight for it. "Tolerance" is the great word. Men even ask for tolerance when they look to God in prayer. But how can any Christian possibly pray such a prayer as that? What a terrible prayer it is, how full of disloyalty to the Lord Jesus Christ!

There is a sense, of course, in which tolerance is a virtue. If by it you mean tolerance on the part of the state, the forbearance of majorities toward minorities, the resolute rejection of any measures of physical compulsion in propagating either what is true or what is false, then of course, the Christian ought to favor tolerance with all his might and main, and ought to lament the widespread growth of intolerance in America today. Or if you mean by tolerance forbearance toward personal attacks upon yourself, or courtesy and patience and fairness in dealing with all errors of whatever kind, then again tolerance is a virtue. But to pray for tolerance apart from such qualifications, in particular to pray for tolerance without careful definition of that of which you are to be tolerant, is just to pray for the breakdown of the Christian religion; for the Christian religion is intolerant to the core.

There lies the whole offense of the Cross – and also the whole power of it. Always the Gospel would have been received with favor by the world if it had been presented merely as one way of salvation; the offense came because it was presented as the only way, and because it made relentless war upon all other ways. God save us, then, from this "tolerance" of which we hear so much. God deliver us from the sin of making common cause with those who deny or ignore the blessed Gospel of Jesus Christ! God save us from the deadly guilt of consenting to representatives in the church who lead Christ's little ones astray; God make us, whatever else we are, just faithful messengers, who present, without fear or favor, not our word, but the Word of God.

But if you are such messengers, you will have the opposition of, not only the world, but increasingly, I fear, of the Church. I cannot tell you that your sacrifice will be light. No doubt it would be noble to care nothing whatever about the judgment of our fellow men. But to such nobility I confess that I for my part have not quite attained, and I cannot expect you to have attained to it. I confess that academic preferments, easy access to great libraries, the society of cultured people, and in general the thousand advantages that come from being regarded as respectable in a respectable world – I confess that these things seem to me to be in themselves good and desirable things. Yet the servant of Jesus Christ, to an increasing extent, is being obliged to give them up. Certainly, in making that sacrifice we do not complain; for we have something with which all that we have lost is not worthy to be compared. Still, it can hardly be said that any unworthy motives of self-interest can lead us to adopt a course which brings us nothing but reproach.

Where, then, shall we find a sufficient motive for such a course as that; where shall we find courage to stand against the whole current of the age; where shall we find courage for this fight of faith? I do not think that we shall obtain courage by any mere lust of conflict. In some battles that means may perhaps suffice. Soldiers in bayonet practice were sometimes, and for all I know still are, taught to give a shout when they thrust their bayonets at imaginary enemies; I heard them doing it even long after the armistice in France. That serves, I suppose, to overcome the natural inhibition of civilized man against sticking a knife into human bodies. It is thought to develop the proper spirit of conflict. Perhaps it may be necessary in some kinds of war. But it will hardly serve in this Christian conflict. In this conflict I do not think we can be good fighters simply by being resolved to fight. For this battle is a battle of love; and nothing ruins a man's service in it so much as a spirit of hate.

No, if we want to learn the secret of this warfare, we shall have to look deeper; and we can hardly do better than turn again to that great fighter, the Apostle Paul. What was the secret of his power in the mighty conflict; how did he learn to fight?

The answer is paradoxical; but it is very simple. Paul was a great fighter because he was at peace. He who said, "Fight the good fight of faith," spoke also of the "peace of God which passeth all understanding;" and in that peace the sinews of his war were found. He fought against the enemies that were without because he was at peace within; there was an inner sanctuary in his life that no enemy could disturb. There, my friends, is the great truth. You cannot fight successfully with beasts, as Paul did at Ephesus; you cannot fight successfully against evil men, or against the devil and his spiritual powers of wickedness in high places, unless when you fight against those enemies there is One with whom you are at peace.

But if you are at peace with the One, then you can care little what men may do. You can say with the apostles, "We must obey God rather than men"; you can say with Luther, "Here I stand, I cannot do otherwise, God help me. *Amen*"; you can say with Elisha, "They that be with us are more than they that be with them"; you can say with Paul, "It is God that justifieth, who is he that condemneth?" Without that peace of God in your hearts, you will strike little terror into the enemies of the Gospel of Christ. You may amass mighty resources for the conflict; you may be great masters of ecclesiastical strategy; you may be very clever, and very zealous too; but I fear that it will be of little avail. There may be a tremendous din; but when the din is over, the Lord's enemies will be in possession of the field. No, there is no other way to be a really good fighter. You cannot fight God's battle against God's enemies unless you are at peace with Him.

But how shall you be at peace with Him? Many ways have been tried. How pathetic is the age-long effort of sinful man to become right with God; sacrifice, lacerations, almsgiving, morality, penance, confession! But alas, it is all of no avail. Still there is that same awful gulf. It may be temporarily concealed; spiritual exercises may conceal it for a time; penance or the confession of sin unto men may give a temporary and apparent relief. But the real trouble remains; the burden is still on the back; Mount Sinai is still ready to shoot forth flames; the soul is still not at peace with God. How then shall peace be obtained?

My friends, it cannot be attained by anything in us. Oh, that that truth could be written in the hearts of everyone of you! Oh, that it could be written in letters of flame for all the world to read! Peace with God cannot be attained by good works, neither can it be attained by confession of sin, neither can it be attained by any psychological results of an act of faith. We can never be at peace with God unless God first be at peace with us. But how can God be at peace with us? Can He be at peace with us by ignoring the guilt of sin? by descending from His throne? by throwing the universe into chaos? by making wrong to be the same as right? by making a dead letter of His holy law? By treating His eternal laws as though they were the changeable laws of man?"

Oh, what an abyss were the universe if that were done, what a mad anarchy, what a wild demon-riot! Where could there be peace if God were thus at war with Himself; where could there be a foundation if God's laws were not sure? Oh, no, my friends, peace cannot be attained for man by the great modern method of dragging God down to man's level; peace cannot be attained by denying that right is right and wrong is wrong; peace can nowhere be attained if the awful justice of God stand not forever sure.

How then can we sinners stand before that Throne? How can there be peace for us in the presence of the justice of God? How can He be just and yet justify the ungodly? There is one answer to these questions. It is not our answer. Our wisdom could never have discovered it. It is God's answer. It is found in the story of the Cross. We deserved eternal death because of sin; the eternal Son of God, because he loved us, and because He was sent by the Father who loved us too, died in our stead, for our sins, upon the Cross. That message is despised today; upon it the visible church as well as the world pours out the vials of its scorn, or else does it even less honor by paying it lip-service and then passing it by. Men dismiss it as a "theory of the atonement," and fall back upon the customary common places about a principle of self-sacrifice, or the culmination of a universal law, or a revelation of the love of God, or the hallowing of suffering, or the similarity between Christ's death and the death of soldiers who perished in the great war.

In the presence of such blindness, our words often seem vain. We may tell men something of what we think about the Cross of Christ, but it is harder to tell them what we feel. We pour forth our tears of gratitude and love; we open to the multitude the depths of our souls, we celebrate a mystery so tender, so holy, that we might think it would soften even a heart of stone. But all to no effect. The Cross remains foolishness to the world, men turn coldly away, and our preaching seems but vain. And then comes the wonder of wonders! The hour comes for some poor soul, even through the simplest and poorest preaching; the message is honored, not the messenger; there comes a flash of light into the soul, and all is as clear as day. "He loved me and gave Himself for me," says the sinner at last, as he contemplates the Saviour upon the Cross. The burden of sin falls from the back, and a soul enters into the peace of God.

Have you yourselves that peace, my friends? If you have, you will not be deceived by the propaganda of any disloyal church. If you have the peace of God in your hearts, you will never shrink from controversy; you will never be afraid to contend earnestly for the Faith. Talk of peace in the present deadly peril of the Church, and you show, unless you be strangely ignorant of the conditions that exist, that you have little inkling of the true peace of God. Those who have been at the foot of the Cross will not be afraid to go forth under the banner of the Cross to a holy war of love.

Where are you going to stand in the great battle which now rages in the church? Are you going to curry favor with the world by standing aloof; are you going to be "conservative liberals" or "liberal conservatives" or "Christians who do not believe in controversy," or anything else so self-contradictory and absurd? Are you going to be coldly aloof when God's people fight against ecclesiastical tyranny at home and abroad? Are you going to excuse yourselves by pointing out personal defects in those who contend for the Faith today? Are you going to be disloyal to Christ in external testimony until you can make all well within your own soul? Be assured, you will never accomplish your purpose if you adopt such a program as that. Witness bravely to the Truth that you already understand, and more will be given you; but make common cause with those who deny or ignore the Gospel of Christ, and the enemy will forever run riot in your life.

There are many hopes that I cherish for you men, with whom I am united by such ties of affection. I hope that you may be gifted preachers; I hope that you may have happy lives; I hope that you may have adequate support for yourselves and for your families; I hope that you may have good churches. But I hope something for you far more than all that. I hope above all that, wherever you are and however your preaching may be received, you may be true witnesses for the Lord Jesus Christ; I hope that there may never be any doubt where you stand, but that always you may stand squarely for Jesus Christ, as He is offered to us, not in the experiences of men, but in the blessed written Word of God.

Many have been swept from their moorings by the current of the age; a church grown worldly often tyrannizes over those who look for guidance to God's Word alone. But this is not the first discouraging time in the history of the church; other times were just as dark, and yet always God has watched over His people, and the hardest hour has sometimes preceded the dawn. So even now God has not left Himself without a witness. In many lands there are those who have faced the great issue of the day and have decided it aright, who have preserved true independence of mind in the presence of the world; in many lands there are groups of Christian people who in the face of ecclesiastical tyranny have not been afraid to stand for Jesus Christ. God grant that you may give comfort to them as you go forth from this seminary; God grant that you may rejoice their hearts by giving them your hand and your voice. To do so you will need courage. Far easier is to curry favor with the world by abusing those whom the world abuses, by speaking against controversy, by taking a balcony view of the struggle in which God's servants are engaged.

But God save you from such a satanic neutrality as that! It has a certain worldly appearance of urbanity and charity. But how cruel it is to burdened souls; how heartless it is to those little ones who are looking to the Church for some clear message from God! God save you from being so heartless and so unloving and so cold! God grant, instead, that in all humility but also in all boldness, in reliance upon God, you may fight the good fight of faith. Peace is indeed yours, the peace of God which passeth all understanding. But that peace is given you, not that you may be onlookers or neutrals in love's battle, but that you may be good soldiers of Jesus Christ.

"And the peace of God, which passeth all understanding, shall keep your hearts and minds through Christ Jesus."
–Philippians 4:7

"Fight the good fight of faith..."   –I Timothy 6:12

Comprehension Questions

1. Describe two ways in which the Apostle Paul was a fighter.
2. Write down a brief description of what it means for a Christian to be tolerant.
3. Why is it impossible for a faithful Christian to consistently avoid controversy?
4. What was the greatest or highest hope that this speaker had for his seminary students?

God's Purposes for Emotion

One of the most common errors in the Christian Church today is the error of confounding religious interest with religious emotion. Interest in pursuing the Christian faith should be our constant duty. Emotion is one of the forms which this interest occasionally assumes. Now many persons confound the two and think that they are in a cold, stupid state, unless their hearts are full of a deep, overwhelming emotion. They struggle continually to awaken and to sustain this emotion and are distressed and disappointed that they cannot succeed. They fail for the obvious reason, that the human heart is incapable of long continued emotion of any kind when in a healthy state. Emotion is given by the Creator for wise and good purposes; but it is intended to be an occasional, not a habitual state of mind, and in general, our duty is to control rather than to cherish it.

For example, a man loves his wife and his little children. He thinks that he may advance their physical well-being in the world by moving to a new home in the West, where he can make his labors far more effectual in laying a foundation for their wealth and prosperity, than he can in the home of his own childhood. He sets off therefore, on the long and toilsome journey, to explore the ground and prepare the way for them to follow. As soon as he arrives at the confines of the new property, his mind is daily engrossed by his labors and cares. Now, he is toiling over the rough and miry road – now hesitating upon the bank of a rapid stream – now making his slow and tedious way through the unbroken forest, his mind intent on studying where and how to build his new home.

During all this time he feels no emotion of love for his wife and children, but his mind is under the continued influence of the strongest possible interest in them. It is love for them which carries him on every step of the way. It is this that animates him; this, that cheers and sustains while he perhaps very seldom pauses in his labors and cares in order to bring them distinctly to his mind and fill his heart with the flowings of a sentimental affection. At length however, at some solitary post-office in a nearby town, he finds a letter from home and pauses for several moments to read its welcome pages.

As he reads sentence after sentence of the message which has found its way to him from his distant home, his ardent affection for the loved ones there, which has, through the day remained a quiet and steady principle of action, awakes and begins to agitate his bosom with more active emotions. And when, at the close of the letter he comes upon a little postscript rudely printed asking, "father to come home soon," it calls to his mind so forceably that round and happy face which smiled upon him from the steps of the door when he came away, that his heart is full. He does not love these absent ones any more than he did before, but his love for them takes for a moment a different form. Nor, is it that his affection is merely in a greater state of intensity than usual at such time; it is in a totally different state, different in its nature and different in its tendency. For while love as a principle of action would carry him forward to labor with cheerfulness and zeal for the future of his family, love as a mere emotion tends to destroy all his interest in going forward, and to lead him to turn round in his path and seek the shortest way back home. He readily perceives this and though the indulgence of such feelings may be delightful, he struggles to put them down. He suppresses the tear which fills his eye, folds up the letter, and jumps in his car. Instead of considering the state of emotion the one to be cultivated as the only genuine evidence of true love, he regards it rather as one to be controlled and suppressed as interfering with his duties and obligations to God and to his family.

Now the discrimination, which it is the design of the foregoing case to set in a strong light, is very often not made in Christianity; but it should be made. True godliness must exist generally as a calm and steady principle of action, changing its form, and manifesting itself as religious emotion only occasionally. The frequency of these emotions and the depth of the religious feeling which they will awaken, depend upon a thousand circumstances, entirely independent of the true spiritual condition of the soul. The physical influences by which we are surrounded – the bodily temperament, the state of health, the degree of pressure of active duty, the social circumstances in which we are placed, the season, the hour, the scenery, a thousand things – may by the combined influence of some or of all of them fill the heart with religious emotion, provided that the principle of biblical faith be already established there. But we must not suppose that religion is dormant and inactive at other times. Religion is, to say the least, quite as active a principle when it leads a man to his work in the cause of God, as when in his retirement, it swells his heart with spiritual joys. They are in fact, two distinct forms which the same principle assumes; and we cannot compare one with the other so as to assign to either the pre-eminence. Neither can exist in a genuine state without some measure of the other. It is, however, undoubtedly the former which is the great test of Christian character. It is the former which we are to strive to establish in our hearts. Christian people can depend upon making steady and certain spiritual progress in just proportion to their obedience to the Word of God, and the sincerity of their prayers.

But in point of fact, a growing number of Christians today, (in their efforts to make progress in personal holiness), very often look almost exclusively to their feelings for direction and instruction rather than looking to the principles and commands contained in the Holy Bible. They think that continued religious emotion is the only right frame of mind, while the human mind is so constituted that continued emotion of any kind is consistent only with insanity. They toil and struggle for emotion but they labor in vain, for emotion of any kind is just the very last thing to come by being toiled and struggled for. The result is, therefore, either a feeling of dejection and confirmed despondency or else the gradual cultivation of a morbid sentimentalism, which has nothing but the semblance of true godliness.

It was Paul the Apostle who testified to the fact that the people of Israel "had a zeal of God, but not according to knowledge." A growing number of professing Christians in this day and age are permitting their emotions or "zeal" to dictate their world view and daily walk with the Lord. Consequently, many of these individuals are frequently blown about by every wind of doctrine and the vain wisdom of men who make their living off the emotional needs of those who are sincerely seeking God. Christian people must never forget that the safest and surest guide to righteousness and true holiness is the Bible. The Bible then must be restored to its rightful place in the minds and hearts of God's covenant people for it is the Christian's surest form of spiritual revelation.

Our business then in our efforts to bring our hearts into a right state in respect to God's kingdom, is to cultivate a steady, healthy, active interest in it – not to struggle in vain for continued religious emotion. If the principle of Godly action reigns over us, it will lead us to exactly the right sort of effort in God's cause; and it will bring to our hearts many happy seasons of sweet emotion in our hours of retirement, meditation and prayer.

The Reputation of George Whitefield

George Whitefield was one of the most respected and influential preachers of colonial America. As a native of Great Britain, this missionary preacher was used by Almighty God to spark great revivals among the colonists and their leaders.

Even leaders like Benjamin Franklin, who were not noted for their allegiance to the Christian faith, publicly declared their admiration for Mr. Whitefield. The following newspaper article, written by Franklin, appeared in *The Pennsylvania Gazette* on July 31, 1746. The article was entitled *Appreciation of George Whitefield.*

On Sunday, the 20th, the Rev. Mr. Whitefield preached twice, though apparently much indesposed to large congregations as he spoke in a new building in this city. The next day he set out for New York.

When we seriouly consider how incessantly this faithful servant (not yet 32 years old) has, for about ten years, labored in his great Master's Vineyard, with an alacrity and fervent zeal, which an infirm constitution, still daily declining, cannot abate; and which has triumphed over the most vigorous opposition from whole armies of jealous preachers and pamphleteers; under whose performances, the pulpits and presses of Great Britain and America, have groaned. We may reasonably think with the learned Dr. Watts, "That Whitefield is a man raised up by providence in an uncommon way, to awaken a stupid and ungodly world, to a sense of the important affairs of Religion and Eternity:" And the lines of Mr. Wesley, concerning another young Methodist, may justly be applied to his dear friend, Whitefield –

Wise in his prime, he waited not for noon,
Convinced that mortals never lived too soon;
As if foreboding here his little stay,
He makes his morning bear the heat of the day.

No fair occasion glides unheeded by,
Snatching the golden moments as they fly,
He by few fleeting hours ensures eternity.

His sermons here this summer have given general satisfaction, and plainly proved the great ability of the preacher. His rich fancy, sound and ripening judgment, and extensive acquaintance with men and books of useful literature, have been acknowledged by every unprejudiced person. Purity of language, an engaging address, and an apt gesture, peculiar to this accomplished orator, considered with his unspotted character in private life, have added force to the plain strong arguments, and pathetic expostulations, wherewith his discourses abounded. And, it cannot be doubted, that many have been awakened to a sense of the importance of religion and others have been built up in their most holy Christian faith under his ministry.

In addition to this article, Franklin wrote a rather humorous story regarding Whitefield's powers of persuasion when soliciting financial contributions to some worthy charity. The following story was written by Benjamin Franklin in his autobiography conveying the incident in his life when he went to hear Whitefield preach on behalf of an orphanage that he was helping to start in Georgia.

Returning northward he preached up this charity and made large collections; for his eloquence had a wonderful power over the hearts and purses of his hearers, of which I myself was an instance. I did not disapprove of the orphanage, but as Georgia was then destitute of materials and workmen, and it was proposed to send them from Philadelphia at a great expense, I thought it would have been better to have built the house here and brought the children to it. This I advised, but he was resolute in his original project, and rejected my counsel. I thereafter refused to contribute. I happened soon after to attend one of his sermons, in the course of which I perceived he intended to finish with a collection and I silently resolved he should get nothing from me. I had in my pocket a handful of copper, paper money, three or four silver dollars, and five pistoles in gold. As he proceeded I began to soften, and concluded to give the coppers. Another stroke of his oratory made me ashamed of that, and determined me to give the silver; and he finished so admirable, that I emptied my pocket wholly into the collector's dish, gold and all. At this sermon there was also one of our club, who being of my sentiments respecting the building in Georgia, and suspecting a collection might be intended, had by precaution emptied his pockets before he came from home; towards the conclusion of the discourse however, he felt a strong desire to give, and applied to a neighbor who stood near him to borrow some money for the purpose. The application was unfortunately to perhaps the only man in the company who had the firmness not to be affected by the preacher. His answer was; "at any other time, friend Hopkinson, I would lend to thee freely; but not now; for thee seems to be out of thy right senses."

Some of Mr. Whitefield's enemies affected to suppose that he would apply these collections to his own private emolument; but I, who was intimately acquainted with him, (being employed in printing his sermons and journals, etc.) never had the least suspicion of his integrity, but am to this day decidedly of opinion that he was in all his conduct, a perfectly honest man. And methinks my testimony in his favor ought to have the more weight, as we had no religious connection. He used indeed sometimes to pray for my conversion, but never had the satisfaction of believing that his prayers were heard. Ours was a mere civil friendship, sincere on both sides, and lasted to his death.

STUDYING CHRISTIAN LITERATURE

George Whitefield will long be remembered as a great man of God, faithful and true to the end. However, one of his greatest achievements as a Christian leader was his ability to gain a reputation with those outside of the Church of Jesus Christ. Few American Christians have better fulfilled the mandate of Scripture that requires church leaders to "have a good report of them which are without; lest he fall into reproach and the snare of the devil." (I Timothy 3:7) God bless the memory of George Whitefield.

Comprehension Questions

1. What country was George Whitefield born in?
2. Who was persuaded to donate to the orphanage founded by George Whitefield in Georgia?
3. What was one of the greatest achievements of George Whitefield?
4. Why do you think that God requires preachers and other Church leaders to have a good reputation for honesty and purity?

Praise for Creation and Providence

I sing the almighty power of God,
    That made the mountains rise;
That spread the flowing seas abroad,
    And built the lofty skies.

I sing the wisdom that ordained
    The sun to rule the day;
The moon shines full at his command,
    And all the stars obey.

I sing the goodness of the Lord,
    That filled the earth with food;
He formed the creatures with his word,
    And then pronounced them good.

Lord, how thy wonders are displayed
    Where'er I turn mine eye;
If I survey the ground I tread,
    Or gaze upon the sky!

There's not a plant or flower below,
    But makes thy glories known;
And clouds arise, and tempests blow,
    By order from thy throne.

Creatures (as numerous as they be)
    Are subject to thy care;
There's not a place where we can flee,
    But God is present there.

In heaven he shines with beams of love,
    With wrath in hell beneath;
'Tis on His earth I stand or move,
    And 'tis his air I breathe.

His hand is my perpetual guard,
   He keeps me with his eye;
Why should I then forget the Lord,
   Who is for ever nigh?

ISAAC WATTS, D.D.
1674-1748

Beethoven and the Blind Girl

It happened in the German city of Bonn. One moonlight evening during the winter I called upon Beethoven, for I wanted him to take a walk, and afterward to sup with me. In passing through a dark, narrow street, he paused suddenly. "Hush!" he said, "what sound is that? It is from Sonata in F!" he said eagerly. "Hark! how well it is played!"

It was a little, plain dwelling, and we paused outside and listened. The player went on; but in the midst of the *finale* there was a sudden break, then the sound of sobbing. "I cannot play any more. It is so beautiful, it is utterly beyond my power to do it justice. Oh, what would I not give to go to the concert at Cologne!"

"Ah, my sister," said her companion, "why create regrets, when there is no remedy? We can scarcely pay our rent."

"You are right; and yet I wish for once in my life to hear some really good music. But it is of no use."

Beethoven looked at me. "Let us go in," he said.

"Go in!" I exclaimed. "What can we go in for?"

"I will play to her," he said, in an excited tone. "Here is feeling, genius, understanding. I will play to her, and she will understand it." And, before I could prevent him, his hand was upon the door.

A pale young man was sitting by the table, making shoes; and near him leaning sorrowfully upon an old-fashioned piano, sat a young girl, with a profusion of light hair falling over her pretty face. Both were cleanly but very poorly dressed, and both turned and stared toward us as we entered.

"Pardon me," said Beethoven, "but I heard music, and was tempted to enter. I am a musician."

The girl blushed, and the young man looked serious, somewhat annoyed.

"I – I also overheard something of what you said," continued my friend. "You wish to hear – that is you would like – that is – Shall I play for you?"

There was something so odd in the whole affair, and something so comic and pleasant in the manner of the speaker, that the spell was broken in a moment, and all smiled involuntarily.

"Thank you!" said the shoemaker; "but our piano is so wretched, and we have no music."

"No music!" echoed my friend. "How, then, does the young lady –"

He paused, and hushed up, for as he looked in the girl's face he saw that she was blind.

"I – I entreat your pardon!" he stammered. "But I had not perceived before. Then you play by ear? But where do you hear the music, since you frequent no concerts?"

"I used to hear a lady practicing near us, when we lived two years in another town. During the summer evenings her windows were generally open, and I walked to and fro outside to listen to her."

She seemed shy; so Beethoven said no more, but seated himself quietly before the piano, and began to play. He had no sooner struck the first chord, than I knew what would follow, how grand he would be that night. And I was not mistaken. Never, during all the years I knew him, did I hear him play as he then played to that blind girl and her brother. He was inspired; and from the instant when his fingers began to wander along the keys, the very tone of the instrument began to grow sweeter.

The brother and sister were silent with wonder and rapture. The former laid aside his work; the latter, with her head bent slightly forward, and her hands pressed tightly over her breast, crouched down near the end of the piano, as if fearful lest even the beating of her heart should break the flow of those sweet, magical sounds.

Suddenly the flame of the single candle wavered, sank, flickered, and went out. Beethoven paused, and I threw open the shutters, admitting a flood of brilliant moonlight. The room was almost as light as before, and the illumination fell strongest upon the piano and the player. But the chain of his ideas seemed to have been broken by the accident. His head dropped upon his breast; his hand rested upon his knees; he seemed absorbed in meditation. It was thus for some time.

At length the young shoemaker rose, and approached him eagerly, yet reverently. "Wonderful man!" he said, in a low tone; "who and what are you?"

The composer smiled. "Listen!" he said; and he played the opening bars of the Sonata in F.

A cry of delight and recognition burst from them both, as they exclaimed, "Then you are Beethoven!"

He rose to go, but we held him back with entreaties:

"Play to us once more – only once more!"

He permitted himself to be led back to the instrument. The moon shone brightly in through the window, and lit up his glorious rugged head and massive figure. "I will improvise a sonata to the moonlight," said he, looking up thoughtfully to the sky and stars. Then his hands dropped on the keys, and he began playing a sad and infinitely lovely movement, which crept gently over the instrument like the calm flow of moonlight over the dark earth.

This was followed by a wild, elfin passage, in triple time – a sort of grotesque interlude, like the dance of maidens at the opera. Then came a swift *finale* – a breathless, hurrying, trembling movement, descriptive of flight and uncertainty, and vague, impulsive terror, which carried us away on its rustling wings, and left us all in emotion and wonder.

"Farewell to you!" said Beethoven, pushing back his chair and turning toward the door, "farewell to you!"

"You will come again?" asked the audience, in one breath.

He paused, and looked compassionately, almost tenderly, at the face of the blind girl. "Yes, yes," he said hurriedly, "I will come again, and give the young lady some lessons. Farewell! I will soon come again!"

They followed us in silence more eloquent than words, and stood at their door till we were out of sight.

"Let us make haste back," said Beethoven, "that I may write out that sonata while I can yet remember it."

We did so, and he sat over it till long past midnight. And this was the origin of the *Moonlight Sonata* with which so many are fondly acquainted.

Ludwig van Beethoven.

The Path of Peace

I trusted in riches, wealth, and fame –
But never sought peace in Jesus' name;
"Good works will save me," this I said –
Never realizing I was spiritually dead.

"Besides, I go to church – once in a while –
And, with pomp and splendor, parade down the aisle.
"But, oh, the joys I have missed from day to day –
Because I have not yielded my all to Christ,
The True and Living Way.

Trust not in riches, wealth, and fame –
But place your trust in the blood of the lamb;
Christ will redeem you from all evil and wrong –
And place within you salvation's song.

Paul Revere's Ride

Listen, my children, and you shall hear
Of the midnight ride of Paul Revere,
On the eighteenth of April, in Seventy-five;
Hardly a man is now alive
Who remembers that famous day and year.

He said to his friend, "If the British march
By land or sea from the town tonight,
Hang a lantern aloft in the belfry arch
Of the North Church tower, as a signal light –
One, if by land, and two, if by sea;
And I on the opposite shore will be
Ready to ride and spread the alarm
Through every Middlesex village and farm
For the country-folk to be up and to arm."

Then he said "Good night," and with muffled oar
Silently rowed to the Charlestown shore,
Just as the moon rose over the bay,
Where, swinging wide at her moorings, lay
The Somerset, British man-of-war;
A phantom ship, with each mast and spar
Across the moon, like a prison bar,
And a huge black hulk, that was magnified
By its own reflection in the tide.

Meanwhile, his friend through alley and street
Wanders and watches with eager ears,
Till in the silence around him he hears
The muster of men at the barrack door,
The sound of arms, and the tramp of feet,
And the measured tread of the grenadiers
Marching down to their boats on the shore.

PAUL REVERE'S RIDE

Then he climbed the tower of the Old North Church,
Up the wooden stairs, with stealthy tread,
To the belfry-chamber overhead,
And startled the pigeons from their perch
On the somber rafters, that round him made
Masses and moving shapes of shade —
Up the trembling ladder, steep and tall,
To the highest window in the wall,
Where he paused to listen and look down
A moment on the roofs of the town,
And the moonlight flowing over all.

Beneath, in the churchyard, lay the dead
In their night-encampment on the hill,
Wrapped in silence so deep and still
That he could hear, like a sentinel's tread,
The watchful night-wind, as it went
Creeping along from tent to tent
And seeming to whisper, "All is well!"
A moment only he feels the spell
Of the place and the hour, the secret dread
Of the lonely belfry and the dead;
For suddenly all his thoughts are bent
On a shadowy something far away,
Where the river widens to meet the bay —
A line of black, that bends and floats
On the rising tide, like a bridge of boats.

Meanwhile, impatient to mount and ride,
Booted and spurred, with a heavy stride
On the opposite shore walked Paul Revere.
Now he patted his horse's side;
Now gazed at the landscape far and near;
Then, impetuous, stamped the earth,
And turned and tightened his saddle-girth;
But mostly he watched with eager search
The belfry-tower of the Old North Church,
As it rose above the graves on the hill,
Lonely, and spectral, and somber, and still.
And lo! as he looks, on the belfry's height,

STUDYING CHRISTIAN LITERATURE

A glimmer, and then a gleam of light!
He springs to the saddle, the bridle he turns,
But lingers and gazes, till full on his sight
A second lamp in the belfry burns!

A hurry of hoofs in a village street,
A shape in the moonlight, a bulk in the dark,
And beneath, from the pebbles, in passing, a spark
Struck out by a steed flying fearless and fleet;
That was all! And yet through the gloom and the light,
The fate of a nation was riding that night;
And the spark struck out by a steed, in his flight,
Kindled the land into flame with its heat.

PAUL REVERE'S RIDE

He has left the village and mounted the steep,
And beneath him, tranquil and broad and deep,
Is the Mystic, meeting the ocean tides;
And under the alders that skirt its edge,
Now soft on the sand, now loud on the ledge,
Is heard the tramp of his steed as he rides.

It was twelve by the village clock
When he crossed the bridge into Medford town.
He heard the crowing of the cock,
And the barking of the farmer's dog,
And felt the damp of the river-fog
That rises after the sun goes down.

It was one by the village clock
When he galloped into Lexington.
He saw the gilded weathercock
Swim in the moonlight as he passed,
And the meeting-house windows, blank and bare,
Gaze at him with a spectral glare,
As if they already stood aghast
At the bloody work they would look upon.

It was two by the village clock
When he came to the bridge in Concord town.
He heard the bleating of the flock,
And the twitter of birds among the trees,
And felt the breath of the morning breeze
Blowing over the meadows brown.
And one was safe and asleep in his bed
Who at the bridge would be first to fall,
Who that day would be lying dead,
Pierced by a British musket-ball.

You know the rest. In the books you have read
How the British regulars fired and fled,
How the farmers gave them ball for ball,
From behind each fence and farmyard wall,
Chasing the redcoats down the lane;
Then crossing the fields to emerge again

STUDYING CHRISTIAN LITERATURE

Under the trees at the turn of the road,
And only pausing to fire and load.

So through the night rode Paul Revere;
And so through the night went his cry of alarm
To every Middlesex village and farm –
A cry of defiance, and not of fear,
A voice in the darkness, a knock at the door,
And a word that shall echo forevermore!
For, borne on the night-wind of the Past,
Through all our history, to the last,
In the hour of darkness and peril and need,
The people will waken and listen to hear
The hurrying hoof-beats of the steed,
And the midnight message of Paul Revere.

Comprehension Questions

1. What was Paul Revere's message?
2. How does Longfellow make you feel the hurry of the rider?
3. What do you consider the most expressive line in the poem?
4. Look up and write the dictionary definition of the following words:

   barrack   grenadier
   impetuous   spectral

80

The Story of Alonzo

Modern child psychologists often tell us that the way to make a child happy is by teaching him how to love himself. The topic of sin is no longer beneficial to stress to a child according to psychologists; only "positive" words should be used to build self-esteem.

It is interesting to note that the Bible never once commands any human being to love himself. On the contrary, the Bible directs us to love God and our neighbor. (Any student of the Bible should already know that the major problem with fallen man is his tendency to love himself too much.)

The real gospel of Christ talks in terms of surrendering ourselves to Jesus. Contrary to this truth stands the self-love crowd who is seeking to encourage our nation's youth to "think more highly of yourselves than you ought to think."

Adults in America today who have a burden for the souls of children must rally around the old rugged cross and point children in the direction of the Savior who bled and died for their sins! The greatest blessing anyone can give to a child is to lead him to a knowledge of the Savior Jesus Christ, and to His love.

The story that follows gives any interested adult a thorough understanding of the inner workings of a child's heart, its deceptions and corruptions, and its greatest need, which is to be freed from the guilt and burden of sin. The primary purpose of the story is to clarify that the greatest need of a child's heart is to secure loving fellowship with Jesus Christ. It is not love of self that will satisfy the great longings of a child's heart. A child becomes truly happy when he is brought to the place where he can see that the love of Christ is the only foundation for real peace and joy.

Alonzo was a young boy who lived in Vermont. His father owned a farm in one of those warm and verdant dells which gave a charm to the scenery of the Green Mountains. The low, broad farmhouse, with its barns and sheds, hay stacks and high woodpiles, made almost a little village as they lay spread out in a sunny opening near the head of the glen. A winding road repeatedly crossing a brook, which meandered among the trees down through the valley, guided the traveller to the spot.

The wide yard was filled with domestic animals and the sheds were stored with utensils of the farm. Lilac trees and rose bushes ornamented the front of the dwelling, and from the midst of a little green lawn on one side of the house a deep clear spring, walled in with moss covered stones, poured up continually from below a full supply of cool, clear water. A group of willows hung over the spring and a well-trod foot path led to it from the house. A smooth flat stone lay before the "end door," as they called it, which led to the spring.

Here, during the second year of his life, Alonzo might have been seen almost every sunny day, playing with buttercups and daisies, or digging with his little shovel in the earth before the door, or building houses out of corn cobs taken from the granary. The next summer, had you watched him, you might have observed that his range was wider and his plans of amusement a little more enlarged. He had a garden, two feet square, where he stuck down green twigs broken from the shrubs around him; he would make stakes with a dull house knife partly for the pleasure of making them, and partly for the pleasure of driving them into the ground. He would ramble up and down the path a little way, and sometimes go with his mother down to the spring to see her dip the bright tin pail into the water and to gaze with astonishment at the effect of the commotion. The stony wall of the spring seemed always to be broken to pieces; its fragments waved and floated about in confusion until they gradually returned to their places of rest. This extraordinary phenomenon astonished him again and again.

One day Alonzo's mother saw him going alone towards the spring. He had grabbed his pail and was going to try the wonderful experiment himself. His mother called him back and instructed him to never go there alone. "If you go there alone," she said, "you will fall in and be drowned."

Alonzo was not convinced by the reason, but he was awed by the command, and for many days he obeyed. At length, however, when his mother was occupied in another part of the house, he stole away softly down the path a little way.

There was a sort of a struggle going on within him while he was doing this. "Alonzo," said Conscience, for even at this early age Conscience had begun to be developed, "Alonzo, this is very wrong."

Conscience must be conquered, if conquered at all, not by direct opposition but by evasion and deceit, and the deceiving and deceitful tendencies of the heart are very early developed.

"I am not going down to the spring," said Alonzo to himself. "I am only going down the path a little way."

"Alonzo," said Conscience, again, "this is wrong."

"Mother will not see me, and I shall not go quite down to the water, so that no harm will be done," said the child to himself in reply, and went hesitatingly on.

"Alonzo," said Conscience a third time, but with a feebler voice, "you should not go any further."

"My mother is too strict with me; there can be no harm in my walking as far as this."

He lingered a little while about halfway down the path, then slowly returned, the dialogue between Conscience and his heart going on all the time. The latter had succeeded so well in its artful policy that when he came back he hardly knew whether he had done wrong or not. It did not seem quite right, and there was a sort of gnawing uneasiness within him, but his heart had succeeded by its evasions in making so much of a question of the whole transaction that he could not really say that it was clearly wrong. Alonzo had been taught that God had made him, and that He watched over him at all times, but somehow or other he did not happen to think of Him at all during this affair. He had also understood something of his obligations to his mother, for her kindness and love to him; but he did not happen to think of her now in this light. The contest consisted simply, on one side, of the low murmurings of Conscience telling him sternly that he was wrong; and on the other, the turnings and shiftings of a deceitful heart trying to quiet, or at least to drown, her disruptive influences.

I have focused particularly upon the philosophy of this early sin, because this was the way in which Alonzo committed all his sins for many years afterwards. Conscience made him uncomfortable while he was transgressing, but his heart kept up such a variety of evasions and queries that whenever he was doing anything wrong, he never seemed to have a distinct idea that it was clearly and positively wrong. For instance, a few days after the transaction described above, his mother had gone away from home to run an errand. His sister, who had the care of him, had left him alone at the door. He took up the pail and began to walk slowly down the path. Conscience, defeated before and familiarized to a certain degree with transgression, allowed him to go without opposition for part of the way, but when she perceived that he was actually approaching the spring, she shook her head and renewed her low, solemn murmuring.

"Alonzo, Alonzo, you must not go there."

"I know I shall not fall in," said Alonzo to himself.

"Alonzo, " said Conscience again, "you must not disobey."

Alonzo tried not to hear her, and instead of answering, he said to himself, "It was many days ago that she told me not to go. She did not mean never."

This was true, yet it may seem surprising that Alonzo could for one instant deceive himself with such an argument. But anything will do to deceive ourselves when we are in the mood. When we are committing sin we love to be deceived about it. Hence, it is very easy for a corrupted heart to justify wrong.

While saying that his mother could not have meant that he must never go, Alonzo leaned over the spring and tremblingly plunged in his pail. The special effect was produced. The stones and moss waved and quivered, to Alonzo's inexpressible delight. His mind was in a state of feverish excitement: Conscience calling upon him, in vain trying to make him hear; Fear whispering eagerly, that he might be seen; Curiosity urging him again and again to repeat his wonderful experiment.

Alonzo was a very little child, and the language in which I am obliged to clothe his thoughts and words correctly describes the thoughts and feelings which really passed within his bosom.

At length, he hastily drew out his pail and went back to the house. Conscience endeavored, when the excitement of the experiment was over, to gain his attention. Nevertheless, his heart was still bent on deceiving and being deceived.

"My mother said," thought he, "that I should fall in and be drowned if I went there, and I did not fall in. I knew I would not fall in."

Thus, instead of thinking of his guilt and disobedience, he was occupied with the thought of the advantage he had gained over his mother; that is, the heart which ought to have been penitent and humbled under the burden of sin was deluding itself with the false colors which it had spread over its guilt, being filled with deceit and self-congratulation.

Year after year passed on, and Alonzo grew in strength and stature; but he continued about the same in heart. Instead of playing on the round, flat door stone, he at length might be seen riding on his father's plough, or tossing about the drying grass in the mowing field, or gathering berries upon the hill side, on some summer afternoon. He was continually committing sins in the manner already described. These sins were different in circumstance and character as he grew older, but their nature, so far as the feelings of the heart were concerned, were the same. There was the same murmuring of Conscience, the same windings and evasions of his heart, the same self-deception, and the same success in leading himself to doubt, whether the act of transgression which he was committing, was right or wrong. His parents in most respects brought him up well. They taught him his duty, and when they knew that he did wrong, they disciplined him seriously, or if necessary, they punished him. Thus his conscience was cherished and he was often deterred by her voice from committing many sins. She held him regularly in check. His parents formed in him many good habits which he adhered to faithfully as habits, and thus so far as the influence of his parents could go he was, in most cases, deterred from the commission of sin.

Other things, equally sinful, he did without scruple. For example, he would have shuddered at stealing even a pin from his sister, but he would by unreasonable wishes and demands give her as much trouble, and occasion her as much loss of enjoyment, as if he had stolen a very valuable article from her. If he had undertaken to steal a little picture from her desk, Conscience would have thundered so terribly that he could not possibly have proceeded, but he could tease and vex her by his unreasonable and selfish conduct without any regret. If his heart had been honest and shrewd in discovering its own real character, these cases would have taught him that his honesty was artificial and accidental, and did not rest on any true foundation. But his heart was neither honest nor shrewd in respect to itself; it loved to be deceived. When he read of a theft in a good story book, he took great pleasure in thinking what a good honest boy he was in comparison.

He would not have forgotten to say his prayers, both morning and night. But, whenever he committed sin during the course of the day, he never thought of going away alone before God to confess it and to ask forgiveness. If his heart had been honest and shrewd in discovering his own character, this would have taught him that his piety was all a mere form, and that he had no real affection for God. His heart, however, was not honest, and though he never thought much about it, he still had an impression on his mind that he was the friend of God and that he regularly worshiped Him. He knew very well that he sometimes committed sin, but he did not suppose that it was often. He often succeeded in blinding or misleading Conscience to make it doubtful. If he could succeed in making a question of it, he would go and commit the sin, with a half-formed idea of examining the case afterwards. But then when the pleasure of the sin was over, he found the true moral character of the transaction to be rather a disagreeable subject to investigate; so he left it in his memory to fester and rankle there. Though he had such a number of these recollections as to give him no little uneasiness and annoyance, he still thought he was a very virtuous and promising young man.

When he was about twelve years old, Alonzo made a discovery which startled and alarmed him. Some young men had formed a plan of ascending a certain mountain summit which projected like a spur from the main range, and which reared its rocky head among the clouds, in full view of his father's farm. They had fixed upon Sunday evening for this purpose, an hour or two before sundown. "A great many people," said one of the boys, "think that the Sabbath ends at sunset, and an hour or so before will not make any great difference. We must climb up in time to see the sun go down." This disposal of the difficulty was abundantly satisfactory to all those who were inclined to go, but Alonzo had some doubts whether it would appear equally conclusive to his father and mother. One thing favored, however: his father was away, having been absent on some business for the town for several days. Alonzo thought that there was at least a possibility that his mother would find the deficiencies in the reasoning made up by a little extra persuasion, and that her consent to his sharing in the pleasure of the excursion would be obtained. At any rate, it was plainly worthwhile to try.

He came in on Saturday afternoon, and standing by the side of his mother, who was finishing some sewing necessary to complete her preparations for the Sabbath, nervously presented his request. She listened to him with surprise, and then told him he must not go.

"It would be very wrong," she said.

"But mother, we shall walk along very still. We will not laugh or play. It will only be taking a little walk after sundown."

Alonzo's mother was silent.

"Come, mother," said the boy, hoping that he had made some impression, "do let me go. Do say yes, just this once."

After a moment's pause, she replied: "Some persons do indeed suppose that the Sabbath ends at sundown, but we think it continues until midnight, and we cannot shift and change the hours to suit our pleasures. Now, with all your resolutions about walking quietly, you know very well that such an expedition, with such companions, will not be keeping holy the Sabbath day. You therefore come to me with a proposal that I will allow you to disobey, directly and openly, one of the plainest of God's commands. It is impossible that I should consent."

While his mother was saying these words, emotions of anger and indignation began to rise and swell in Alonzo's bosom. Foreseeing how the sentence would end, he began to walk off towards the door and, just before the last words were uttered, he was gone. He shut the door violently, muttering to himself, "It is always just so."

In a state of wretchedness and sin (which my readers must conceive of if they have ever acted as Alonzo did), he walked out of the house and sank down upon a bench which he had made in the little orchard. Here he gave full flow for a few minutes to the torrent of boiling passion which had so suddenly burst out of his heart. In a short time, however, the excitement of his feelings subsided a little, and there came suddenly a sort of flash of moral light which seemed to reveal to him for an instant the true character of the transaction.

Something within him seemed to say, "What an unreasonable, ungrateful, wicked boy you are, Alonzo. Here is your mother, as kind a mother as ever lived. You owe her your very being. She has taken care of you for years, without any return, and has done everything to make you happy; and now, because she cannot consent to let you do what is most clearly wrong, your heart is full of anger, malice, and revenge. What a heart! Love and duty are forgotten, and every feeling of gratitude for long years of kindness is obliterated by one single interference with your wicked desires."

This reflection occupied but an instant in passing through Alonzo's mind. It flashed upon him for a moment, and was gone. The dark, heavy clouds of anger rolled over his soul again. He sat upon the bench in moody silence.

After several minutes, he again began to see that he was very wrong; such feelings towards his mother were, he knew, unreasonable and sinful, and he determined that he would not indulge them. So he rose and walked through a small gate into the yard where a large pile of long logs were lying, one of which had been rolled down and partly cut off. He took up the axe and went to work. But he soon learned that it was one thing to see that his feelings were wrong, and another thing to feel right. His mind was in a sort of chaos. Floating visions of the party ascending the hill, vexation at his disappointment, uneasiness at the recollection of his unkind treatment of his mother, all mingled together in his soul. "I wish I could feel right towards mother about this," he said to himself; but somehow or other, there seemed gathering over his heart a kind of dogged sullenness which he could not break or dispel. He concluded it was best to forget the whole affair for the present. So, he laid down the axe and began to pick up some chips and sticks to carry in for kindling the morning fire. He secretly determined that when he went in and met his mother again he would not show his impatience and anger, but would act "just as if nothing had happened."

Just as if nothing had happened! How, after such an act of disrespect, ingratitude, and disobedience, could he act as if nothing had happened! One would think that Alonzo would have great trouble with this self-centered plan.

But Alonzo did not make any such reflection. His heart

clung to his sin and loved to be deceived by it. It seemed to him impossible to feel the relenting of true, heartfelt penitence, the love and gratitude which he knew his mother deserved, and especially that cheerful acquiescence in her decision which he knew he ought to feel. So he concluded to forget all about it. The poisoned fountain which had so suddenly burst forth in his heart was covered up again, smoothed over, yet ready to boil out anew upon any new occasion.

This and a few other similar occurrences led Alonzo to think that there might be deeper sources of moral difficulty in his heart than he had been accustomed to imagine, but he did not think much about it. His life passed on without much thought or regard for his character or his prospects as a moral being. He had, however, a sort of standing suspicion that there was something wrong, but he did not stop to examine the case. The little uneasiness which this suspicion caused was soothed and quieted a good deal by a sort of prevailing idea: that there was a great deal that was very excellent in his conduct and character. He was generally considered a good boy. He knew this very well, and one of the grossest of the forms of deceitfulness which the heart assumes is to believe that we deserve all that others give us credit for, even where the good qualities in question are merely the most superficial and shallow pretence. There is no manner of deceit quite so destructive to one's moral excellence as self-deceit.

An incident occurred about this time which almost opened Alonzo's eyes to the true character of some of his virtues. During the winter months he went to school, and the good qualities which he fancied he exhibited there were among those on which he most prided himself. One afternoon, as he was walking home with a green satchel full of books slung over his shoulder, he stopped a few minutes at the brook which crossed the road and looked down over the bridge upon the smooth dark colored ice which covered the deep water. It looked so clear and beautiful; he went down and cautiously stepped upon it. It was so transparent that it seemed impossible that it could be strong. He sat down on a stone which projected out of the water, and while he was there his teacher came along, and stopping on the bridge he began to talk with him. Alonzo and the teacher were on very good terms, and after talking together a few minutes at the brook they both walked along together.

Their way was a cross path through the woods, which led by a shorter course than the main road, to the part of the town where they were both going.

As they were stepping over a low place in the log fence where their path diverged from the road the teacher said, "Alonzo, I am glad to see you carrying your books home."

"I like to study my lessons at home in the evenings," said Alonzo with a feeling of secret satisfaction.

"Well, Alonzo, what would you say if I should tell you I could guess exactly what books you have in your satchel?"

"I don't know," Alonzo replied, "perhaps you saw me put them in."

"No, I did not."

"Well, you can tell by the shape of the books which you can see by looking at the satchel."

"No," said the teacher, "I see you have either your writing book or your Atlas, but I could not tell which by the appearance of the satchel. I see that there is by the side of it one middle sized book, too, but merely its size will not tell whether it is your Arithmetic, your Geography, or your Grammar."

"Well, what do you think they are?"

"I think they are your writing book and your spelling book."

There was in Alonzo's countenance an appearance of surprise and curiosity. He said the teacher was right, and asked him how he knew.

"I know by your character."

"By my character!" said Alonzo, "What do you mean by that?"

"I will tell you, though I think it will give you pain rather than pleasure. You are one of the best boys in my school, you give me very little trouble, and you are generally diligent in your duties – obedient and faithful. Now, have you ever thought what your motives are for this?"

"No sir, I have never thought about them particularly. I want to improve my time and learn as much as I can, so as to be useful when I am a man."

Alonzo thought that ought to be his motive, and so he fancied that it was. He did not mean to tell a falsehood. He did not say it because he wished to deceive his teacher, but because his heart had deceived him. It is so with us all.

"You think so, I have no doubt. But now I wish to ask you one question. What two studies do you think you are most perfect in?"

Alonzo did not like to answer, though he knew that he prided himself much on his handsome writing and on his being almost always at the head of his class in spelling. At length he said, with a modest air, that he thought he "took as much interest in his writing and in his spelling lessons, as in anything."

"Are there any studies that you are less advanced in than these?"

"Yes, sir."

"Well," said the teacher, "now I want to ask you another question. How is it that the writing book and the spelling book, which represent the two studies in which you have made the greatest proficiency, and in which you, of course, least need any extra efforts, are the very ones which you are bringing home to work on in the evenings?"

THE STORY OF ALONZO

Alonzo did not answer immediately. In fact, he had no answer at hand. He thought that if he was inclined to study out of school hours, he had a right to take any books home that he pleased; however, he did not say so.

"And I should like to ask you one more question," said the teacher. "In what study do you think you are most deficient?"

"I suppose it is my Arithmetic," replied Alonzo, recollecting how he disliked, and avoided as much as possible, everything connected with calculation.

"And do you ever carry home your Arithmetic to study in the evening?"

Alonzo shook his head.

"Now you know that there are few subjects more important to a man than a knowledge of figures. How does it happen then, if your motive is to fit yourself for usefulness and happiness when a man, that the very study in which you are most deficient is the very one in which you never make any voluntary effort?"

There was a little pause, during which Alonzo looked serious. He felt very unhappy. It seemed to him that his teacher was unkind. He was purposely bringing his books home to study his lessons for the next day in order to please the teacher, and to be blamed just because he had not planned to bring his arithmetic instead of his spelling was very hard. Tears came to his eyes, but he strove to suppress them and said nothing.

"I know, Alonzo," continued the teacher, "that these questions of mine shall trouble you. I have not, however, asked them for the sake of troubling you, but for the purpose of letting you see into your heart and learn a lesson of its deceitfulness. I want you to think of this tonight when you are alone, and perhaps I will some day talk with you again."

So saying, they came out into the road again near the teacher's residence. They bid one another goodbye, and Alonzo walked on alone.

"He means," thought Alonzo, "that if I honestly wanted to improve, I should take greater interest in the studies in which I am deficient." As this thought floated through his mind it brought after it a dim, momentary vision of the pride, vanity, and love of praise which he suddenly saw revealed as the secret spring of all those excellences at school on which he had prided himself. But seeing all those fancied virtues of industry, love of learning, and desire to be conscientious and faithful, wither at once under the influence of two simple questions and turn into vanity, afforded him no pleasant subject of reflection. He was, therefore, glad to see a load of wood coming into his father's yard as he approached it, and he hastened to help him unload it. He thus got rid of the disagreeable subject without actually deciding whether the teacher was right or wrong.

The affair, however, shook and weakened his faith in the good traits of his character. He did not come to the distinct conclusion that they were all hollow and superficial, but he had a sort of vague fear that they might prove so. This was another sort of uneasiness laid up in his heart, a part of the burden of sin which he bore without thinking much of it.

Thus Alonzo lived. From twelve he passed on to fifteen, and from fifteen to twenty. He became a strong, athletic young man, known and esteemed for his industry, frugality, and steadiness of character. The time drew near which was to terminate his minority, and at this age his moral condition might be summed up thus:

First, the external excellences of his character arose from the influence of his excellent education. This would have been no disparagement to Alonzo if they had been of the right kind. However, they resulted only from the restraints imposed by the opinions of those around him, from the influence of his conscience which had been cultivated by his parents, and ultimately from the discomfort which occurred when he acted directly counter to the power of habit. His industry, for instance, was based upon the last, his regard for the Sabbath upon the second, and his temperance and steadiness mainly upon the positive influence of others.

Second, he made no regular systematic effort to improve his character. In fact, he felt little interest in any plan of this kind. He was quite interested in the various plans of cultivation and improvement on his father's farm, but his heart was chiefly set upon the amusements with which the young people of the neighborhood had involved themselves in the hours when work was done: the sleigh ride, the singing school, the fishing party, and the hiking. In the evening he was occupied with some one of these enjoyments, and the next day at his work he was busy planning the next – thus life glided on. I do not mean that he was entirely careless about his character and prospects as a moral being; he did sometimes feel a little uneasiness about them. Such discoveries as I have already described gave him an occasional glimpse of the secrets of his heart. As to his character, he knew it was superficially fair. He prided himself a good deal upon the appearance it presented towards others, and he did not see how he could improve it much without making a thorough work among the motives and feelings of the heart. This he could not but strongly shrink from, so he passed quietly along and thought about other things.

Finally, there was no connection between his soul and God. I mean no spiritual connection, no communion, no interchange of thought or feeling. He was taught to repeat a prayer morning and evening, and this practice he continued, considering it one of his duties. As he grew up from boyhood, however, he often neglected it in the morning, until at length he omitted it then altogether; and he gradually found an increasing reluctance to say it at night. He often omitted it, not intentionally, exactly – he forgot it; or, he was very tired and went immediately to sleep. These omissions, however (which, by the way, were far more frequent than he imagined), did not trouble him as much as it might have been expected that they would, for he began to think that the practice was intended for children and that he was getting too mature for such things. When he did remember this duty, it was only a form. There was no communion or connection between him and God. So far as the feelings of his heart were concerned, he lived in independence of his Maker. God was irrelevant.

Such was Alonzo's condition during the winter before he was to be twenty-one. One evening during that winter a meeting was appointed at a local schoolhouse. A stranger was to preach. On such occasions the schoolhouse was always filled. The congregation came from the farmers' families for several miles around: curiosity regarding the stranger, the pleasure of a winter evening's expedition, the light from the great blazing wood fire beaming upon a hundred bright and cheerful countenances, and in at least some cases, an honest desire to know and do duty, constituted the motives which drew the assembly together. At six o'clock, Alonzo harnessed a strong, fleet, well-fed horse onto a colorfully painted sleigh, helped his father and mother into the back seat, and mounted himself upon a higher one in front; away they went jingling down the valley. They were lost to sight by the turnings of the road among the trees, and the sleigh-bells, sounding fainter and fainter, soon died away upon the ear.

A little before nine, Alonzo might have been seen returning slowly up the valley. The moon had risen and it shone through the trees, casting a beautiful white light upon the snowy wreaths which hung upon them. The horse walked along slowly, and Alonzo was making crosses with his whip-lash upon the smooth surface of the snow which bordered the road. He was lost in thought. The subject of the sermon was the importance of preparation for another world; and it happened, from some cause or other, that Alonzo's mind was in such a calm, contemplative state that evening that the discourse made a strong impression. It was not an impression made by any extraordinary eloquence. The preacher, in a quiet, simple manner presented truths which Alonzo had heard numerous times before, though heretofore they had, as it were, stopped at the ear. This night, they seemed to penetrate to his heart. He came out of the meeting thoughtful. He rode home silently. There seemed to be a new view opened before his mind. The future world appeared a reality to him; it looked near, and he wondered why he was not making a preparation for it. His father and mother rode in silence, too, each unconscious of the thoughts of the other but both thinking of their son. A rare and divine influence was moving upon the hearts of all.

These serious thoughts passed away the next day, but they left behind a more distinct impression than he had been accustomed to feel: that he had a great work to do before he left the world, and that was a work which he had not yet begun.

He was careful to say the prayer of his childhood that night, with great seriousness, and he made a great effort to think about what it meant while he was repeating it. It is true that there is a great, and one would suppose, sufficiently obvious distinction between having the meaning of a prayer in the mind, and having the feelings and desires it expresses in the heart. But Alonzo did not perceive this distinction. He thought very distinctly of the meaning of the several successive petitions and confessions, and that was all; but it was enough to satisfy a deceiving and deceitful heart, and Alonzo dismissed his cares on the subject of his preparation for death as he went to sleep, feeling that he had made a good beginning.

Alonzo's attention was occupied early the next morning by an excursion into the forest for a load of wood with his father, and he entirely forgot his new religious resolutions until the evening. This discouraged him a little. However, he again offered his prayer with an effort to keep its meaning in his mind, though that effort was less successful than on the evening before. His thoughts would slip away from his control, and while he was saying, "my sins have been numerous and aggravated," or "lead me not into temptation," he would find that his mind was dwelling upon the past scenes of the day; it would be off in the forest where he had been at work or surveying the smooth slopes of hay in the barn loft or dwelling with pleasure upon his favorite horse feeding in the stall.

Alonzo was so dissatisfied with his prayer that he began again before he got through, though with not much better success than before. He was upset with himself that he could not confine his attention more easily. He could not understand the nature of his problem. The obvious explanation was a heart alienated from God and governed by its own spontaneous tendencies. Willingly deceived, he was spiritually blind.

However, Alonzo's deceitful heart had succeeded so well that he thought his second prayer would do, and he gradually fell asleep.

Weeks passed on, and Alonzo made feeble efforts to be a religious man. He said nothing of his feelings to anyone. In fact, he would not have anybody know that he had any intention of serving God. Whether it was because he was ashamed to be seen in the service of such a Master, or because he thought that his new feelings were of so high a degree of moral excellence that modesty required he should conceal them, we do not say. He was, at any rate, very careful to conceal them.

He made, naturally, little progress. Weeks and months passed away, and it seemed to him that he remained in the same place. The truth was that there was a current carrying him down which he did not perceive, but whose effects at distant intervals were very evident. He moved like the little water skipper whose motions he had often watched on his father's brook, who now and then makes a convulsive and momentary effort to ascend but who is borne continually backwards by a current steady and unceasing in its flow so that, notwithstanding his leaps, he drifts insensibly down towards the gulf behind him.

Alonzo was also like the skipper in other respects. He distinctly saw his own repeated efforts, but the slow, gentle, continual operation of the current was unperceived. His face was turned up the stream, too, where all was smooth and sunny and beautiful. He did not see the dark gulf that yawned behind.

In a word, Alonzo made but little progress. The work was all uphill. He perceived that on the whole he was not advancing, and yet he could scarcely tell why. There were several difficulties, the operation of which he felt, but there was something mysterious and unaccountable about them.

First, he was continually forgetting all his good intentions. He would, for example, reflect sometimes on the Sabbath – upon

THE STORY OF ALONZO

his duties and obligations, and would resolve to be watchful all the coming week to guard against sin and to keep his heart right. But he found it very hard to control the conduct of one day by the resolutions of the preceding. Saturday night would come and he would wake up, as it were, from his dream of business and pleasure and find that his spiritual work had been entirely neglected and forgotten during the week. Half ashamed, and half vexed with himself, he would renew good resolutions to be again neglected and forgotten as before. What could he do? There was no lack of good intention in his hours of solitude, but how to give these intentions an arm long enough to reach through the week; how to make the resolutions of retirement binding upon the conduct during the business and bustle of life was a great frustration to him. If he did not think of his resolutions at the right time, of course he could not keep them, and he was unable to discipline his soul so it would think of them at the right time.

There was another difficulty which very much perplexed and troubled Alonzo in his attempts to reform himself. Sometimes it seemed impossible for him to control his wrong feelings. When he became upset and irritated, as he sometimes did about his work, or when out of humor on account of some restraint which his mother laid upon him, he was conscious that his feelings were wrong and he would struggle against them with all his strength, but he could not conquer them. He thought he succeeded partially, but he was deceived. It was even worse than he supposed. For all the effect of his struggling was only to restrain the outward manifestation of his feelings; they still burned on in his heart. They were too strong for him, he perceived; and then in his despondency he would get lost in the metaphysical difficulties of the question: namely, how far he could be blamed for what it seemed to him he could not help.

Thus, in ordinary temptations Alonzo never could think of his resolutions, and in extraordinary ones he never could keep them. He knew not what to do, yet he was not very anxious about it. There was indeed a vague idea floating in his mind that there was a great work to be done, a work which he was yet only partially performing. He determined to take hold of it in earnest soon. The winter was so cold that he could not conveniently spend as much time alone as he wished. He thought that when the warm spring evenings came he could enjoy more solitude; spring, therefore, would be a more convenient season. When spring came they were pressed with work, and Alonzo looked forward for a time of a little greater leisure. But when planting was done there was haying, and after haying, harvesting. Then Alonzo thought that in a few months he should be free, and that he would make such arrangements as to have the more perfect command of his own time. Thus he passed on, thinking that he was watching for an opportunity to do his duty. But he was deceived. The secret was an innate dislike and repugnance for the work of repentance.

There was a strange inconsistency in his ideas. When he tried to purify and reform his heart, he found that he could not do it. Still, he had an impression, vague and undefined yet fixed and confided in, that he could perform the task easily at any time; therefore it was of little consequence that he waited for a more convenient season.

This postponement of a thorough attention to the work did not give him any particular uneasiness, for he was conscious that though he was not doing his duty quite in earnest enough, he still was not entirely neglecting it.

Alonzo's father had purchased for him a small farm a mile or two from his own. For some months, Alonzo had been very interested in his preparations for taking possession of it when he turned twenty-one; then, for many months afterwards, his whole soul was engrossed in his plans and labors for repairing the premises, getting his stock in good order, and putting the first seed into the ground. During these months he remained a member of his father's family, his own little farmhouse being empty and desolate. Occasionally, however, a piece of furniture was brought there and he would carry it in and fix it in its place, and then survey it again with a look of satisfaction. First came a stained birch bureau, then a half dozen chairs, then a bed; a few simple implements for the kitchen followed, and a load of wood was piled up in the yard. In a short time, the house began to look as if it was really intended to be occupied.

Finally, lights were seen one evening by the distant neighbors in both the rooms, for there were but two. Busy preparations were going forward, and at eight o'clock Alonzo drove up to his door in his own sleigh and handed out, first his sister, and then the bride, whom he had brought to share with him the responsibilities of his new home.

Alonzo led his horse away to the barn, took off the harness, and fastened him to his crib, previously filled to the top with hay. While doing this, he could not help thinking of his obligations to God for the circumstances of prosperity, and the prospects of happiness under which his life had been commenced. He thought he ought to be grateful. But this, as he afterwards found, was a different thing from actually being grateful. At any rate, he could not help thinking of his obligations to God, and this reminded him of the question whether he should begin the important exercise of evening family prayer that first night in his new home.

"It is your duty to do it," said Conscience.

"You will not do it properly. You will be embarrassed and perplexed; you cannot begin tonight," said Distrust.

"Still," said Conscience again, "it is your duty to do it."

"You had better wait a day or two until you get settled. It will be much easier, and more pleasant then," said a lying spirit of evasion and delay.

"It is your duty to do it tonight," murmured Conscience again.

Distracted by the discordant thoughts within him, Alonzo cut short their clamor by saying to himself that he could not begin that night, and hurried in; and the murmurs of conscience grew feebler, and soon died completely away.

Alonzo was not to blame for his double-mindedness; he was not to blame for shrinking from embarrassment, or for considering the duty before him a real trial. However, if he had actually been grateful to God for His goodness, instead of merely thinking that he ought to be so, he would have strived to fulfill this duty towards Him, even if it had been ten times as painful to perform.

Alonzo found it harder and harder to begin, the longer he postponed it. A month passed away, and the duty continued to be neglected. It was his design to read the Bible every day, but it seemed rather awkward to sit down before his wife and read it silently and alone, so he gradually neglected that. At night as he went to bed he usually offered a brief prayer, which was a sort of compromise to Conscience to induce him to let her rest in peace. He did not, however, feel happy in this mode of life. Uneasiness and anxiety rankled in his heart more and more. One evening, after hearing a plain and heartfelt sermon from his minister in the schoolhouse near his farm, he heard him announce with pleasure, what in New England is called an inquiry meeting, the next evening at his house. The design of such a meeting is to afford an opportunity for more plain and direct religious instruction to those who feel a personal interest in it, rather than the formal discourse offered to a large assembly.

Alonzo and his wife both resolved to go, and early in the evening they took their seats with twenty others around their pastor's fireside. Such a meeting is one of great interest and solemnity. It is understood that all present feel a direct personal interest in respect to their own salvation, and they come together with a stillness and solemnity, which scarcely any other assembly exhibits.

The pastor sat by the side of the fire. First he read a hymn; it was not sung. Then he offered a short and simple prayer. He then addressed the little assembly much as follows:

"The most important question which you can ask about yourselves is, 'Am I the friend or the enemy of my Maker?' Now, there is probably not one here who really feels that he is his Maker's enemy, and yet, it is very possible that there are at least some here who are truly God's enemies.

"God justly requires us all to love Him; that is, to feel a

personal affection for Him and to act under the influence of it. They who do not, He considers as not belonging to His spiritual family. They are His enemies. Not that they are employed directly and intentionally to oppose Him – they make perhaps no demonstrations of actual hostility – but in heart they dislike Him. To determine, therefore, whether we are the friends or the enemies of God, we must ascertain whether our secret hearts are in a state of love or of dislike towards Him.

"Perhaps some of you are saying to yourselves while I make these remarks, 'I am sure I love God in some degree, though I know I do not love Him as much as I should. I pray to Him, I try in some things to do my duty, I am (in some degree at least) grateful for his goodness, and I cannot perceive in myself any evidence of a feeling of dislike or hostility.'"

The pastor was right, at least in one instance, for these were exactly the thoughts which were passing through Alonzo's mind.

"Now, it is a difficult thing to tell," he continued, "what the state of our hearts is; or rather, it is a very common thing to be deceived about it. I will tell you how.

"First, we mistake approbation for love. We cannot help approving God's character. We cannot deny His excellence of justice, mercy, and holiness, any more than we can the directness of a straight line which we look upon. Approbation is the decision of the intellect or of the moral sense, which is entirely independent from the convictions of the heart. I once asked a young man whether he thought he loved God. 'O yes,' he said, 'I certainly think our Maker is worthy of all our praise and gratitude.' He was completely blind to the distinction, you see. He thought his Maker was worthy. Of course, he could not help thinking so. The question is not whether God is worthy of love and gratitude, but whether we really render these feelings in our hearts. Now, it is very possible that if you look honestly into your hearts, you will find that all your supposed love for God is only a cold, intellectual admission of the excellence of His character. This may exist without any personal feelings of affection towards Him.

"The second delusion is similar. We pray and we make an effort to confine our attention to our prayers, or as we term it, to think of what we are saying. This we mistake for really feeling the desires which we express. I do not doubt that many of you are in the habit of prayer, and that you often strive to confine your mind to what you are saying. Now you may do all this, without having in the heart any real desire for the forgiveness, the holiness, and the other blessings you seek. In fact, the very effort you make to confine your mind proves, or rather indicates very strongly, that the heart is somewhere else; for the mind goes easily where the heart is, and stays there with very little effort.

"There is another delusion, similar to the previous one; that is, thanking God without gratitude. We see that He is our benefactor and that He deserves our gratitude. We say this and feel satisfied with it, never reflecting that this is a very different thing from actually feeling gratitude.

"For instance, we may rise in the morning, look out upon the pleasant landscape before us, and think of our comfortable home, our friends, and all our means of happiness, which we are now to enjoy for another day. We feel a kind of complacency in them which, connected with our knowing that they come from God, we mistake for gratitude. We thus often think we are grateful, when the only feeling is a pleasant recognition of the good enjoyed. The difference is shown in this, that this latter feeling has no effect upon the conduct, whereas real gratitude will lead us to take pleasure in doing our Benefactor's will. Even a painful duty will become a pleasant one, for we always love to make a sacrifice for one who has been kind to us, if we are really grateful to him."

Alonzo here recollected the evening when he took possession of his new home, thinking that he was grateful to God for it, while yet "he could not" do that evening what he knew was God's will.

"In a word," continued the pastor, "we mistake the convictions of the understanding and the moral sense for the movements of the heart; whereas, the former may be all right, and the latter all wrong. I will tell you now some of the indications that a person dislikes God in his heart, even if his understanding is right in respect to His character and His favors:

"He dislikes God when his feelings do not go forth spontaneously and pleasantly towards Him. A parent once said to his child, 'Have you not sometimes felt, when thinking of some person whom you loved and who was away from you, as if your heart went out to that person; and then, it seemed as if the distance between you was lessened, though it was not in reality? On the other hand, when you think of a person whom you do not like, your heart draws back and shrinks coldly from him.' Now just tell me in which of these ways is your heart affected when you think of God."

Alonzo recollected how readily, when he was at work on the hill-side or in the distant forest, his thoughts and affections would roam away to his wife and his home, and hover there. He saw clearly that his heart never once sought God in this manner.

"Another evidence of our disliking God is when we escape from His presence as soon as we can. We cut short our prayers, and our thoughts come back with a spring to our business or our pleasures as if we had kept them on God for a few minutes by force; also, when the Sabbath is a weariness, and secret communion with God is a hassle."

Alonzo felt that the pastor was describing his feelings, exactly.

"Also, it is evidenced when we hold back a little from cordial acquiescence in God's justice and in His fearful decision to punish sin, both as exhibited in His daily dealings with mankind and in the Bible. We shrink from some things in His administration, just as one condemned prisoner is shocked at what he calls the cruelty of the government in executing a convicted felon.

"Now do you, when examined by these tests, love God or dislike him?"

It was plain from the appearance of the assembly that they felt condemned. The pastor perceived that they pleaded guilty. He closed his remarks with these words: "You ought to love God. He commands you to do it. You should have loved him all your lives; you ought to love him now. He will forgive all the past for His Son's sake, if you will now simply turn your hearts to Him. Seek peace with your Maker without delay."

"I will do it," thought Alonzo, as they kneeled once more to offer their parting prayer. The pastor uttered expressions of penitence, gratitude, affection, but Alonzo perceived that, notwithstanding his determination, his heart did not follow. The more he tried to force himself to love God, the more clearly he perceived the distinctions which the pastor had been drawing, and the more painfully evident it was to him that he had no heart to love God. He rose from his knees with a thought, half impatience and half despair: "I do not love Him, and I cannot love Him. What shall I do?"

For many weeks, Alonzo was quite discouraged and distressed. He saw more and more clearly that he did not love God, and that he never had loved Him. Conscience upbraided him and he had little peace. Yet he would not come and yield his heart to his Maker. He thought he wished to do it, as if it were possible for a person to wish to love, without loving. He struggled, but struggling did no good. What God commands us to do is to love Him, not to struggle against our hatred of Him. He set a double watch over his conduct: he was more regular in his prayers, more attentive to the Scriptures, and to every means of instruction; but all seemed to do no good. His heart was still alienated from God, and it seemed to him to become alienated more and more.

There were three great difficulties which he experienced, and which perplexed and troubled him exceedingly.

First, it really seemed to him that he could not change his heart; he could not force himself to love God and repent of sin. He also could not help the wrong and wicked feelings which often raged within him, on occasions of peculiar temptation. I am aware that the theological philosophers disagree on this subject, but it really seemed to Alonzo that his wicked heart was too strong for him. This thought, however, did not make him comfortable. Conscience upbraided him the more for being in such a state of heart towards God.

Second, the more he thought of the subject, and the more he tried to make himself fit for heaven, the more hollow and superficial and hypocritical he found all his supposed goodness to be. The Law of God claiming his heart had come home to his apprehension, and brought a new standard before him. His supposed gratitude and penitence, his prayers, and all the virtues on which he had prided himself, resolved themselves into elements of corruption and sin under the powerful analysis of the Holy Spirit.

Third, in trying to correct his sinful habits, his progress in discovering his sins went on far in advance of his success in purifying himself from them, so that in his attempts to reform his heart he was continually alarmed at new and unexpected exposures. In fact, the Law of God had come home to him, and as oil upon the fresh surface of a variegated wood brings out the dark stains which had before been invisible, it exposed corruptions and sins in his heart which he had never supposed to be slumbering there. He was alive without the Law once, but when the Commandment came, sin revived and he died. His heart sunk within him as he saw his sad spiritual condition. In a word, Alonzo opened his eyes to the fact that the excellences of character which circumstances had produced in him were external and superficial, and that he was in heart the enemy of God and the miserable, helpless slave of sin.

Though he was thus, in some degree, aware of the condition of his heart, that condition did not alter. The trouble with him was that he still disliked God and loved the world and sin, but he feared a judgment to come. However, instead of throwing himself fully upon God and giving Him his heart, he still kept away, alienated and miserable. He had certain excuses with which he unconsciously deceived himself, and he was gradually lulling his conscience to rest. Then one day, he had a private interview with his pastor where he presented his excuses and they were answered. These excuses, and the replies made by the pastor to them, were in substance somewhat as follows:

"Sir, I do feel that I am a most miserable sinner, but I do not know what to do. I have been seeking religion for many years, and the more I seek it the further I seem to be from it."

"What more then, can you do?" said the pastor.

"I am sure I do not know," responded Alonzo.

"Then why does your heart fail to rest quietly in the consciousness of having been faithful to the utmost in duty? God requires no more."

Alonzo hung his head. He perceived the absurdity of his excuse.

"No," said his pastor, "you show by that remark how easily and completely the heart deceives itself. Upbraided as you are by conscience for guilt in disliking and disobeying God, reproached so severely and continually that you cannot rest, you yet say to me that which implies that you have done and are doing all which God requires."

Alonzo sighed. It was too true.

"I know it," he said. "It is just so. I continually find some new proof of the corruption and deceitfulness of my heart. I want to change it, but it seems to me that I cannot."

"You speak as if your heart were one party and you another; and as if you were right, and all the blame rested upon your heart, as an enemy that had planted itself by some means into your bosom. Now what is your heart? It is simply yourself; your moral character and moral feelings. To talk of a contention between yourself and your heart is a complete absurdity, for the parties in the contest are one and the same thing. The struggle, if there is any, is between the claims of God's Law urged by his Spirit, on the one side, and you or your heart resisting on the other. He commands you to give him your heart – that is, yourself, your affections, and your love; yet you do not do it."

"I know it, but it seems to me that I cannot help it. I am conscious that my affections are not given to God; that they will cling to the world and sin, and I cannot help it," cried Alonzo.

"The feelings, however, which you cannot help, you admit to be wrong feelings," said the pastor.

"Yes sir, I feel and know they are wrong, and that is what makes me miserable."

"Then you are more guilty than I supposed. What should you say if you knew of a man who said that he had such an uncontrollable desire to steal or to kill that he could not help but continually commit these crimes? Should you think him worse or better than those who sinned occasionally under strong temptation?"

"But I struggle against the feelings, and cannot conquer them," said Alonzo.

"And suppose such a man as I have described should meet you in a lonely place, and should tell you that he must rob and murder you; that he had been struggling against the urge but it was too strong for him. What would you think of him? Why plainly, that he was a man of extraordinary depravity. The greater the struggle, the greater the evidence of the wickedness which could not be overcome. Our duty is to feel right towards God, not to struggle with wrong feelings," responded the pastor.

"I feel that that is true. But what can I do to change? It does seem to me that I want to repent of sin and forsake it... but... but..."

"But you do not, and therefore it is impossible that you should want to. There is no force applied to you to make you continue in sin. If there was, your conduct would not be sin. To wish to repent, without repenting, is as impossible and absurd as to wish to be sorry for something for which you are really glad. I have no doubt you really think you wish to repent, but I think you deceive yourself. What you wish for is some of the results which you suppose would follow from repentance. This is what the desires of your mind rest upon; but repentance itself looks disagreeable and repulsive, and as you cannot gain those results in any other way, you are troubled and distressed."

Alonzo saw at once by a glance within that this was true. He longed for peace of mind, relief from the reproaches of conscience, the reputation and the standing of a Christian here, and assurance of safety and happiness hereafter; but he perceived that he did not long for penitence itself. It was a disagreeable means of obtaining a desirable end. He was silent for a few moments, and then he said with a sigh, "Oh, how I wish I could begin life anew. I would live in a very different manner from what I have done."

"That remark shows how little you know after all, of your own character and of the way of salvation. It is not by purifying ourselves, and thus making ourselves fit for heaven, or by any such ideas as should suggest the plan of beginning life anew. If you should begin, you would undoubtedly be again as you have been," said the pastor.

Alonzo saw that this was true. He was ashamed that he had expressed such a wish, and at length asked, in a sorrowful desponding tone, whether his pastor could say anything to aid or guide him.

"I do not know that I can," was the reply. "The difficulty is not the lack of knowledge, but the lack of a heart to do it. If you had the right desires, your difficulties would all be over in a moment; but as you have not, I cannot impart them. Since you are thus bent on sin, God alone can change you.

"However," continued the pastor, "I will ask you one question. Do you clearly understand what this verse means: For they, being ignorant of God's righteousness, and going about to establish their own righteousness, have not submitted themselves to the righteousness of God; for Christ is the end of the law for righteousness to every one that believes."

"No sir, I have never thought of it particularly," said Alonzo.

"You feel in some degree the hopelessness of your condition if God should leave you to yourself. You have been neglecting your highest duty all your days, and in your efforts to seek religion you have been endeavoring to set yourself right with an idea of thus recommending yourself to God's favor. You have been discouraged and disheartened by this hopeless labor, for the farther you proceed in your efforts to repair your character, the more deep and extended do you find the proofs of its inherent corruption and depravity.

"You are like the man attempting to repair a house gone thoroughly to decay," continued the pastor, and as he said these words he took down from a little set of shelves behind him a small volume from which he read the following passage:

> The sinner going about to establish a righteousness of his own, is like a man endeavoring to repair his house which had thoroughly gone to decay. When he begins there is a tolerably fair exterior. It appears as if a few nails to tighten what is loose, a little new flooring, and here and there a fresh sill, will render all snug again; and that by means of these, together with wallpaper and paint to give the proper superficial decoration, all will be well, or at least, that his building will be as good as his neighbor's. When he begins, however, he finds that there is a little more to be done than he had expected. The first board that he removes in order to replace it with a better, reveals one in a worse condition behind it. He drives a nail to tighten a clapboard, and it slumps into decayed wood behind, taking no hold. He takes away more, by little and little, hoping at every removal to come to the end of what is unsound, but he finds that the more he does, the more disheartened and discouraged he feels. His progress in learning the extent of the decay keeps far in advance of his progress in repairing

it, until at last he finds to his disappointment that every beam is gone, every rafter worm-eaten and decayed, the posts pulverized by dry rot, and the foundation cracked and tottering. There is no point to start from for making his repairs; no foundation to build upon. The restoration of the edifice to strength and beauty can never be accomplished; if it could, the expense would far exceed his financial means. His building only looks the worse for his having broken its superficial continuity. He has but revealed the corruption which he never can remove or repair.

"Now does not this correspond with your efforts and disappointments during the last few months?"

"Exactly," said Alonzo.

"And your case is hopeless if God leaves you to yourself. You cannot be saved. It is not that you cannot come and be the child of God if you wish to, but you cannot come because you do not possess the will to love Him.

"Now, this being your condition, you need a Savior. There is one for you. If you wish, you can come and unite yourself with Him. If you do, through His sufferings and death you may be freely forgiven. The responsibility, the liability so to speak, for the past will be cut off. The Savior assumes all that burden and you may go free. By coming and giving yourself up wholly to Him you bring your past life as it were to a close, and begin a new spiritual life which comes from union with Him. The burden of past guilt is like a heavy chain which you have been dragging along until it is too heavy to be borne any longer. Union with Christ sunders it at a blow, and you go forward free and happy, forgiven for all the past, and for the future enjoying a new spiritual life which you will draw from Him. In a word, you abandon your own character, with the feelings with which a man would abandon a wreck, and take refuge with Jesus Christ who will give you the power to receive Him and procure for you forgiveness for the past and strength for the future, by means of His own righteousness and sufferings."

Alonzo had heard the way of salvation by Christ explained a hundred times before, but it always seemed a mysticism to him, as it always does to those who have never seen their sins and felt the utter hopelessness of their moral condition. As long as man is deceived about his true character, he desires no Savior. But when his eyes are opened by God and his deep seated corruptions are exposed, when he feels the chains of sin holding him with a relentless grip in hopeless bondage, then he finds that utter self-abandonment and humble reliance upon a Divine Redeemer whose past sufferings ransomed him, and who will supply new spiritual life to guide him in the future. He finds this prospect opens to him a refuge just such as he needs.

As Alonzo walked home from this interview, his heart dwelt with delight on the love of Christ to men in thus making arrangements for taking lost sinners into such an union with Him. His heart was full. There was no struggling to feel this love and gratitude. It was the warm, spontaneous movement of his soul which no struggling could have suppressed. He longed for an occasion to do something to evidence his gratitude. It was evening, and he looked forward with delight to the opportunity of calling together his family to establish family prayers. He almost wished that the exercise was twice as embarrassing as it was, for he longed to tell his family about the new spirit of love which burned within him, regardless of the consequences.

As he walked along, his heart clung to the Savior with a feeling of quiet happiness. In former days, he thought he loved Him; now he knew he did. He saw "God in Christ, reconciling the world unto Himself," and the Savior whom he saw there was all in all.

When he opened his Bible, old familiar passages which had always seemed strange and unintelligible to him, shone with new meaning:

"Christ has redeemed us from the curse of the law, being made a curse for us." "Being justified by faith, we have peace with God by our Lord Jesus Christ." "I am crucified with Christ, nevertheless I live, but the life I now live in the flesh, I live by faith in the Son of God, who loved me and gave himself for me."

Alonzo made greater efforts to do his duty after this than he did before, but it was for a different object and in a different way. Then, he was trying to establish his own righteousness, so as to fit himself for heaven. He abandoned this altogether now, having hope only in Christ – undeserved mercy in Christ. He made great efforts to grow in grace and to do good to others, but it was now simply because he loved to do it. Previously, he made these efforts as an unpleasant but a supposed necessary means to a desired end. Now, he hoped to secure that end in another way, and he made these efforts because they were delightful on their own account. He was, in fact, a new creature – a "new creature in Christ Jesus"; changed not by his vain efforts to establish his own righteousness, but by the regenerating influences of the Holy Spirit, altering fundamentally the desires and affections of his inmost soul.

Reader, in going forward through this volume (which will explain to you the way to do good) – if your aim is secretly or openly to fit yourself by your good deeds for the approbation of God, and thus to procure the pardon for your sins; the farther you go and the greater the effort you make, the more discouraged and disheartened you will be. Your progress in discovering the corruption and depravity of your heart will keep far in advance of your success in correcting or repairing it. The hopeless task may as well be abandoned in the beginning as at the end. Come first to the Savior. Give up yourself, your character, and all the hopes you may have founded upon it. Unite yourself with Christ as the branch is united to the vine; to be sustained by one common vitality. This will of course be a new life to you, a spiritual life without which all excellence is superficial, all hopes of eternal happiness baseless, and all real peace and enjoyment unknown.

Concord Hymn

Emerson wrote this poem to celebrate the completion of the monument which marks the spot on which the Battle of Concord was fought, April 19, 1775. This monument is the work of the American sculptor, Daniel C. French. The "Concord Hymn" was sung at the celebration, April 19, 1836.

> By the rude bridge that arched the flood,
>   Their flag to April's breeze unfurled,
> Here once the embattled farmers stood,
>   And fired the shot heard round the world.
>
> The foe long since in silence slept;
>   Alike the conqueror silent sleeps;
> And time the ruined bridge has swept
>   Down the dark stream which seaward creeps.
>
> On this green bank, by this soft stream,
>   We set today a votive stone,
> That memory may their deed redeem,
>   When, like our sires, our sons are gone.
>
> Spirit, that made those freemen dare
>   To die, and leave their children free,
> Bid time and Nature gently spare
>   The shaft we raise to them and Thee.

Comprehension Questions

1. In what sense was the first shot at the Battle of Concord the shot "heard round the world"?
2. How does this poem help the memory "to redeem the deed?"
3. Why do we observe Memorial Day?
4. The last stanza tells us to whom the shaft of honor was raised; which of these is the greater, the "freemen" or the Spirit?"

The American Experiment

Daniel Webster (1782-1852) stands out as America's foremost orator. His eloquence, his clear thinking, and the force of his personality made him equally great, whether answering an opponent in the Senate or delivering less passionate orations on anniversary occasions. He was the champion of the idea of complete union among the states. His service in the Senate, representing not only the people of Massachusetts, but all who believed with him in "Liberty and Union, now and forever, one and inseparable," and his service as Secretary of State in President Tyler's cabinet, made him one of America's great statesmen.

It was the extraordinary fortune of Washington that, having been intrusted in revolutionary times with the supreme military command, and having fulfilled that trust with equal renown for wisdom and for valor, he should be placed at the head of the first government in which an attempt was to be made on a large scale to rear the fabric of social order on the basis of a written constitution and of a pure representative principle. A government was to be established, without a throne, without an aristocracy, without castes, orders, or privileges; and this government, instead of being a democracy existing and acting within the walls of a single city, was to be extended over a vast country of different climates, interests and habits, and of various communions of our common Christian faith. The experiment certainly was entirely new. A popular government of this extent, it was evident, could be framed only by carrying into full effect the principle of representation or of delegated power; and the world was to see whether society could, by the strength of this principle, maintain its own peace and good government, carry forward its own great interests, and conduct itself to political renown and glory.

THE AMERICAN EXPERIMENT

At the period of the birth of Washington there existed in Europe no political liberty in large communities except in the provinces of Holland, and except that England herself had set a great example, so far as it went, by her glorious Revolution of 1688. Everywhere else despotic power was predominant, and the feudal or military principle held the mass of mankind in hopeless bondage. The king was the state, the king was the country, the king was all. There was one king, with power not derived from his people, and too high to be questioned, and the rest were all subjects, with no political right but obedience. All above was intangible power; all below was quiet subjection. A recent occurrence in the French chamber shows us how public opinion on these subjects is changed. A minister had spoken of the "king's subjects." "There are no subjects," exclaimed hundreds of voices at once, "in a country where the people make the king!"

Gentlemen, the spirit of human liberty and of free government, nurtured and grown into strength and beauty in America, has stretched its course into the midst of the nations. It must change, it is fast changing, the face of the earth. Our great, our high duty is to show, in our own example, that this spirit is a spirit of health as well as a spirit of power; that its benignity is as great as its strength; that its efficiency to secure individual rights, social relations, and moral order is equal to the force with which it prostrates principalities and powers. The world, at this moment, is regarding us with a willing, but something of a fearful, admiration. Its deep and awful anxiety is to learn whether free states may be stable as well as free; in short, whether wise, consistent, and virtuous self-government is a vision for the contemplation of theorists, or a truth established, illustrated, and brought into practice in the country of Washington.

Comprehension Questions

1. This selection is taken from an address, "The Character of Washington," delivered at a public dinner in Washington, D.C., on February 11, 1832, the centennial of Washington's birthday. Why was a discussion of the "American Experiment" especially appropriate on such an occasion?

STUDYING CHRISTIAN LITERATURE

2. Find lines in the first paragraph in which Daniel Webster defines this experiment. Explain the two distinctive features of the experiment.
3. Why was the use of "the principle of representation" so necessary in the American experiment in free government?
4. In the last paragraph what prophecy does Webster make? To what extent has this prophecy come true?

Christ Has Risen

Let's sing praises to God today,
    As our hearts break forth in joy to say –

        Hallelujah! Hallellujah!
        Christ has risen from the grave!

Oh, shout the message loud and clear,
    For He's removed our every fear –

        Hallelujah! Hallellujah!
        Christ has risen from the grave!

Good news! Good news! re-echo the sound
    To countless thousands, the world around –

        Hallelujah! Hallellujah!
        Christ has risen from the grave!

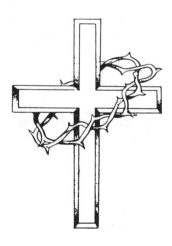

The Life of John Bunyan

As there is but one English poet great enough to express the Puritan spirit, John Milton, so there is but one commanding prose writer, John Bunyan. Milton was the child of the Renaissance, inheritor of all its culture, and the most profoundly educated man of his age. Bunyan was a poor, uneducated tinker. From the Renaissance he inherited nothing; but from the Reformation he received an excess of that spiritual independence which had caused the Puritan struggle for liberty. These two men, representing the extremes of English life in the seventeenth century, wrote the two works that stand today for the mighty Puritan spirit. One gave us the only epic since *Beowulf*; the other gave us our only great allegory, which has been read more than any other book in our language except the Bible.

Life of Bunyan. Bunyan is an extraordinary figure; we must study him, as well as his books. Thankfully we have his life story in his own words, written with the same lovable modesty and sincerity that marked all his work. Reading that story now, in *Grace Abounding*, we see two great influences at work in his life. One, from within, was his own vivid imagination, which saw visions, allegories, parables, revelations, in every common event. The other, from without, was the spiritual ferment of the age, the multiplication of strange sects – Quakers, Free-Willers, Ranters, Anabaptists, Millenarians – and the untampered zeal of all classes, like an engine without a balance wheel, when men were breaking away from authority and setting up their own religious standards. Bunyan's life is an epitome of that astonishing religious individualism which marked the close of the English Reformation.

He was born in the little English village of Elstow, near Bedford, in 1628, the son of a poor tinker. For a little while the boy was sent to school, where he learned to read and write after a fashion; but he was soon busy in his father's shop, where, amid the glowing pots and the fire and smoke of his little forge, he saw vivid pictures of hell and the devils which haunted him all his life. When he was sixteen years old his father married the second time, whereupon Bunyan ran away and became a soldier in the Parliamentary army.

The religious ferment of the age made a tremendous impression on Bunyan's sensitive imagination. He went to church occasionally, only to find himself wrapped in terrors and torments by some fiery itinerant preacher; and he would rush violently away from church to forget his fears by joining in Sunday sports on the village green. As night came on the sports were forgotten, but the terrors returned, multiplied like the evil spirits of the parable. Visions of hell and the demons swarmed in his brain. He would groan aloud in his remorse, and even years afterwards he bemoans the sins of his early life. When we look for them fearfully, expecting some shocking crimes and misdemeanors, we find that they consisted of playing ball on Sunday and swearing. The latter sin, sad to say, was begun by listening to his father cursing some obstinate kettle which refused to be tinkered, and it was perfected in the Parliamentary army. One day his terrible swearing scared a woman, "a very loose and ungodly wretch," as he tells us, who reprimanded him for his profanity. The reproach of the poor woman went straight home, like the voice of a prophet. All his profanity left him; he hung down his head with shame. "I wished with all my heart," he says, "that I might be a little child again, that my father might learn me to speak without this wicked way of swearing." With characteristic vehemence Bunyan hurls himself upon a promise of Scripture, and instantly the reformation begins to work in his soul. He casts out the habit, root and branch, and finds to his astonishment that he can speak more freely and vigorously than before. Nothing is more characteristic of the man than this sudden seizing upon a text, which he had doubtless heard many times before, and being suddenly raised up or cast down by its influence. He was, even at a young age, mighty in spirit.

With Bunyan's marriage to a good woman the real reformation in his life began. While still in his teens he married a girl as poor as himself. " We came together," he says, "as poor as might be, having not so much household stuff as a dish or spoon between us both." The only dowry which the girl brought to her new home was two old, threadbare books, *The Plain Man's Pathway to Heaven,* and *The Practice of Piety.* Bunyan read these books, which instantly gave fire to his imagination. He saw new visions and dreamed terrible new dreams of lost souls; his attendance at church grew exemplary; he began slowly and painfully to read the Bible for himself, but because of his own ignorance and the contradictory interpretations of Scripture which he heard on every side, he was tossed about like a feather by all the winds of doctrine.

The record of the next few years is like a nightmare, so terrible is Bunyan's spiritual struggle. One day he feels himself an outcast; the next the companion of angels; the third he tries experiments with the Almighty in order to put his salvation to the proof. As he goes along the road to Bedford he thinks he will work a miracle, like Gideon with the fleece. He will say to the little puddles of water in the horses' tracks, "Be ye dry;" and to all the dry tracks he will say, "Be ye puddles." As he is about to perform the miracle a thought occurs to him: "But go first under yonder hedge and pray that the Lord will make you able to perform a miracle." He goes promptly and prays. Then he is afraid of the test, and goes on his way more troubled than before.

After years of such struggle, chased about between heaven and hell, Bunyan at last emerges into a saner atmosphere, even as Pilgrim came out of the horrible Valley of the Shadow. Soon, led by his intense feelings, he becomes an open-air preacher, and crowds of laborers gather about him on the village green. They listen in silence to his words; they end in groans and tears; scores of them amend their sinful lives. For the Anglo-Saxon people are remarkable for this, that however deeply they are engaged in business or pleasure, they are still sensitive as barometers to any true spiritual influence, whether of priest or peasant; they recognize the "accent of the Holy Ghost," and in this recognition of spiritual leadership lies the secret of their democracy. So this village tinker, with his strength and sincerity, is presently the acknowledged leader of an immense congregation, and his influence is felt throughout England. It is a tribute to his power that, after the return of Charles II, Bunyan was the first to be prohibited from holding public meetings.

Concerning Bunyan's imprisonment in Bedford jail, which followed his refusal to obey the law prohibiting religious meetings without the authority of the established Church, there is a difference of opinion. That the law was unjust goes without saying; but there was no religious persecution, as we understand the term. Bunyan was allowed to worship when and how he pleased; he was simply forbidden to hold public meetings, which frequently became fierce denunciations of the Established Church and government. His judges pleaded with Bunyan to conform with the law. He refused, saying that when the Spirit was upon him he must go up and down the land, calling on men everywhere to repent. In his refusal we see much heroism, a little obstinacy, and perhaps something of that desire for martyrdom which tempts every spiritual leader. That his final sentence to indefinite imprisonment was a hard blow to Bunyan is beyond question. He groaned aloud at the thought of his poor family, and especially at the thought of leaving his little blind daughter:

I found myself a man encompassed with infirmities; the parting was like pulling the flesh from my bones... Oh, the thoughts of the hardship I thought my poor blind one might go under would break my heart to pieces. Poor child, thought I, what sorrow thou art like to have for thy portion in this world; thou must be beaten, must beg, suffer hunger, cold, nakedness, and a thousand calamities, though I cannot now endure that the wind should blow upon thee.

And then, because he thinks always in parables and seeks out most curious texts of Scripture, he speaks of "the two milch kine that were to carry the ark of God into another country and leave their calves behind them." Poor cows, poor Bunyan! Such is the mind of this extraordinary man.

With characteristic diligence Bunyan set to work in prison making shoe laces, and so earned a living for his family. His imprisonment lasted for nearly twelve years; but he saw his family frequently, and was for some time a regular preacher in the

Baptist church in Bedford. Occasionally he even went about late at night, holding the proscribed meetings and increasing his hold upon the common people. The best result of this imprisonment was that it gave Bunyan long hours for the working of his peculiar mind and for study of his two only books, the King James Bible and Foxe's *Book of Martyrs*. The result of his study and meditation was *The Pilgrim's Progress,* which was probably written in prison, but which for some reason he did not publish till long after his release.

The years which followed are the most interesting part of Bunyan's strange career. The publication of *Pilgrim's Progress* in 1678 made him the most popular writer, as he was already the most popular preacher, in England. Books, tracts, sermons, nearly sixty works in all, came from his pen; and when one remembers his ignorance, his painfully slow writing, and his activity as an itinerant preacher, one can only marvel. His evangelistic journeys carried him often as far as London, and wherever he went crowds thronged to hear him. Scholars, bishops, statesmen went in secret to listen among the laborers, and came away wondering and silent. At Southwark the largest building could not contain the multitude of his hearers; and when he preached in London, thousands would gather in the cold dusk of the winter morning, before work began, and listen until he had made an end of speaking. "Bishop Bunyan" he was soon called on account of his missionary journeys and his enormous influence.

What we most admire in the midst of all this activity is his perfect mental balance, his charity and humor in the strife of many sects. He was badgered for years by petty enemies, and he arouses our enthusiasm by his tolerance, his self-control, and especially by his sincerity. To the very end he retained that simple modesty which no success could spoil. Once when he had preached with unusual power some of his friends waited after the service to congratulate him, telling him what a "sweet sermon" he had delivered. "Aye," said Bunyan, "you need not remind me; the devil told me that before I was out of the pulpit."

For sixteen years this wonderful activity continued without interruption. Then, one day when riding through a cold storm on a labor of love, to reconcile a stubborn man with his own stubborn son, he caught a severe cold and appeared, ill and suffering but rejoicing in his success, at the house of a friend in Reading. He died there a few days later, and was laid away in Bunhill Fields burial ground, London, which has been ever since a *campo santo* to the faithful.

Works of Bunyan. The world's literature has three great allegories: Spenser's *The Faerie Queene,* Dante's *Divina Commedia,* and Bunyan's *Pilgrim's Progress.* The first appeals to poets, the second to scholars, the third to people of every age and condition. Here is a brief outline of the famous work:

"As I walked through the wilderness of this world I lighted on a certain place where was a den [Bedford jail] and laid me down in that place to sleep; and, as I slept, I dreamed a dream." So the story begins. He sees a man called Christian setting out with a book in his hand and a great load on his back from the city of Destruction. Christian has two objects – to get rid of his burden, which holds the sins and fears of his life, and to make his way to the Holy City. At the outset Evangelist finds him weeping because he knows not where to go, and points him to a wicket gate on a hill far away. As Christian goes forward his neighbors, friends, wife and children call to him to come back; but he puts his fingers in his ears, crying out, "Life, life, eternal life," and so rushes across the plain.

Then begins a journey in ten stages, which is a vivid picture of the difficulties and triumphs of the Christian life, Every trial, every difficulty, every experience of joy or sorrow, peace or temptation, is put into the form and discourse of a living character. Other allegorists write in poetry and their characters are shadowy and unreal; but Bunyan speaks in terse, idiomatic prose, and his characters are living men and women. There are Mr. Worldly Wiseman, a self-satisfied and dogmatic kind of man, youthful Ignorance, sweet Piety, courteous Demas, garrulous Talkative, honest Faithful, and a score of others, who are not at all the bloodless creatures of the romance novels but men real enough to stop you on the road and to hold your attention. Scene after scene follows, in which are pictured many of our own spiritual experiences. There is the Slough of Despond into which we all have fallen, out of which Pliable scrambles on the hither side and goes back grumbling, but through which Christian struggles mightily till Helpful stretches him a hand and drags him out on solid ground and bids him go on his way. Then come Interpreter's house, the Palace Beautiful, the Lions in the way, the Valley of Humiliation, the hard fight with the demon Appolyon, the more terrible Valley of the Shadow, Vanity Fair, and the trial of Faithful. The latter is condemned to death by a jury made up of Mr. Blindman, Mr. Nogood, Mr. Heady, Mr. Liveloose, Mr. Hatelight, and others of their kind to whom questions of justice are committed by the jury system. Most famous is Doubting Castle, where Christian and Hopeful are thrown into a dungeon by Giant Despair. And then at last the Delectable Mountains of Youth, the deep river that Christian must cross, and the city of All Delight and the glorious company of angels that come singing down the streets. At the very end, when in sight of the city and while he can hear the welcome with which Christian is greeted, Ignorance is snatched away to go to his own place; and Bunyan quaintly observes, "Then I saw that there was a way to hell even from the gates of heaven as well as from the city of Destruction. So I awoke, and behold it was a dream!"

Such, in brief, is the story, the great epic of a Puritan's individual experience in a rough world, just as *Paradise Lost* was the epic of mankind as dreamed by the great Puritan who had "fallen asleep over his Bible."

The chief fact which confronts the student of literature as he pauses before this great allegory is that it has been translated into seventy-five languages and dialects, and has been read more than any other book save one in the English language.

As for the secret of its popularity, Taine says, "Next to the Bible, the book most widely read in England is the *Pilgrim's*

Progress... Protestantism is the doctrine of salvation by grace, and no writer has equaled Bunyan in making this doctrine understood." And this opinion is echoed by the majority of our literary historians. It is perhaps sufficient answer to quote the simple fact that *Pilgrim's Progress* is not exclusively a Protestant study; it appeals to Christians of every name. When it was translated into the languages of Catholic countries, like France and Portugal, only one or two incidents were omitted, and the story was almost as popular there as with English readers. The secret of its success is probably simple. It is, first of all, not a procession of shadows repeating the author's declamations, but a real story, the first extended story in our language. Our Puritan fathers may have read the story for religious instruction; but all classes of men have read it because they found in it a true personal experience told with strength, interest, humor – in a word, with all the qualities that such a story should possess. Young people have read it, first, for its intrinsic worth, because the dramatic interest of the story lured them on to the very end; and second, because it was their introduction to true allegory. The child with his imaginative mind – the man also who has preserved his simplicity – naturally personifies objects, and takes pleasure in giving them powers of thinking and speaking like himself. Bunyan was the first writer to appeal to this pleasant and natural inclination in a way that all could understand. Add to this the fact that *Pilgrim's Progress* was the only book having any story interest in the great majority of English and American homes for a full century, and we have found the real reason for its wide reading.

The Holy War, published in 1665, is the first important work of Bunyan. It is a prose *Paradise Lost* and would undoubtedly be known as a remarkable allegory were it not overshadowed by its great rival. *Grace Abounding to the Chief of Sinners*, published in 1666, twelve years before *Pilgrim's Progress*, is the work from which we obtain the clearest insight into Bunyan's remarkable life, and to a man with historical or antiquarian tastes it is still excellent reading. In 1682 appeared *The Life and Death of Mr. Badman*, a realistic character study which is a precursor of the modern novel; and in 1684 the second part of *Pilgrim's Progress,* showing the journey of Christiana and her children to the city of All Delight. Besides these Bunyan published a multitude of treatises and sermons, all in the same style – direct, simple, convincing, expressing every thought and emotion perfectly in words that even a child can understand. Many of these are masterpieces, admired by workingmen and scholars alike for their thought and expression. Take, for instance, *The Heavenly Footman*; put it side by side with the best work of master writers and the resemblance in style is startling. It is difficult to realize that one work came from an ignorant tinker and the other from a great scholar, both engaged in the same general work. As Bunyan's favorite book was the Bible, we have here a suggestion of its influence in Puritan literature in general. John Bunyan was truly a trophy of God's grace, for his life is an enduring testimony of the transforming power of the Christian faith.

JOHN BUNYAN

The Assurance of Salvation

Watered-down doctrines are preached today,
By those who are leading thirsty souls astray;
Many today given the assurance of salvation
Are still lost in sin – their soul in damnation.

Repentance true brings life anew
Through faith in Jesus Christ alone –
The work of salvation, the Holy Spirit must bring,
And this He will do – "eternal security," we shall sing!

It may take a day or a month or a year,
But assurance will come, please do not fear;
Christian workers are wrong if assurance *they* give –
For only the Godhead knows if a soul really lives.

Let us preach the Holy Scriptures –
May the Word be carefully read;
God will not give assurance
To one whose heart is dead.

The Puritan Age

In its broadest sense the Puritan movement in England may be regarded as a second and greater Renaissance, a rebirth of the moral nature of man following the intellectual awakening of Europe in the fifteenth and sixteenth centuries. In Italy, whose influence had been uppermost in Elizabethan literature, the Renaissance had been essentially pagan and sensuous. It had hardly touched the moral nature of man, and it brought little relief from the despotism of rulers. One can hardly read the horrible records of the Medici or the Borgias, or the political observations of Machiavelli, without marveling at the moral and political degradation of a cultured nation. In the North, particularly among the German and English people, the Renaissance was accompanied by a moral awakening, and it is precisely that awakening in England, "that greatest moral and political reform which ever swept over a nation in the short space of half a century," which is meant by the Puritan movement. We shall understand it better if we remember that it had two chief objects: the first was personal righteousness; the second was civil and religious liberty. In other words, it aimed to make men honest and to make them free.

Such a movement should be cleared of all the misconceptions which have clung to it since the Restoration, when the very name of Puritan was made ridiculous by the jeers of the gay courtiers of Charles II. Though the spirit of the movement was profoundly religious, the Puritans were not a religious sect; neither was the Puritan a narrow-minded and gloomy dogmatist, as he is often pictured even in the modern history books. Famous Englishmen such as Pym, Hampden, Eliot and Milton were Puritans; and in the long struggle for human liberty there are few names more honored by freemen everywhere. Oliver Cromwell and Thomas Hooker were Puritans; yet Cromwell stood like a rock for religious tolerance; and Thomas Hooker, in Connecticut, gave to the world the first written constitution, in which freemen, before electing their officers, laid down the strict limits of the offices to which they were elected. That is a Puritan document, and it marks one of the greatest achievements in the history of government.

OLIVER CROMWELL.

From a religious view point Puritanism included all shades of belief. The name was first given to those who advocated certain changes in the form of worship of the reformed English Church under Elizabeth. However, as the ideal of liberty rose in men's minds from their study of the Scriptures, the king of England and his evil counselors began to openly oppose what they perceived to be a threat to their power base. The opposition quickly galvanized the followers of Puritan thought into a great national movement. It included English churchmen as well as militant Separatists, Calvinists, Covenanters, Catholic noblemen – all bound together in resistance to despotism in Church and State, and with a passion for liberty and righteousness such as the world has never since seen. Naturally such a movement had its extremes and excesses, and it is from a few zealots and fanatics that most of our misconceptions about the Puritans arise. Life was stern in those days, too stern perhaps, and the intensity of the struggle against despotism made men narrow and hard. In the triumph of Puritanism under Cromwell a few severe laws were passed, some simple pleasures were forbidden, and an austere standard of living was forced upon an unwilling people. So the criticism is made that the wild outbreak of immorality which followed the restoration of king Charles was partly due to the unnatural restrictions of the Puritan era. The criticism has some merit; but we must not forget the whole spirit of the movement. That the Puritan prohibited certain types of dancing and horse racing is of small consequence beside the fact that he fought for liberty and justice, that he overthrew despotism and made a man's life and property safe from the tyranny of rulers. A great river is not judged by the foam on its surface, and certain austere laws and doctrines which we have ridiculed are but froth on the surface of the mighty Puritan current that has flowed steadily, like a river of life, through English and American history since the Age of Elizabeth.

Changing Ideals. The political upheaval of the Puritan period (1620-1660) is summed up in the terrible struggle between the king and Parliament, which resulted in the death of king Charles at the block and the establishment of the Commonwealth under Cromwell. For centuries the English people had been wonderfully loyal to their sovereigns; but deeper than their loyalty to kings was the old Saxon love for personal liberty. At times, as in the days of Alfred and Elizabeth, the two ideals went hand in hand; but more often they were in open strife, and a final struggle for supremacy was inevitable. The crisis came when James I, who had received the right of royalty from an act of Parliament, began by the assumption of *divine right*, to ignore the Parliament which had created him. Of the civil war which followed in the reign of Charles I, and of the triumph of English freedom, it is unnecessary to write here. The blasphemy of a man's divine right to rule his fellow-men was ended. Modern England began with the charge of Cromwell's brigade of Puritans at the great battle of Naseby.

Religiously the age was one of even greater ferment than that which marked the beginning of the Reformation. A great ideal, the ideal of a national church, was pounding to pieces, like a ship in the breakers, and in the confusion of such an hour, the action of the various sects was like that of frantic passengers, each striving to save his possessions from the wreck. The Catholic church, as its name implies, has always held true to the ideal of a united church, a church which like the great Roman government of the early centuries, can bring the splendor and authority of Rome to bear upon the humblest village church to the farthest ends of the earth. For a time that mighty ideal dazzled the German and English reformers; but the possibility of a united Protestant church perished with Elizabeth. Then, instead of the world-wide church which was the ideal of Catholicism, came the ideal of a purely national Protestantism. This was the ideal of Laud and the reactionary bishops, no less than of the scholarly Richard Hooker, of the rugged Scotch Covenanters, and of the Puritans of Massachusetts Bay. It is intensely interesting to note that Puritans, turning to Scotland for help, entered into the solemn Covenant of 1643, establishing a national Presbyterianism, whose object was:

> To bring the churches of God in the three kingdoms to uniformity in religion and government, to preserve the rights of Parliament and the liberties of the Kingdom; . . . that we and our posterity may as brethren live in faith and love, and the Lord may delight to live in the midst of us.

In this famous Covenant we see the national, the ecclesiastical, and the personal dream of Puritanism, side by side in all their grandeur and simplicity.

Years passed, years of bitter struggle and heartache, before the impossibility of uniting the various Protestant sects was generally recognized. The ideal of a national church died hard, and to its death is due all the religious unrest of the period. Only as we remember the national ideal, and the struggle which it caused, can we understand the amazing life and work of Bunyan, or appreciate the heroic spirit of the American colonists who left home for a wilderness in order to give the new ideal of a free church in a free state its practical demonstration.

Many individuals in modern America, ignorant of the true contributions of the Puritans to western culture, continue to perpetuate the myth that Puritanism was the height of human folly. It is nothing less than ironic that the ignorant people just referred to are often the very ones who accuse the Puritans of being "narrow minded" and "non-intellectual." It is time for all twentieth century Americans, especially Christians, to throw off the unscholarly and prejudicial lies of humanistic historians who have perverted the true history of the Puritans.

JOHN MILTON

Choice Quotes from Shakespeare

Adversity

Sweet are the uses of adversity,
Which, like the toad, ugly and venomous,
Wears yet a precious jewel in his head;
And this our life exempt from public haunt,
Finds tongues in trees, books in the running brooks,
Sermons in stones, and good in everything.
Shakespeare, As You Like It

Reputation

Good name in man and woman, dear my lord,
Is the immediate jewel of their souls:
Who steals my purse steals trash; 'tis something, nothing;
'Twas mine, 'tis his, and has been slave to thousands;
But he that filches from me my good name
Robs me of that which not enriches him
And makes me poor indeed.
Shakespeare, Othello

Fear of Death

Cowards die many times before their deaths;
The valiant never taste of death but once.
Of all the wonders that I yet have heard,
It seems to me most strange that men should fear;
Seeing that death, a necessary end,
Will come when it will come.
Shakespeare, Julius Caesar

Washington's Farewell Address

Excerpt from Washington's farewell address to the people of the United States, given September 19, 1796.

Interwoven as is the love of liberty with every ligament of your hearts, no recommendation of mine is necessary to fortify or confirm the attachment. The unity of government which constitutes you one people, is also now dear to you. It is justly so, for it is a main pillar in the edifice of your real independence, the support of your tranquility at home, your peace abroad; of your safety, of your prosperity, of that very liberty which you so highly prize. But as it is easy to foresee that, from different causes and from different quarters, much pains will be taken, many artifices employed, to weaken in your minds the conviction of this truth, as this is the point in your political fortress against which the batteries of internal and external enemies will be most constantly and actively (though often covertly and insidiously) directed, it is of infinite importance that you should properly estimate the immense value of your national union to your collective and individual happiness, that you should cherish a cordial, habitual, and immovable attachment to it, accustoming yourselves to think and speak of it as of the palladium of your political safety and prosperity, watching for its preservation with jealous anxiety, discountenancing whatever may suggest even a suspicion that it can in any event be abandoned, and indignantly frowning upon the first dawning of every attempt to alienate any portion of our country from the rest, or to enfeeble the sacred ties which now link together the various parts.

Of all the dispositions and habits which lead to political prosperity, religion and morality are indispensable supports. In vain would that man claim the tribute of patriotism who should labor to subvert these great pillars of human happiness, these firmest props of the duties of men and citizens. The mere politician, equally with the pious man, ought to respect and to cherish them. A volume could not trace all their connections with private and public felicity. Let it simply be asked, Where is the security for property, for reputation, for life, if the sense of religious obligation desert the oaths, which are the instruments of investigation in courts of justice? And let us with caution indulge the supposition that morality can be maintained without religion. Whatever may be conceded to the influence of refined education on minds of peculiar structure, reason and experience both forbid us to expect that national morality can prevail in exclusion of religious principle.

Promote, then as an object of primary importance, institutions for the general diffusion of knowledge. In proportion as the structure of a government gives force to public opinion, it is essential that public opinion should be enlightened by religious principles.

The Bold Sound of the Trumpet

This address, by Wayne C. Sedlak, discusses the importance of learning how to pray imprecatory prayers. Rev. Sedlak is the pastor of the Covenant Reformed Church of Brookfield, Wisconsin.

Just a few years ago, a plane crashed in southern Africa. On board was the Marxist dictator of Mozambique, Samora Machel. To Christians throughout southern Africa, his name was synonymous with the burning of thousands of churches, as well as the slaughter of several hundred thousand people. His sworn objective was to eradicate Christian cultural influence. In this regard, he was highly successful. Machel now sought to **"export"** his murderous program to Malawi, a small pro-Christian country. He met with other Marxist leaders in the region to plan the invasion. However, on the night of his return trip, numerous churches began to pray, **"imprecatorily"** against him according to the pattern set forth in the Psalms (Ps. 7:9-13,17). At the very time prayers were being lifted up to God, Machel's plane was becoming engulfed in what many remember as the most violent thunderstorm they had ever experienced. As a result, Machel and his henchmen met violent deaths, his plans were fully exposed, Malawi was spared and to this day is a free country.

Imprecation is an instrument which God uses to uphold righteousness. Imprecation is defined as that act of imploring God to execute His righteous indignation against persecutors and other malicious transgressors.

Imprecation has a long history behind it. Men of faith such as Moses, Joshua, Samuel, David, the Apostle Paul and our Lord Jesus, used imprecation by way of pronouncements or prayer. However, it must be noted that the Lord does not honor just any prayer His people may raise—especially of this type. Psalm 66 states: *"If I regard iniquity in my heart the Lord will not hear me"*

(Ps. 66:18). Our walk with the Lord must be one of integrity of spirit without the base alloy of lawless compromise. For example, before asking the Lord to judge the rage of his persecutors, David was conscious that if he has been unjust toward others, then God would allow him to be dishonored and oppressed by his persecutors (Ps. 7:5).

In other words, the Lord only honors the imprecations of believers of upright character. One wonders if the church in America today can possibly lift up effectual prayer in defense of righteousness in light of its own sins of backbiting, tale-bearing, harshness and defrauding of one another across the length and breadth of the ecclesiastical landscape of this nation (I Thess. 4:6-12).

It is clear from Scripture that imprecation is not the plaything of someone's petty vengeance. Imprecation is exclusively a function of "**interposition**." Interposition is that mandate of righteous ethic that "**stands in the gap**" between the malice of the oppressor and his intended victim. Such prayer is lifted up by those who are at risk *because they are exercising Christian love by "standing in the gap"*. Thus, David called unto God (Ps. 59:3-5) to chastise such terrible persecutors. Nehemiah prayed for the confusion of the conspiracy of Sanballet and Tobiah and was answered marvelously (Neh. 6:12-16).

Paul was opposed by Elymas the sorcerer and counselor of state as he was proclaiming Christ's righteousness to the Roman governor. To thwart such opposition, Paul, *"being filled with the Holy Spirit,"* imprecated him (Acts 13:8-12). The result was his blinding by the Lord. In all of these cases, righteousness was at risk, and those defending it faced powerful opposition. It was for this reason that Samora Machel was cast down. Likewise many of us in Wisconsin believe that God answered our imprecatory prayers aimed specifically against abortionists over the past eight months. Within that period of time, six doctors quit murdering unborn babies or died. Some call it happenstance. We believe otherwise, and we trust God will continue to answer such prayers.

When God is pleased to answer such prayers, He gives

specific reasons in His Word. The psalmist lists one such reason: *"God shall shoot at them with an arrow, suddenly shall they be wounded...* ***and all men shall fear and shall declare the work of God; for they shall wisely consider His deeds"*** (Ps. 64:7,9). This was precisely the result Paul's imprecation had upon the Roman governor: *"Then the deputy, when he saw what was done, believed, being astonished..."*

Imagine! A Roman magistrate believed on the Lord, being astonished at God's powerful judgment. What restraint and awe could be the churches' inheritance if magistrates knew that on a given Sunday all the pulpits would cry out against their evils and implore God's judgment for their oppression, corruptions and deceptions.

However, if this is done, we must have the wisdom to do so biblically:

1. Individuals and groups must be named according to their malice and persecutions (Neh. 6:14). The reason for this is simple. Such prayer functions as judicial indictment, charging them publicly. God then assesses sentence publicly.

2. We must pray that they fall into the pit they have dug for others (Ps. 9:16; 35:7-8). This point alone is emphasized in Scripture, because it links their malice publicly to God's righteous sentence against them.

3. We must pray that their declarations (public speeches, laws, legal proceedings, publications, etc.) come back to haunt them (Ps. 64:7-8). In a sense, we are praying that they judge themselves by their own words.

4. We pray that their actions against the righteous be confounded. This, of course, hedges the upright but also makes clear whose side the Lord has chosen (Ps. 13).

5. Knowing that they secretly **"lie in wait,"** we pray that they be exposed for their secret agenda so that even their

friends refuse to associate with them.

6. We must pray that God will "**divide their tongues**," i.e., that their united counsels will become a veritable confusion – rife with divisions and dissension among their own ranks (Ps. 65:8). Such divided counsel will inevitability result in frustrations (theirs, not ours, for once), despair and, best of all, *failure.*

7. We must pray that the hearts of the upright be encouraged. Over the past twelve years, I have seen many Christians despair of having any further impact – and quietly give up. *Righteous imprecation is the bold sound of the trumpet* and, when answered, emboldens heroic interposition to advance against the kingdom of darkness.

In fact, the reason that 90 out of 150 Psalms (60%) include imprecations of varying types and degrees is to encourage God's people in the fight against powerful adversaries. In August 1989, this writer had the unique experience of seeing beleaguered South African Christians encouraged when God struck down the notorious Marxist, Oliver Tambo, in answer to our prayers there (lifted up that very day).

8. Finally, imprecation in prayer must be coupled with imprecation in action. Christ specifically commanded imprecatory demonstration against evildoers (Mark 6:11). The Lord even commands some good deeds as a function of imprecation (Rom. 12:20). Church courts are also designed to call forth such exacting judgment and accountability when repentance is not forthcoming (Matthew 18:17; II Thess. 3:10-14). Such directives, and many, many more, are provided in detail throughout the Scriptures.

Let us, therefore, implore God's mighty hand through prayer and act accordingly that we might be the instruments of righteous victory in spirit and in truth.

Mr. Kleinhorst's Auction

The crowd pressed closer to the auctioneer, straining to hear the item being bid on.

Mary and William stretched tall on their tiptoes to see what the auctioneer was holding up. From atop Dad's shoulders Melody saw it first. It looked like a big letter **U**.

"What is it, Daddy?" Melody asked.

Dad twisted his head to see clearly. The auctioneer held it up in his right hand, a microphone in the other.

"Here we have a brass horseshoe, a lucky horseshoe. Yep! Mr. Kleinhorst's lucky horseshoe, "the auctioneer cried in his singsong voice.

From across the crowd a man motioned to the auctioneer.

"I see that hand," the auctioneer said. "Four dollars. Four dollars. Five dollars. Okay. Six dollars. Six dollars. Who'll give six dollars? Anybody? Anybody? Six dollars. Who'll give me six dollars? I see that hand. Seven dollars. Seven dollars. Seven dollars. Who'll give me seven dollars? Anybody? Seven dollars for Mr. Kleinhorst's lucky horseshoe. Seven dollars. Seven dollars. Seven dollars. No? Six-fifty. Six-fifty. Six-fifty." The voice droned on. "Sold for six dollars to the man in the blue coat. What's your number, mister?"

The man in the blue coat held up a card with the number 52 on it.

"Okay, next we have an antique pitchfork. Looks like it's pitched quite a bit of hay in its day. You don't see them like this anymore, folks..." the auctioneer's voice went on.

MR. KLEINHORST'S AUCTION

"Let's go, you guys," Dad said. "We already have what we came for." Dad pointed to the china teapot they had chosen for Mom's birthday present. "Remember," he said. "It's a surprise."

"No problem, Dad," Mary stated clearly.

William and Mary nodded their heads vigorously.

They made their way through the crowd. Gingerly William carried the teapot to the car.

"What was that about the lucky letter U?" Melody asked.

"Oh," Dad said as he shrugged his shoulders. "Some people believe in doing things like hanging a horseshoe in a doorway or carrying a rabbit's foot in their pocket to supposedly bring good luck. Sometimes they may touch the horseshoe or rub the rabbit's foot or even talk to those things and recite something. They think these things will bring them good luck in the future."

"That sounds weird," Mary observed.

"Well," Dad said. "It is weird. Putting your trust in anything other than the God who made heaven and earth is wrong. Putting a horseshoe above a doorway and reciting things to it is what the Bible means when it talks about worshiping graven images."

"A graven image?" William thought about that for awhile.

"You mean," Mary said, "like the second commandment? Thou shalt not make unto thee any graven image..."

"Someone must have been paying attention during the Bible lesson," Dad commented. "Maybe not everyone who puts up a lucky horseshoe realizes that's what they are doing, but that doesn't excuse them. The Bible says it very plainly."

"What about the man who bought Mr. Kleinhorst's lucky horseshoe?"

"Well, if he puts it up in the house, recites things to it and believes it is going to bring him good luck, he is wrong."

"That's too bad," Mary said.

"I don't understand why everybody doesn't follow God's rules. They are pretty easy to understand," Melody said.

"Well," Dad said. "They are easy to understand when a person has been given the eyes to see God's truth – but the fact is we all struggle with spiritual blindness and sin. The only reason why any of us can know and obey God's commands is because God has freely given the gift of understanding. Let's pray that the Lord would open the spiritual eyes of the man who is trying to buy good luck from an auctioneer."

The New Year

Ring out, wild bells, to the wild sky,
   The flying cloud, the frosty light;
   The year is dying in the night;
Ring out, wild bells, and let them die.

Ring out the old, ring in the new;
   Ring, happy bells, across the snow;
   The year is going, let him go;
Ring out the false, ring in the true.

Ring out the grief that saps the mind
   For those that here we see no more;
   Ring out the feud of rich and poor;
Ring in redress to all mankind.

Ring out a slowly dying cause,
   And ancient forms of party strife;
   Ring in the nobler modes of life,
With sweeter manners, purer laws.

Ring out the want, the care, the sin,
   The faithless coldness of the times;
   Ring out, ring out my mournful rhymes,
But ring the fuller minstrel in.

Ring out false pride in place and blood,
   The civic slander and the spite;
   Ring in the love of truth and right;
Ring in the common love of good.

Ring out old shapes of foul disease;
   Ring out the narrowing lust of gold;
   Ring out the thousand wars of old;
Ring in the thousand years of peace.

STUDYING CHRISTIAN LITERATURE

Ring in the valiant man and free,
    The larger heart, the kindlier hand;
    Ring out the darkness of the land;
Ring in the Christ that is to be.

America's Closet Christians

*"Herein is my Father glorified, that you bear much fruit;
so shall you be My disciples."*
(John 15:8)

It has been reported that there are about 95 million Americans who claim to be "born again." Maybe that's high. Maybe not.

Based on the response to a 1987 Gallup Poll, 70% of American adults said that they belonged to a church. If so, that would figure out to 121 million persons. Of those responding to the survey, 53% said religion was very important to their lives. That would be about 92 million.

Granted, not all churches in America are Christian. And, not all religions in the land are Christ-centered. But it is reasonable to assume that the predominant faith in the nation is Christian (the U.S. Statistical Abstract reported that in 1990 "Christian church adherents" totalled 111.7 million, about 49.3% of the population).

Let's be very conservative. Let's say there are about 25 million "born-again" Christians in the land. Twenty five million! That's more than enough to change the nation. In fact, ten million – even five million – active, Christ-centered, Bible-based, praying, "on fire" Christians could have a major impact on this nation.

IF...

...if those five million took a stand for Jesus – and pressed for restoration of Bible-based standards in the American society. Really worked toward that goal. Not just with occasional rallies. Not just in annual conventions. Not just in seminars and workshops. But studying day-after-day, in the persistent, consistent pursuit and application of a total Christian world and life view.

If we should start to live – really live and apply – our Christian faith; if we would study and pray and apply the full dimensions of God's Word; if we would make our faith manifest not only in words but also in good works...

...if, as our Savior commands, we would let our light – *His light* – shine through our lives and our deeds, we could turn our nation around. We could turn it back to God. Jesus made it clear in Matthew 4:4 that He has only *one* standard for truth and law, and it is binding upon *all* men. "It is written, Man shall not live by bread alone, but by every word that proceedeth out of the mouth of God."

* * *

God's people are responsible for the government of the nation. God assures us of that. He does. Check the alternatives. Read Deut. 11:26-28. Or, II Chron. 7:14 and II Chron. 7:19, for starters.

God expects us to work as hard to preserve and maintain liberty under God as our founding fathers did to establish it in the first place. Are we as Christians in this republic doing that? Today? Are we assuming, fulfilling, our role in the governance of this nation as we should?

Well, look at some numbers.

According to a *New York Times/NBC* voting-pattern study, in 1984 only 15 million Christians – just about 50 percent of those Christians registered to vote – bothered to go to the polls. And, according to Rev. Tim LaHaye of *Family Life Seminars*, in 1986 only 42.5 percent of Christians eligible to vote bothered to do so. The recent voting records from the 1992 election reveal that little has changed in this regard.

Maybe we have only ourselves to blame for the growing gap between God and Government. Maybe, by sins of omission, we are allowing the "active others" who know not the Lord to take over the affairs of government and the souls of men.

We are losing by default the Christian role and influence in what Rev. Richard John Neuhaus calls "the public square." Thus, wrote Neuhaus, "We exclude from public discourse precisely the moral visions that are held by the great majority of the American people."

The immoral minority is taking advantage of the Christians' sloth. They are active; they are engaged in the battle. And, because they are, they are preempting the field and setting the nation's course and agenda.

Take the sodomites, for example. Not too long ago they came out of their closets. Now, they are exerting an increasing influence on our institutions – on government (and politics), academia, the "news" media, and even some churches. They have an impact far beyond their numbers; and impact that bodes ill for the nation.

If a few hundred thousand sodomites – maybe a million at most – can do this to the nation, what could ten, or even five, million Biblical Christians accomplish – if they stopped hiding their light under a bushel. If they came out of the closet?

* * *

Consider a Closet:

A closet is for hiding. For getting things out of sight. For storing things that aren't in use. Things that are out of style. Things that are embarrassing. Things that you don't want around when company comes calling.

A closet is not for Christians (except for prayer – Matthew 6:6)

Jesus said: "You are the light of the world." (Matthew 5:14).

The "light of the world" does not shine forth when it is shut up in a closet.

Jesus said: "Neither do men light a candle and put it under a bushel, but on a candlestick; and it gives light unto all who are in the house" (Matthew 5:15).

In fact, He urged: "Let your light so shine before men that they may see your good works, and glorify your Father which is in heaven" (Matthew 5:16).

What could be more explicit? More direct?

We are not to be "closet Christians"! Not if we have truly made Jesus our Savior and our King.

Our Savior prayed, "As Thou has sent Me into the world, even so have I sent them into the world" (John 17:18). He did not pray that The Father take His own out of the world; his prayer was that God would protect them from evil.

Jude, servant of Christ and brother of James, urged the Christians of his day: "Contend for the faith!" (Jude 2). How much contending can we do sitting in a closet?

And, the Apostle Paul wrote to Titus: Christ rescued us from iniquity to purify unto Himself "a special people zealous of good works" (Titus 2:14).

What good works can we do if we confine our faith to a closet? We can pray, yes. But, we are to be both doers of His word and not hearers only. (James 1:22).

* * *

Faith does have – will have, must have – consequences!

IF...

...if it is a "go-forth" faith, a "get-up-and-go" faith, a "change-the-world" faith.

Remember the two on the road to Emmaus? Not long after our Lord's burial and resurrection? How Jesus walked with them and talked with them and supped with them? And when their eyes were opened and they knew Him? "Did not our hearts burn within us, while He talked with us by the way, and while He opened to us the scriptures?" (Luke 24:32).

When we "know" Jesus, when our eyes are opened to His glory, to His truth, to His word and His love, do not our hearts burn within us? How can anyone having had such a life-changing, all-consuming experience be a closet Christian?

Go! said our Lord, our Master. **Go!** Make disciples of all the nations. Teach them to obey all that I have taught you. And I will be with you, alway!

To claim to be a Christian without following Christ, without obeying His commandments, is to take His name in vain. To profess to love Christ while being a "closet Christian" is to deny The Lord!

The All-Seeing God

Almighty God, thy piercing eye
   Strikes through the shades of night;
And our most secret actions lie
   All open to thy sight.

There's not a sin we commit,
   Nor wicked word we say,
But in thy dreadful book 'tis writ,
   Against the judgment day.

And must the crimes that I have done
   Be read and published there;
Be all exposed before the sun,
   While men and angels hear?

Lord, at thy foot ashamed I lie;
   Upward I dare not look;
Pardon my sins before I die,
   And blot them from thy book.

Remember all the dying pains
   That my Redeemer felt,
And let his blood wash out my stains,
   And answer for my guilt.

Oh may I now for ever fear
   To indulge a sinful thought;
Since the great God can see and hear,
   And writes down every fault.

No Other Gods

"I can't believe it," Mary squealed excitedly. "A cousin! I've never had a cousin before!" Mary danced happily around the kitchen table as she distributed napkins to each place setting.

"What's a cousin?" Melody asked, looking up from the dishwasher where she was unloading silverware.

"A cousin," William said matter-of-factly, "is the offspring of one of our aunts or uncles."

"What's an offspring?" Melody asked.

"A child," Mary said, delighted that she could add something to the conversation.

"I wonder when we'll see her," William said aloud.

The children's chores were disturbed when a burst of cold air rushed in as their father hurried inside. He wore a long face.

"When can we go to the hospital to see our cousin?" Mary demanded.

Dad shook his head from side to side. "I don't know, sweetheart," he said. Sadly he sat down in a kitchen chair and pulled his gloves from his hands.

"What is it?" Mom asked as she hurried to the table.

"It's the baby," Dad said. "It has some breathing problems. It's in the neonatal intensive care unit."

"What's a neonatal?" William asked.

NO OTHER GODS

"A neonatal intensive care unit is a place where brand new babies with problems stay. There are all kinds of machines hooked up to the baby."

"Oh, no," Mom moaned.

"Yes," Dad said. "All Uncle Bob and Aunt Lillie can say is that the doctors will do something. They don't seem to understand that the baby is in God's hands or that God is the author of life. They are putting all their faith in the doctors."

"But, Dad," William said. "God tells us in the Bible: 'Thou shalt have no other gods before me'."

"Yes," Dad agreed. "That is the first commandment God gave Moses. How easy it is to forget sometimes! We should trust in God first. Sometimes God will use doctors, but we should always trust in God first."

"We should pray for them and the baby," Mom suggested gently.

"Good idea," Dad said. "Let's gather the whole family together at the table and lift up our cousins, all of them, before the throne of grace. It's time to assemble at the family altar."

A few moments later, everyone gathered around the kitchen table and bowed their heads.

155

The Priority of Education

"We are putting what we earn into our children's minds, instead of into houses and clothes," said little Mrs. Findley as she smoothed the hair of small Ben, who leaned against her knee. "We think it a better investment."

"My husband agrees with me regarding the priority of education. He didn't at first. He said we couldn't educate the children because we were poor, but now he is as ambitious for them as I am."

"Tell me about it," I said, and this is the story she told me as we sat on the shady porch one pleasant afternoon.

"When I was a child we lived back in the woods, and father was poor. My own mother was dead, and while my stepmother did the best she could for me, there were smaller children to take care of and always so much to do. Father wanted me to go to school, but when I was needed at home to help, he could never see any other way but that I must stay and work. Then, too, he hadn't money to buy my school books.

"When I was twelve years old, my brother and I chopped a load of wood, hauled it to town, and sold it for money to buy a grammar and history book. We hacked the wood up some, but we got it into sticks and we got the books.

"It was that way when I needed the first book for my children, Glen and Joette; there was no money to buy the book, so I took in a washing and got the money. I've always been ashamed to take in laundry and do that type of work. It was not well done, because I was in such poor health that I had to hold myself up by the tub while I scrubbed; but that book just had to come and it came.

"You see, after I married, we lived in Joplin, Missouri and my husband worked in the mines. Jess had been earning $4.50 a day, but it took it all to live; so when we came back to the hills, we had only our bare hands.

Starting Home Education

"Well, I started the children to work in their new book, and every day we had lessons. I taught them first a word, then the letters in it; and they had them ready for use in another word. When they learned a name, I showed them the object; when they learned an action word, we acted it. For instance, when they read the word 'jump,' we jumped; and how they did enjoy saying their lessons to daddy in the evening, especially when he'd let them beat him.

"When Glen was seven years old and Joette six, I started them to school ready for the fourth grade work. The superintendent did not think my children could handle fourth grade and insisted that they begin in the third grade; but after only one day there, they were promoted to the fourth.

"The first year they went to school only two months, then finished their grades at home. The next year they went two months and finished at home. The following year they went four months and were obliged to stop because of sickness, but again they finished the grades at home. Since then they have gone regularly, and at thirteen and fourteen years old have finished the first year in high school and the fifth set in bookkeeping.

"Violet has been more difficult to teach than the others, because she likes to sew and play with her dolls better than to study. People said she was stupid and that I never would be able to push her as I had the others; but she was only different and just as smart, if not smarter. She just would not keep her mind on her books until she found she must and would be punished if she didn't. I know what her talent is, but she has to have her books, too; and she will sew all the better for having 'book learning.'

"Besides, I had made up my mind that through my children

I would raise the standard of the family. It couldn't be bettered morally except through further Bible study and prayer but it could be raised educationally; and so Violet, as well as the rest, must study her books. I knew her well and gave her special attention so she is going right along with the others.

I believe it would be much better for everyone if children were given their start in education at home. No one understands a child as well as his mother, and children are so different that they need individual training and study. A teacher with a roomful of pupils cannot do this. At home, too, they are in their mother's care. She can keep them from learning immoral things from other children. At home the expense is much less, for in school there are a great many expenses that are difficult for poor people to meet.

"The children are well started in getting their education. None of the family has ever graduated from high school, but my children will, and some of them will go to college too.

"Jess says I aim too high, but I tell him I'll shoot straight; for when a thing has to be done, it's done And if people say the Jess Findley family were poor, they'll say, too, that the children were well educated; for that is where we are putting our life's work – into their heads.

"We are doing something worthwhile, for in raising the standard of our children's lives we are raising the standard of four homes of the future, and our work goes on and on, raising the moral and educational standard of the community and of future generations."

When Mrs. Findley had finished her story, I mentally took note of one thought which has escaped so many of us. It was not the old story of an education always being within the grasp of those who really seek it; but that in raising the standard of the Findley home, the standard of four homes of the future had been elevated to the point which we like to think of as a representative "American Home." Here, mother love had combined with the vision of future usefulness in the service of God, resulting in the finest service to which any parent can aspire.

Memories of Home

Out in the meadow, I picked a wild sunflower, and as I looked into its golden heart, such a wave of homesickness came over me that I almost wept. I wanted Mother, with her gentle voice and quiet firmness; I longed to hear Father's jolly songs and to see his twinkling blue eyes; I was lonesome for the sister with whom I used to play in the meadow picking daisies and wild sunflowers.

Across the years, the old home and its love called to me, and memories of sweet words of counsel came flooding back. I realize that all my life the teachings of those early days have influenced me, and the example set by Father and Mother has been something I have tried to follow, with failures here and there, with rebellion at times; but always coming back to it as the compass needle to the star.

So much depends upon the homemakers. I sometimes wonder if they are so busy now with other things that they are forgetting the importance of this special work. Especially did I wonder when reading recently that there were a great many child suicides in the United States during the last year. Not long ago we had never heard of such a thing in our own country, and I am sure that there must be something wrong with the home of a child who commits suicide.

Because of their importance, we must not neglect our homes in the rapid changes of the present day. For when tests of character come in later years, strength to the good will not come from the modern improvements or amusements few may have enjoyed but from the quiet moments and the "still small voices" of the old home.

Nothing even can take the place of this early home influence; and as it does not depend upon externals, it may be the

STUDYING CHRISTIAN LITERATURE

possession of the poor as well as of the rich, a heritage from all fathers and mothers to their children.

The real things of life that are the common possession of us all are of the greatest value – worth far more than automobiles or radios, more than lands or money – and our whole store of these wonderful riches may be revealed to us through such a common, beautiful thing as a wild sunflower.

The best inheritance that any parents can leave for their children is the memory of a loving Christian home.

The Law of Sowing and Reaping

Some small boys went into my neighbor's yard this spring and with slingshots killed the wild birds that were nesting there. Only the other day, I read in my daily paper of several murders committed by a nineteen-year-old boy.

At once there was formed a connection in my mind between the two crimes, for both were crimes of the same kind, though perhaps in differing degree – the breaking of laws and the taking of life cruelly.

For the cruel child to become a hard-hearted boy and then a brutal man is only stepping along the road on which he has started. A child allowed to disobey without punishment is not likely to have much respect for law as he grows older. Not that every child who kills birds becomes a murderer nor that everyone who is not taught to obey goes to prison.

The Bible says, "Train up a child in the way he should go: and when he is old, he will not depart from it." (Proverbs 22:6) The opposite is also true, and if a child is started in the way he should not go, he will go at least some way along that road as he grows older. It will always be more difficult for him to travel the right way even if he finds it.

The first laws with which children come in contact are the commands of their parents. Few fathers and mothers are wise in giving these, for we are all so busy and thoughtless. But I am sure we will all agree that these laws of ours should be as wise and as few as possible, and, once given, children should be made to obey or shown that to disobey brings punishment. Thus they will learn the lesson every good citizen and every good man and woman learns sooner or later – that breaking a law brings suffering.

If we break a law of nature, we are punished physically; when we disobey God's law, we suffer spiritually, mentally and usually in our bodies also. Man's laws, being founded on the ten commandments, are really mankind's poor attempt at interpreting the laws of God, and for disobeying them there is a penalty. The commands we give our children should be our translation of these laws of God and man, founded on justice and the law of love, which is the Golden Rule.

And these things enter into such small deeds. Even insisting that children pick up and put away their playthings is teaching them order, the law of the universe, and helpfulness, the expression of love.

The responsibility for starting the child in the right way is the parents' – it cannot be delegated to the schools or to the state, for the little feet start on life's journey from the home.

The Good Shepherd

"He shall gather the lambs with His arm, and carry them in His bosom, and shall gently lead those that are with young."
Isaiah 40:11b.

Who is He of whom such gracious words are spoken? He is THE GOOD SHEPHERD. *Why* doth He carry the lambs in His bosom? Because *He hath a tender heart, and any weakness at once melts His heart.* The sighs, the ignorance, the feebleness of the little ones of His flock draw forth His compassion. *It is His office,* as a faithful High Priest, to consider the weak. Besides, *He purchased them with blood, they are His property:* He must and will care for *that* which cost Him so dear. Then He is *responsible for each lamb*, bound by covenant engagements not to lose one. Moreover, *they are all a part of His glory and reward.*

But how may we understand the expression, "He will *carry* them?" Sometimes He carries them by *not permitting them to endure much trial*. Providence deals tenderly with them. Often they are "carried" by being filled with *an unusual degree of love,* so that they bear up and stand fast. Though their knowledge may not be deep, they have great sweetness in what they do know. Frequently He "carries" them by giving them *a very simple faith*, which takes the promise just as it stands, and believingly runs with every trouble straight to Jesus. The simplicity of their faith gives them an unusual degree of confidence, which carries them above the world.

"He carries the lambs *in His bosom.*" Here is *boundless affection*. Would He put them in His bosom if He did not love them much? Here is *tender nearness*: so near are they, that they could not possibly be nearer. Here is *hallowed familiarity:* there are precious love-passages between Christ and His weak ones. Here is *perfect safety*: in His bosom who can hurt them? They must hurt the Shepherd first. Here is *perfect rest and sweetest comfort.* Surely we are not sufficiently sensible of the infinite tenderness of Jesus!

STUDYING CHRISTIAN LITERATURE

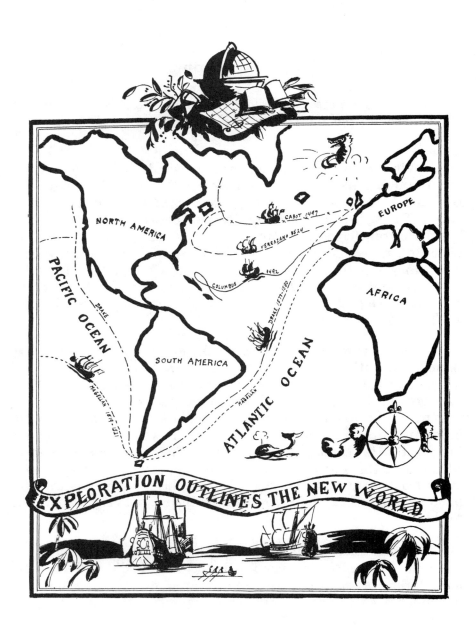

Queen Isabella's Resolve

Time--- January, 1492

Scene-Discussion of the proposed voyage of Christopher Columbus involving Queen Isabella of Spain, a trusted advisor named Don Gomez, and Columbus. They are discussing these issues in the private chamber of Queen Isabella located at the Royal Palace.

Characters

Queen Isabella   Don Gomez
           Christopher Columbus

Don Gomez. I have come, my queen, to speak with you regarding the plans of Columbus.

Isabella. And so, Don Gomez, it is your conclusion that we ought to dismiss the proposition of this worthy adventurer.

Don Gomez. His scheme, your majesty, seems to me fanciful in the extreme; but I am a plain, matter-of-fact man, and do not see visions and dreams like some.

Isabella. And yet Columbus has given us cogent reasons for believing that it is possible to reach the eastern coast of India by sailing in a westerly direction.

Don Gomez. Admitting that his theory is correct, namely, that the earth is a sphere, how would it be possible for him to return, if he once descended that sphere in the direction he proposes? Would not the coming back be all uphill? Could a ship accomplish it with even the most favorable wind?

Columbus. Will your majesty allow me to suggest that, if the earth is a sphere, the same laws of adhesion and motion must operate at every point on its surface; and the objection of Don Gomez would be quite as valid against our being able to return from crossing the Strait of Gibraltar.

Don Gomez. This gentleman, then, would have us believe the monstrous absurdity, that there are people on the earth who are our opposites, who walk with their heads down, like flies on the ceiling.

Columbus. But, your majesty, if there is a law of attraction which makes matter gravitate to the earth, and prevents it from flying off into space, may not this law operate at every point on the round earth's surface?

Isabella. Truly, it so seems to me; and I perceive nothing absurd in the notion that this earth is a globe floating or revolving in space.

Don Gomez. May it please your majesty, the ladies are privileged to give credence to many wild tales which we plain, simple men cannot admit. Every step I take confutes this visionary idea of the earth's rotundity. Would not the blood run into my head if I were standing upside down? Were I not fearful of offending your majesty, I would quote what the great Lactantius says.

Isabella. We are not vain of our science, Don Gomez; so let us have the quotation.

Don Gomez. "Is there anyone so foolish," he asks, "as to believe that there are people with their feet opposite to ours, that there is a part of the world in which all things are topsy-turvy, where the trees grow with their branches downward, and where it rains and snows up-ward?"

Columbus. I have already answered this objection. If there are people on the earth who are our opposites, it should be remembered that we are theirs also.

Don Gomez. Really, that is the very point wherein people with common sense, like myself, abide by the assurance of our own senses. We know that we are not walking with our heads downwards.

Isabella. To cut short the discussion, you think that the enterprise which the sailor from Genoa proposes is one unworthy of our serious consideration, and that his theory of an unknown shore to the westward of us is a fallacy?

Don Gomez. As a plain, matter-of-fact man, I must confess that I so regard it. Has your majesty ever seen an ambassador from this unknown coast?

Isabella. Don Gomez, do you believe in the existence of a world of spirits? Have you ever seen an ambassador from that unknown world?

Don Gomez. Certainly not. By faith we look forward to it.

Isabella. Even so by faith does Columbus look forward, far over the misty ocean, to an undiscovered shore.

Columbus. Your majesty is right; but let it be added that I have reasons, oh! most potent and resistless reasons, for the faith that is in me; the testimony of many navigators who have picked up articles that must have drifted from this distant coast; the nature of things admitting that the earth is round; the reports current among the people of one of the Northern nations, that many years ago their mariners had sailed many leagues westward till they reached a shore where the grape grew abundantly. These and other considerations have made it the fixed persuasion of my mind that there is a great discovery reserved for the man who will sail patiently westward, trusting in God's good providence, and turning not back till he has achieved his purpose.

Don Gomez. Then truly we should never hear of him again. Speculation! mere speculation, your majesty! When this gentleman can bring forward some solid facts that will induce us practical men to risk money in forwarding his enterprise, it will then be time enough for royalty to give it heed. Why, your majesty, the very boys in the streets point at their foreheads as he passes along.

Isabella. And so you bring forward the frivolity of boys, jeering at what they do not comprehend, as an argument why Isabella should not give heed to this great and glorious scheme? Ay, sir, though it should fail, still it has been urged in language so intelligent and convincing by this grave and earnest man, whom you think to under-value by calling him an adventurer, that I am resolved to test the "absurdity," as you style it, and that forthwith.

Don Gomez. Your majesty will excuse me if I remark, that I have from your royal consort himself the assurance, that the finances are so exhausted by the late wars that he cannot consent to advance the necessary funds for fitting out an expedition of the kind proposed.

Isabella. Be *mine,* then, the privilege! I have jewels by the pledging of which I can raise the amount required; and I have resolved that they shall be pledged to this enterprise without any more delay.

COLUMBUS. Your majesty shall not repent your heroic resolve. I will return, your majesty; be sure I will return, and lay at your feet such a jewel as befits a noble queen, an imperishable fame – a fame that shall couple with your memory the benedictions of millions yet unborn, in places yet unknown to civilized man. There is an uplifting assurance in my mind, a conviction that your majesty will live to bless the hour you came to this decision.

DON GOMEZ. A mere assumption! A plain, rational man, like myself, must take leave of your majesty, if my practical common sense is to be met and superseded by presumption. An ounce of fact, your majesty, is worth a ton of presumption.

ISABELLA. That depends altogether upon the source of the presumption, Don Gomez. If it comes from the Fountain of all truth, shall it not be good?

DON GOMEZ. I humbly take my leave of your majesty. It is obvious that you believe that this plan has been inspired by Almighty God and I cannot and will not try to argue against that. Good day, my lady.

Comprehension Questions

1. What objections did Don Gomez assert regarding the proposed voyage of Columbus?
2. Why did Columbus believe that he would return safely from his voyage?
3. How did Queen Isabella propose to raise the funds to help Columbus set sail?
4. How did Don Gomez react to the decision of the Queen to help finance the voyage of Columbus?

The King Of Love

"My Beloved put in His hand by the hole of the door, and my bowels were moved for Him." Solomon's Song 5:4

Knocking was not enough, for my heart was too full of sleep, too cold and ungrateful to arise and open the door, but the touch of His effectual grace has made my soul bestir itself. Oh, the long-suffering of my Beloved, to tarry when He found Himself shut out, and me asleep upon the bed of sloth! Oh, the greatness of His patience, to knock and knock again, and to add His voice to His knockings, beseeching me to open to Him! How could I have refused Him! Base heart, blush and be confounded! But what greatest kindness of all is this, that He becomes His own porter and unbars the door Himself! Thrice blessed is the hand which condescends to lift the latch and turn the key. Now I see that nothing but my Lord's own power can save such a naughty mass of wickedness as I am; ordinances fail, even the gospel has no effect upon me, till His hand is stretched out. Now, also, I perceive that His hand is good where all else is unsuccessful; He can open when nothing else will. Blessed be His name, I feel His gracious presence even now. Well may my bowels move for him, when I think of all that He has suffered for me, and of my ungenerous return. I have allowed my affections to wander. I have set up rivals. I have grieved Him. Sweetest and dearest of all beloveds, I have treated Thee as an unfaithful wife treats her husband. Oh, my cruel sins, my cruel self! What can I do? Tears are a poor show of my repentance; my whole heart boils with indignation at myself. Wretch that I am, to treat my Lord, my All in All, my exceeding great joy, as though He were a stranger. Jesus, Thou forgivest freely, but this is not enough; prevent my unfaithfulness in the future. Kiss away these tears, and then purge my heart and bind it with sevenfold cords to Thyself, never more to wander.

Christians Can Change the World

If God can change you – then God can use you to change some part of this world.

That this fallen world needs changing is beyond question. When our newspapers and films glamorize selfishness, greed and rebelliousness; when criminals escape justice by legal technicalities and "clever lawyers"; when one half of this world is under totalitarian dictatorships and persecution; when perversion and venereal disease, divorces and abortions, pornography and the occult, terrorism and suicides are increasing – then we know that this world needs to be changed.

As John Wesley declared:

"Give me a hundred men who fear nothing but God, and who hate nothing but sin, and who know nothing but Jesus Christ and Him crucified, and I will shake the world."

Elijah dared to stand alone against the 450 false prophets of Baal and the 400 false prophets of Asherah, and challenge their heresy and idolatry. Elijah's faith in God made him strong and bold enough to oppose the majority who were wrong. And Elijah changed history that day on Mount Carmel – by exposing falsehood and turning the people of Israel back to God. (I Kings 18).

Wycliff, Huss, Luther and Calvin changed the course of human history by daring to study the Bible, and boldly speaking out against the unbiblical teachings and corrupt abuses of the medieval Roman Church.

Missionaries like William Carey changed history by taking the Gospel to India, translating the Bible into numerous local dialects and by ending the Hindu practice of burning alive the widow of each deceased man on his funeral pyre. Hudson Taylor launched a movement that sent thousands of missionaries to China. David Livingstone boldly blazed a trail through the uncharted regions of Central Africa, which ended the Islamic slave trade, inter-tribal warfare and the grip of witchcraft over those tribes. C.T. Studd galvanized hundreds into the mission field and thousands into the Kingdom of God in the Congo. Jim Elliot died for Christ among the Auca Indians of Ecuador, and Richard Wrumbrand stood for Christ while he suffered in the prisons of Communist Romania.

Eastern and tribal thought has a cyclical view of history. Repetition and the "inevitability of history" is so ingrained in non-Christian thought that they see themselves as suffering history rather than affecting or making history. They see themselves as caught up in the process of history and at the mercy of the forces of nature, the spirits, their ancestors (all external forces), and only a part of the community.

This is in contrast to the Christian world view which sees a linear development of history which starts at creation, goes through the flood, the giving of the Law at Mount Sinai, the incarnation of Christ, His crucifixion and resurrection, Pentecost, and will culminate in the Second Coming of Christ and the Judgment. Hence Christians say: *"Only one life, it will soon be past – only what's done for Christ will last."*

Each day is unique, every opportunity must be used. Time is limited in the Christian world view. The Christian sees himself as significant because he is an individual created by God with a particular mission or purpose in life. This emphasis on the individual is unique to Christianity among the major world religions. We must each individually stand before God on the day of Judgment and give an account of our faith and conduct. Each of us must repent for our own sins and exercise personal faith in Christ for forgiveness and freedom. The personal relationship of the individual to Christ is at the heart of Christianity.

In Christian thought; nature is subject to us, able to be developed and used. We are able to affect the course of history because we are the *"change agents"* of an Almighty and Sovereign God. We believe that through the power of God's answers to our prayers and through our obedience to His commands and principles in Scripture – we can change this world.

The Bible teaches us to have a holy dissatisfaction with second best, a bold faith to trust God for great things, to step out and change what is wrong, and establish what is right.

It is this faith that enabled Christians to step out and change history, ending the child sacrifices, cannibalism, voodooism, polygamy, slavery and widow-burning of heathen religions. Such Christians changed their world.

Are you such a Christian who claims: *"I can do all things through Christ who strengthens me."* (Philippians 4:13).

If you are, remember: *You cannot have victory without a battle.* Sacrifice and risk are essential. We can never win if we keep avoiding problems; we must solve problems by facing them and dealing with them. The future belongs to the brave and the bold, to those who are willing to *act* upon their faith.

A CASE OF INDECISION—DANGER ON BOTH SIDES.

The Case of the Missing Keys

"Has anyone seen my car keys?"

"I haven't seen them!" Kelly called from the back bedroom.

"Did you check the kitchen table?" asked Kevin from the living room.

"Yes, but they aren't there." Mother checked the kitchen table, once again. Then, she bent down to examine the floor and the kitchen chairs. A small furry creature named Spike rubbed against her legs and purred as she stood up. "It's the strangest thing! They can't have just disappeared."

"Did you look in your purse?" Kelly asked as she entered the kitchen. Spike ran from Mother to Kelly and meowed softly as he rubbed his head on Kelly's shoe.

"Yes, they aren't there, either. I know I put the car keys on the table when I returned from the grocery store, just as I always do." Mother glanced at Spike as he ran to the corner of the kitchen, momentarily distracted.

"Hmmm, this sounds like a case for Sherlock Holmes," Kevin said theatrically, striking a pose upon entering the room.

"Kevin, this is no time for jokes, this is serious."

"I am serious, Mom! We should study the problem the way Sherlock Holmes would."

Mother sighed. Of course, she was happy that Kevin liked the Sherlock Holmes book she bought him, but his constant reference to the fictional sleuth was beginning to annoy everyone.

"What's Spike doing?" Kelly asked, pointing to the calico cat. He was facing the corner of the kitchen and reaching one paw up under the cabinet.

"Who knows? Perhaps he saw a water bug."

"Ughhh!" Kelly shivered, "I hope not. I can't stand them!"

"Back to our case," Kevin interjected, "let's retrace your steps. Start from the very beginning. You went to the grocery store..."

"Alright," Mother sighed, again. "I drove to the grocery store at 3 o'clock yesterday afternoon. When I returned home, I opened the trunk of the car and carried two bags of groceries into the house. I set both bags on the table, and I placed the car keys on this corner," Mother pointed to a specific spot on the table.

The three of them studied the conspicuously empty spot on the table. When Spike meowed, they simultaneously looked up at him. He was sitting perfectly still, head tilted to one side, as if he was listening to something, staring intently at the corner of the floor.

"That is the strangest cat!" Kevin observed. "Maybe he heard a mouse!"

"A what?" Kelly shrieked.

"Kevin, don't tease your sister! You know we don't have mice!"

Kevin grinned at his mother, then put on his serious, Sherlock Holmes face again. "Back to the case ... did you notice if the keys were still on the table when you prepared dinner?"

Mother thought before answering. "I don't remember seeing them. I placed the tray of dishes and silverware right here," she pointed to the center of the table, "before setting the dining room table. But, now that I think of it, I don't believe the keys were there at that time."

"Ah-ha!" Kevin stepped forward, triumphantly. "So we can place the time of the crime between 4 p.m. and 6 p.m.!" He paced back and forth with his arms folded, thoughtfully. "Kelly, do you remember seeing the car keys when you took the tray into the dining room?"

Kelly reflected momentarily, then replied, "No, I don't think they were there."

"Exactly! We've confirmed the approximate time of the theft. Now, who entered the kitchen during that 2-hour interval?"

"I was here, of course," Mother responded, "and Kelly came in to help me." She thought intently. "No, no one else came into the kitchen, to my knowledge."

"Let's review the facts, again." Kevin stopped pacing and faced his mother. "You came home approximately 4 p.m. and placed the car keys on the corner of the kitchen table." Kevin reached into his pocket and drew out a set of house - and locker-keys on a chain with a miniature football attached. Spike looked up at the sound of the keys jangling. "You set the keys here!" Kevin placed his keys in the appropriate spot. Spike ran to rub against Kevin's leg as Kevin continued expounding. "And, somehow, within the next two hours, they simply disappeared!"

Three sets of eyes stared at the keys. Spike jumped up on the chair closest to Kevin's keys and sniffed at them.

"That appears to be the way it was," Mother mused.

Suddenly, Spike placed one paw alongside Kevin's keys and swept them to the floor, where they fell with a resounding clang. The three looked at each other, then back at Spike, who jumped down from the chair and proceeded to bat the keys back and forth towards the corner of the kitchen. Kevin held up one hand as Kelly bent to retrieve the keys. "Wait!" he said softly.

THE CASE OF THE MISSING KEYS

Of one accord, the three of them followed the playful cat as he buffeted Kevin's keys into the same corner he had been watching so intently. Once the keys were trapped, Spike lay down on his side and expertly lifted the keys with one paw up under the overhanging cabinet.

Mother, Kelly and Kevin exchanged a look of amazement when the keys disappeared! Spike sat up and calmly began to lick his paw.

"Case solved!" Kevin pronounced with a flourish. He ran to where Spike sat grooming himself and unceremoniously pushed him aside. Kevin knelt and felt under the cabinet. "Did you know there's an opening here?" It's between the two cabinets."

"Can you reach inside?" Mother asked. Kelly shuddered.

"Yes," Kevin replied in a muffled voice as he moved his shoulders to a different angle. Suddenly, he withdrew his hand and produced two sets of keys. "Ta-dum!"

STUDYING CHRISTIAN LITERATURE

Spike moved closer to sniff at the dust-laden keys.

"There's more," Kevin chuckled, retrieving a ping-pong ball and two barrettes. "Apparently, this is Spike's secret hideaway."

Spike looked from his treasures to Kevin. Then, he disdainfully arose and walked away.

Tomorrow, he would find a new hide-out — one that even Sherlock Holmes would be unable to find!

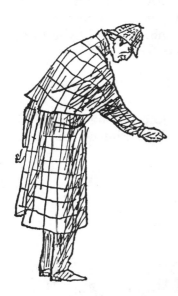

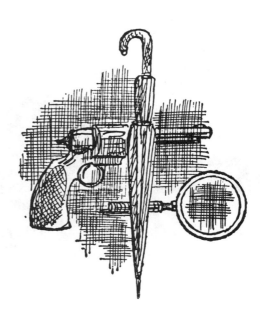

How to Be Happy

It is often assumed that all people know how to be happy. In reality, however, few individuals are ever provided with the understanding they need regarding how to be happy. The following comments will provide insight into this often neglected subject.

First of all, if you wish to be happy – if you wish to have any real peace, any steady and substantial enjoyment – you must make up your mind decidedly whether you will be the child of God or not. If you expect Him to take you under His care, you must be his: really, honestly, and thoroughly, not merely in pretence and in form. If you find, therefore, that in looking into your heart you are not happy, it is very probable that the cause may be that you are not really and fully at peace with God. You have only declared a truce, and then resumed hostilities. Of course you cannot expect to enjoy a quiet and a happy heart. You may, however, depend upon the fact that your days must be days of uneasiness and misery until you come and make yourself wholly the Lord's. To secure your happiness then, your first duty is to most faithfully and thoroughly examine your spiritual condition, to confess and to crucify your dearest sins, and to cast yourself upon the merits and atonement of your Savior. Then you will be prepared to go on to the next step.

The next step in the order of importance, is to see that all your worldly affairs are in order. The special power of organization in increasing success has often been praised, but it has, if possible, a still greater power to promote happiness.

People talk about the cares of business, the perplexities of their daily lot, and the endless intricacies in which they find themselves involved; but they are, nine times out of ten, the cares of mismanagement and the perplexities of confusion. The burdens of human life are often doubled, and sometimes rendered ten-fold greater than they otherwise would be, because people are unorganized. The proof of this is that when a man, either from some natural discipline of the mind or the effect of early education, acquires the habit of order and method, he can accomplish more than twice as much as ordinary men; and of all the men in the community, he is most likely to have time for any new and sudden call. Now, if he can do twice as much, with no more care and hurry, it is plain that he could perform the ordinary work of man with a far more quiet and peaceful mind. This is unquestionable. The facts are notorious, and the inference from them immediate and irresistible.

But let us look more particularly at the manner in which disorganization and confusion, in the management of worldly business, affects the peace and happiness of the heart. There are few persons so correct in this respect that they will not find a testimony within them to the truth of what I shall say. Let us take the following case as the basis of our illustration.

James is a school boy. His affairs, though not quite so intrinsically extensive and important as those of an accountant, are still important to him. He has his business, his cares, his disappointments; the conditions of success and happiness are the same with him as with all mankind.

James' first duty in the morning (I speak only of his worldly duties here) is to rise at six o'clock and start a fire in his father's wood-burning furnace. James hears the clock strike six, but it is cold, and he shrinks from his morning's task; he lies still, postponing the necessary effort. His mind is all the time dwelling upon it and dreading it, and his conscience goading and worrying him with the thought that he is doing wrong. Thus fifteen minutes pass most wretchedly. The mistake he makes is in imagining two evils: a little sensation of cold on his face and limbs while dressing, and the nagging of a disturbed conscience. So he quietly waits, suffering the latter for fifteen or twenty minutes, until the lapse of time makes it too intolerable to be borne any longer, and then he slowly forces himself out of his bed. He then finds that he still has to bear the first evil after all. Instead of taking the least of the two evils, he has taken both, and the bitterest first.

Many of my readers will condemn James' folly – but be not in haste. Do you never in any way procrastinate duty? Look over your mental memorandum, and see if there is anything upon it that you have been putting off because you have been dreading it. If so, you are like James completely. He who procrastinates duty which he knows must be done, always chooses both evils, beginning with the bitterest portion.

James has in fact chosen three evils, for the recollection of this neglect of duty will continue all the morning. For hours there will be an uneasiness in his mind, whose cause and origin he may not distinctly understand, though he might find it if he would search for it. He feels restless and miserable, though he knows not exactly why.

When James comes down to his work, he finds no proper preparation made. The wood which should have been carefully prepared the evening before is out under the snow. The fire has gone out and his tinderbox cannot be found. He does not remember where he left it, so of course he has to search for it at random. When he finds it, the matches are gone, the flint is worn out, and only a few shreds of tinder remain. Perplexed and irritated at the box, instead of being penitent for his own sinful negligence, he toils for a long time; and at last meets with partial success in kindling his morning fires, an hour after the proper time. The family, however, does not distinctly call him to account for his negligence, for the family which produces such a character will generally be itself as shiftless as he. Still, though he expects to sustain no immediate accountability, he feels uneasy and restless, especially as he finds that his postponed and neglected morning's work is encroaching upon the time he had allotted to his morning's school lesson.

For James is a school boy, and the lesson which he is to be called upon to recite, as soon as he enters school in the morning, he had postponed from the evening before. It ought to have been studied during the half hour before breakfast, which he expected that he should find. Acting without a plan and without goals he is, of course, disappointed; and when he rises from his breakfast table, he seems surprised to find that it is time for school to begin. He hurries away to find his books, hat, and coat, for every morning they have to be found. He goes about the house with angry feelings, scowling brow, and fretful tone, displeased with everybody and everything except the proper object of displeasure – himself.

He hurries to school. It is a bright and beautiful winter morning, and everything external tends to either calm the mind to peaceful happiness or to awaken emotions of joy. But James cannot be happy. Even if he should now begin to be faithful in duty, it would be many hours before the turbulent sea of commotion which he has raised in his heart would subside. He is worried, restless, anxious, and unhappy. He sees the external circumstances in which he is placed as the source of his sufferings, instead of looking for their cause within.

I need not follow him through the day. Everyone will see that with such habits, he must be miserable. And yet James is not a bad boy, in the common sense of the word. He has few vices. He will not steal. He will not lie. He loves his father and mother, and never directly disobeys them or does anything intentionally to give them pain. Perhaps my readers would be surprised to have me tell them that he is a Christian. He is, nevertheless, a sincere Christian. He has repented of his sins and made his peace with God, and he lives in the daily habit of communion with God. In his hours of retirement and prayer he experiences many seasons of high enjoyment, and yet he generally leads a very wretched life. A constant, irritating uneasiness corrodes his innermost soul, and he knows not why. In fact, he seldom inquires why. He has borne it so long and so consistently that he has no idea that serenity, peace of mind, and steady happiness are within the reach of the human soul in this world. Thus he goes on, accomplishing very little and suffering a great deal. Now the reader must remember that it is the suffering that we are now considering; our object is not to show how a lack of discipline and organization interferes with success in life, but how it destroys happiness.

Very many of my readers will probably find, by careful self-examination, that though your circumstances and condition may be totally different from those of James, your characters are substantially like his. Disorder, irregularity, and perhaps confusion reign in your affairs. Instead of acting on a general plan, having your business well arranged, your accounts settled, and your work in advance, you act from impulse and temporary necessity. Instead of looking forward – foreseeing duty and providing for its claims, regularly and methodically – you wait until it forces itself upon you, and then waste your time and your spirits. You neglect or postpone unpleasant duties, leaving them to burden your mind and mar your peace and happiness, until at length you are forced to attend to them because some new thorn of irritation pricks in your side.

So, whatever may be the reader's situation and condition in life, if he wishes to be happy, let him regulate his affairs. If you have uncertain, unsettled accounts open, which you have been dreading to examine, go and explore the cases thoroughly and have them closed. If there are plans which you have been intending to accomplish, but which you have been postponing, summon your resolution and carry them at once into effect, or else determine to abandon them and dismiss them from your thoughts.

The mind of a young and ardent man becomes loaded with crude, half-formed designs, unfinished plans, and duties postponed. He is like a child unaccustomed to the world, who takes a walk on a pleasant summer's day. Every object seems valuable, and he picks up a pebble here, a stick there, and gathers a load of pretty flowers in this place and that, until he becomes so encumbered with his treasures that he can hardly go on. They are constantly slipping and dropping from his hands, and become a source of perplexity and anxiety to him because he cannot retain them all. So it is with us. Every plan which reason forms or imagination paints, we think we must execute; but after having made a new beginning, a new project which we are equally eager to secure enters our heads. In a short time, we become encumbered with a mass of intellectual lumber which we cannot carry and are unwilling to leave. Consider what you can and will execute, and take hold of the execution of them now. Abandon the rest, so that you may move forward with a mind that is free and uncluttered.

This, then, is the second great rule for securing personal happiness. Look over your affairs, and arrange and methodize everything. Define in your own mind what you have to do, and dismiss everything else. Take time for reflection, and plan all your work so as to go on smoothly and quietly so that the mind may be ahead of all its duties, choosing its own way, and going forward in peace.

There is one point in connection with this subject of the management of worldly affairs which should not be passed by, and which is yet an indispensable condition of human happiness. I mean the duty of every man to bring his expenses and his financial liabilities fairly within his control. There are some cases of a peculiar character, and some occasional emergencies, perhaps, in the life of every person, which constitute exceptions; but this is the general rule.

The plentifulness of money depends upon its relation to our expenditures. A big city banker with an annual income of $200,000 may be pressed for money, and be harassed by it to such a degree as to make life a burden; while a common laborer on a railroad in New England may have a plentiful supply with only twenty dollars a day, in the dead of winter. Reduce your expenditures, your style of living, and your business far below your financial means, so that you may have money in plenty.

Perhaps there is nothing which so grinds the human soul and produces such an insupportable burden of dependency as financial pressure. Nothing more frequently drives men to suicide. There is, perhaps, no danger to which men in an active and enterprising community are more exposed. Almost all are eagerly reaching forward to a station in life a little above what they can well afford, or struggling to do a business a little more extensive than they have capital or steady credit for. Thus all through life they keep just above their means; and just above, by even a small excess, is inevitable misery.

If your aim is happiness, reduce your style of living and

HOW TO BE HAPPY

your responsibilities of business to such a point that you shall easily be able to reach it. Do this, I say, at all costs. If you cannot have money enough for your purposes in a house with two rooms, take a house with one. For there is such a thing as happiness in a single room, with plain furniture and simple fare; but there is no such thing as happiness, with responsibilities which cannot be met and debts increasing, without any prospect of their discharge. If your object is power, the credit of belonging to good society, or the most rapid accumulation of property, and you are willing to sacrifice happiness for it, I might perhaps give you different advice. But if your object is happiness, then this is the only way.

The principles which we have just considered, as the means of attaining personal happiness, relate to both young people and adults. Let us share this time-proven and biblically sound advice on the subject of happiness with our families, and be quick to act upon this advice ourselves.

Comprehension Questions

1. What was the first necessary step towards securing happiness that was mentioned by the author?
2. Do you think, after reading this selection, that God will bless someone with happiness who is unorganized and without discipline? Explain your answer.
3. What does it mean to procrastinate?
4. Why do you think the author believed that it was important for people who desired happiness to live within their financial means?

The Good Samaritan

Amy first saw the old woman on Thursday morning as she walked to school. From a distance, there appeared to be a heap of rags piled in front of Wilson's Hardware Store window. But, then the rags moved, lifted a dirty head and stared at her over a gray muffler draped across her nose and mouth. Amy could still feel the shiver that went down her spine! To avoid contact, she had crossed the street.

What, Amy wondered, could bring a human being down so low? When Amy arrived at school, she put the old woman out of her mind.

On Friday morning, however, Amy returned and found herself looking for the vagrant. The pile of rags were in the same place as the day before. This time, Amy didn't cross the street, but she approached cautiously.

The matted gray head lifted slowly as Amy neared. Once again, the woman's eyes chilled Amy's heart.

"Can I have a quarter?" a voice crackled from under the muffler.

"I'm sorry," Amy quickly replied, matching her steps to her words, "I don't have any money." She gave the woman a wide berth and hurried up the walk.

Amy glanced back fearfully, but the vagrant had returned to her former position. Amy noticed that the woman was sitting on an air vent for heat. Her steps slowed, then stopped. She had no money, that was true, but she did have a large bag of lunch. Amy's mother prepared a lunch fit for a football player, every day. And, no matter how often Amy talked about it, the lunch never diminished in size. She gave most of it to her friends. Or, worse,

THE GOOD SAMARITAN

Amy sometimes threw part of her lunch away.

With a new resolve, Amy turned around and walked back to where the old woman sat. She opened her lunch bag and shoved a banana, a candy bar and a sandwich towards the pile of rags. "Here!" she said, nervously.

The old woman's head jerked up. Slowly, a trembling hand took the sandwich, then the candy bar, then the banana. Without a word, the woman held them to her chest and bent her head over them.

Amy hurried away and tried to put the old woman out of her mind, once again. But, it was no use.

"Are you crazy?" Erica exclaimed when Amy told her about her morning encounter. "Don't you know that those homeless people are dangerous?" Erica looked at her friend with disbelief. "She could have hurt you!"

"I don't think she can stand up, much less hurt me," Amy replied. "I'm going to tell someone about her. She needs help." As Amy looked around the cafeteria, she caught sight of her principal. "I'll see you later," she said hastily, rising to intercept Mr. Adams as he left the cafeteria.

Amy liked and respected Mr. Adams. He seemed to be a man of high principles, and he really listened to his students. He listened very carefully, now, as Amy explained her concern for the old vagrant.

"Does she seem threatening in any way?"

"No, not at all," Amy hurriedly responded. "At first, I was afraid of her because of her appearance. But, she gave me no reason to fear her." Amy pictured the old woman in her mind. "She has such pain in her eyes. That's what got to me. I don't know if she's in physical pain or if it's emotional. I just wanted to take some of the pain away."

"I think we should call the police," Mr. Adams said.

"But, I don't want to see her locked up! She isn't hurting anyone." Amy searched Mr. Adams' face. "Isn't there somebody else we can call?"

Mr. Adams hesitated, then nodded his head. "You're right! Come to the office, we'll contact Pastor Davidson who runs the local shelter for homeless people. He can guide us to the correct person."

Amy sat across the desk from Mr. Adams and listened to his phone conversation.

"Yes, one of my students found her sitting on the air vent in front of Wilson's Hardware Store at 3915 Central Avenue." Mr. Adams listened carefully and nodded. "I understand." He glanced at Amy. "Can you let me know what happens to her?" He nodded, once more. "Thank you! I appreciate your help. You have my name and phone number."

After he hung up, Mr. Adams stood and walked around his desk. "He suggested that his office should call the police so they could pick up the old woman," Mr. Adams said, raising his hand to silence Amy, "so she can be taken to County Hospital for a complete examination. That's the proper procedure. While the doctors are examining her, the police will check their missing persons' reports; it's possible that she's confused and lost, and someone might be looking for her."

"I never thought of that!" Amy nodded in agreement.

"I asked Pastor Davidson to let me know what the outcome is," Mr. Adams continued. "Why don't you stop by my office before you leave, this afternoon. Perhaps we'll have some information by then."

Mr. Adams took Amy's hand and shook it warmly. "Thank you for taking time to help this woman. Most people would have walked away."

THE GOOD SAMARITAN

Amy returned to her classroom reflecting upon her recent discussion. She had confessed to Mr. Adams that she had walked past the poor woman on Thursday and had avoided the area entirely on her way home Thursday afternoon. His response was, "But, you went back ...that's the main thing!"

The afternoon seemed exceptionally long, but finally the dismissal bell rang. Amy raced to her locker, grabbed her books, coat, and gloves, and ran to Mr. Adams' office. Through the window, Amy could see Mr. Adams talking on the telephone. When he caught sight of her, he motioned for Amy to enter.

"That's wonderful!" Mr. Adams smiled at Amy as she took a seat across from him. "Her name is Amy Stuart," Mr. Adams said. "Yes, I'll tell her. Thank you, once again."

Mr. Adams hung up and smiled broadly at Amy. "The old woman's going to be all right," he informed her. "Her name is Martha Iverson. She wandered away from a nursing home in Jefferson County several days ago. They have no idea how she got here. You found her just in time! She's suffering from hypothermia and was on the verge of a diabetic coma; your lunch probably saved her life."

Amy lowered her head, "Why didn't I stop and help her Thursday?"

Mr. Adams lifted Amy's chin and looked into her brimming eyes. "You've been taught all of your life to stay away from strangers. This is a dangerous world, and you took the appropriate precautions. But, you listened to your heart, as well. Once you had determined there was no immediate danger to you, you stopped to help her." Mr. Adams gripped Amy's shoulders. "You are a Good Samaritan! I'm proud of you."

As Amy walked home, she passed the now-empty spot in front of the hardware store. It was amazing how everyone had missed finding Mrs. Iverson! The newspaper and television news programs had shown her picture, but no one would have recognized her, the way she looked when Amy found her.

STUDYING CHRISTIAN LITERATURE

Somehow, she had been overlooked by the police on their regular patrols. She must have moved to another location before Mr. Wilson opened his store, or he would have spotted her.

At any rate, the old woman had a name and was being taken care of, now. Mr. Adams told Amy that Mrs. Iverson's daughter was going to send her a letter, thanking her for helping her mother. She still didn't feel exactly like a Good Samaritan, but she wasn't a Levite, either.

Amy resolved to keep her eyes open, from now on, and watch for opportunities to help street people. In fact, she planned to talk to her pastor, Sunday morning, about starting a 'Help the Homeless' program at her church. Amy walked faster. Why wait until Sunday? She could call the pastor, this afternoon! The sooner the better!

Until Death Do Us Part

Christy polished the silverware, thoughtfully, rubbing the same piece over and over.

"I think that spoon is polished sufficiently, don't you?"

"What?" Christy looked up in confusion.

"You've just spent several minutes polishing one spoon. So you have something on your mind?"

Christy gravely observed her mother before answering. "I was just thinking of Grandma's and Grandpa's fiftieth wedding anniversary."

"It's certainly an extraordinary celebration, in this day and age," her mother agreed.

"But why?" Christy laid the spoon and cloth aside and leaned forward. "Why do so many marriages fail, now?"

Christy's mother studied her face. "Do you have a specific marriage in mind?"

Christy bit her lower lip. "Denise's parents are getting a divorce," she said softly.

"Oh, dear!" Dropping her cloth, Christy's mother reached across the table to take her daughter's hand. "How is Denise taking it?"

Christy sighed deeply. "About the same way I would take it if you and Dad got a divorce!" Christy looked imploringly into her mother's eyes. "You won't, will you?"

"Good heavens, no!" Christy's mother gripped her hand reassuringly. "Your father and I made a lifetime commitment, when we got married. We'll never get a divorce!

"I'll bet that's what Denise's parent said, too!" Christy said flatly.

"I can't speak for anyone else, but I promise you, your father and I will be married until death do us part."

"How can you be so sure?"

Christy's mother could see that the silver wasn't going to be polished, that morning. She pushed everything aside and stood up. "Let's go have a cup of tea and talk about it."

Fifteen minutes later, they were both seated at the kitchen table sipping their tea. "Some people jump into marriage irresponsibly," Christy's mother asserted. "They get caught up in the excitement of the moment... the glamour, the attention and the romantic atmosphere. It's difficult to keep a cool head in that situation."

"Do you think that's what happened to Denise's parents?"

"It happens to a great many couples. You know, it takes a long time to learn to love a person. What you feel at first is infatuation. When the excitement is over and life is back to normal, that's when some people experience marital difficulties. They don't want to have to work at marriage; they want the initial infatuation to go on forever... in other words, they don't want to mature." Christy's mother sipped her tea. "Sadly, many people today are more interested in meeting their own personal needs that in building strong Christian marriages."

"My Sunday School teacher talked about that. She said people have gotten away from biblical teachings, and that's why so many marriages have failed."

"She's absolutely right!" Christy's mother walked to the

small desk in the corner of the kitchen and retrieved a book. When she returned to the table, Christy saw it was one of her mother's Bibles. She quickly turned to a heavily underlined passage. "Ephesians advises wives to submit to their husbands as to the Lord and tells the husband to love their wives just as Christ loved the church and gave his life for it." Christy's mother held the Bible up and tapped it. "This is the instruction book! It has all of the answers. I wonder if Denise's parents ever turned to the Bible for help?"

"I don't remember ever seeing a Bible in their home," Christy commented. She studied the well-worn book. "Do you think they would take offense if I gave them a Bible?"

"Their marriage is drowning, and this is a lifeline; how can we withhold it?" Christy's mother stood and offered her beloved Bible to her daughter. "Why don't we visit Denise's parents, right now, and if they're willing, we can ask Pastor Dalton to join us." She placed a hand on Christy's shoulder and quoted, "Man must not separate what God has joined together."

STUDYING CHRISTIAN LITERATURE

Suddenly, Christy felt a surge of hope. Following a prayer to open the minds and hearts of Denise's parents, Christy and her mother left the house together, arm in arm, equipped with an old, worn Bible and a strong desire to share the Word of God. As they went, the wedding vow kept running through Christy's mind, "...for better or worse, for richer or poorer, in sickness and in health, until death do us part..."

Whoa, Car!!!

"Tell us more about Great-Grandpa Vernie," Gary urged.

"Yes, Grandma, please tell us a story," Scott and Stephanie joined in. Several cousins nodded in happy anticipation.

"Well, let's see..." Great-Grandmother Catherine leaned back in her ancient oak rocking chair and thought for a moment. Then, she smiled. "Would you like to hear about the time Vernie first learned how to drive?"

"Yes... please," the children chimed in. They arranged themselves on the floor close to Grandma's chair, leaving enough room for her to rock slowly, to and fro. Grandmother's stories were better than television... better than the movies... because they were true stories about their ancestors. Great-Grandfather Vernie had died when Gary was five, and he vaguely remembered him as a small man with twinkling blue eyes, a completely bald head, and very large hands. Probably due to the fact that Grandpa Vernie had been a farmer. Gary's sister and brother were too young to remember Grandpa, so they had to rely on old photographs.

"Now, back in our time," Grandma began, as she always did, "you didn't have to take a test to get a driver's license. In fact, they didn't even have drivers' licenses then. People just bought a car and taught themselves how to drive."

"How did they know about the driving laws?" Stephanie asked.

"Well, there really weren't any driving laws, in the early days. All of that came later."

"But, how did he know what to do when the electric lights came on?" cousin Cody asked.

"Oh, we didn't have electric lights, then, either. We didn't have highways, stop signs, parking meters or paved roads." Grandma laughed and rocked slowly, staring into space, watching scenes of days gone by in her mind's eye. "Our roads were dirt-packed, or muddy, if it rained. Although, there were a few gravel roads, as I recall."

"Don't interrupt!" Gary instructed the others. If Grandma got sidetracked, they would never hear about Grandpa Vernie's first driving lesson.

"Let's see... where was I?"

"Grandpa Vernie had just bought his first car," Gary prompted.

"Yes, Vernie bought an old model-T Ford from his cousin. It was Sunday when his cousin drove it over to our farm, and we all gathered around to admire it. Not many people owned cars, back then, and we were all very excited... much like you probably were when you saw your first television set."

"Well, actually, Grandma, televisions were invented long before we were born," cousin Dan reminded her.

"Oh, that's right! That would have been before your time," Grandma mused. "So many things have happened during my life!"

"So, Grandpa Vernie got into the car?" Gary prompted, again.

"Yes, Vernie climbed into the old model-T Ford and sat up as high as he could." Grandma glanced around at the eager faces, "He wasn't very tall, you know. So, he sat up ramrod straight and took the wheel in his hands. His cousin gave him a few preliminary driving instructions and proceeded to walk around to the passenger side. But, before he could climb in, the car started lurching forward. Everyone scattered out of Vernie's way and his cousin started running after him, shouting for Vernie to turn off the motor."

WHOA, CAR!!!

Grandma stopped rocking and looked at the children knowingly. "Everyone else thought the car took off by itself," she nodded, "but I knew better. Vernie was a proud man, and he just wanted to prove that he could do it, alone." She chuckled and sat back, again rocking slowly. "Well, it was quite a sight... Vernie was hanging onto the steering wheel with a look of astonishment on his face. The clouds of dust made it hard for his cousin to see where he went, but the rest of us were standing up on the front porch, and we could see Vernie making wide circles around the barn. After a few minutes, Vernie knew he was in trouble; he had mastered the skill of driving, but, he had forgotten to ask how to stop the vehicle! His cousin continued to shout instructions to Vernie, but the old car was so noisy that Vernie couldn't hear him." Grandma laughed softly at the memory. "But, you know , we could hear Vernie's voice above the racket. He was shouting 'Whoa, car! Whoa, there, old car!' as if he was talking to our old plow horse!"

The children laughed delightedly, and the adults, who had entered the room while the story was in progress, were laughing in appreciation, too. "I remember that story," Uncle Eddie nodded.

"But, Grandma, how did Grandpa Vernie finally stop the car?" Scott asked, when the laughter died down.

"He just rode around and around until it ran out of gas," Grandma replied with a grin, "which was close to midnight!"

Once again, the room was filled with laughter... and memories.

Perseverance of the Saints

"Therefore, my beloved brethren, be ye steadfast, unmovable, always abounding in the work of the Lord, forasmuch as ye know that your labour is not in vain in the Lord." I Corinthians 15:58

Of all the qualities that could be attributed to Christians in the United States at the end of the twentieth century, one that would likely not be mentioned would be perseverance.

A story is told of a famous mine owner in California who drove a tunnel a mile long through strata that he thought contained gold. Months later, he began to become discouraged because he had not struck the vein of gold, having already spent thousands of dollars in pursuit of it. Finally, in spite of some hopeful signs that he was getting close to the precious metal, he quit. Another company undertook the project, following in the footsteps of this mine owner, and drove the tunnel two yards further and struck the ore.

So, in this case, and often in life itself the gold of life may be but a short distance off. There are countless failures in life due to not going far enough.

For the Christian, the Bible is a deep mine of treasured truth. Yet how often God's people miss out on the richest knowledge and wisdom because they keep too near the surface. The key to finding the richest blessings from God's Word is to "go deeper" into the Scriptures. But how do servants of God do this?

Drilling into the depths of the Bible means reading it. Meditating on its truths, applying its instruction, and memorizing key verses. The result will be abundant spiritual wealth for daily living. Furthermore, as we persevere in our mining of God's Word, we not only "get" for ourselves but we are also able to "give" to others. This spiritual wealth enables us to bless, help, and influence fellow believers who are struggling with spiritual poverty. It also equips us to defend the honor of God's truth when it is attacked.

We must seek if we would find. We must knock and keep on knocking – then and *only* then will it be opened unto us. God will never bless a seeker who is passive and lukewarm – we must persevere!

Ask God to give you the gift of perseverance as you seek to grow in the knowledge and grace of our Lord Jesus Christ. Pray that He might give you opportunities to enrich others with the riches He so freely gives to all who hunger and thirst after righteousness. Above all, keep on keeping on; the reward may lie but a yard ahead.

"Till I come, give attendance to reading, to exhortation, to doctrine. Neglect not the gift that is in thee, which was given thee by prophecy, with the laying on of the hands of the presbytery. Meditate upon these things; give thyself wholly to them; that thy profiting may appear to all. Take heed unto thyself, and unto the doctrine; continue in them: for in doing this thou shalt both save thyself, and them that hear thee."

I Timothy 4:13-16

PERSEVERANCE.

The Importance of Family Worship

"BEHOLD, how good and how pleasant it is for brethren to dwell together in unity. It is like the precious ointment upon the head, that ran down upon the beard, even Aaron's beard, that went down to the skirts of his garments. As the dew of Hermon, and as the dew that descended upon the mountains of Zion; for there the Lord commanded the blessing, even life for evermore." (Psalm 133).

Family unity and peace is a blessing which cannot be overrated. This selection is designed to show that it is directly promoted by family worship.

The deliberate and consistent assembly of a whole household for the purpose of praise and worship of God, provides more than simply the means of bringing the several members together. There are striking differences among families in regard to the simple quality of cohesion. While some are a bare collection of so many particles, without mutual attraction, others are consolidated into a unity of love. Many scattering influences are at work. Some of these may be attributed to a lack of system and regularity; some to late hours; some to peculiarities of business; some to fashion; and some to the influences of vice. From one or several of these influences we see domestic harmony impaired. Parents and children meet only at their meals, and not even at all of these. The tardy inmates of the house descend in the morning at any hour, and at long intervals, and the evening is often despoiled of the charm of home. In such circumstances we are persuaded the links of affection are tarnished, if not worn away. In proportion as the subjects of mutual obligation live apart, they will cease to care for one another. No customs of society are laudable or safe which tend, in any considerable degree, to separate parents from children, and brothers from sisters. It is good to bring together the coals on the domestic hearth. Hence we have always looked with unqualified satisfaction on the New England custom of gathering all the members of a family, however remote, under the paternal roof on the day of annual thanksgiving. There is a sacred virtue in even beholding the face of an aged father and a gentle beloved mother. On this very principle, the president of a prestigious college, justly celebrated for his influence on young men, was accustomed, when he saw the first sign of rebellion in a student, to call him to his study, and kindly propose to him a simple visit to his parents. We do not wonder that the effect was often magical.

Family worship assembles the household twice every day, and that in a deliberate and solemn manner. No individual is missing. This is the law of the house from childhood to old age. The observance is as stated as the daily meals. Other employments and engagements are made to bow to this, until it becomes the irreversible rule of the little commonwealth. Such assemblies provide opportunities for each family member to look upon one another's faces and exchange kind words and gentle wishes. Such influences, which may seem rather trivial, rise to inestimable magnitude when multiplied through all the days of long years, that is, over the entire progress of family life. By those who have enjoyed them, they can *never* be forgotten. Such households stand in open contrast to those where parents and children, in haste and disorder, and with many interruptions, snatch their daily bread, without so much as a word of discussion, thanks, or prayer.

Some good results, in respect of harmony, ensue, when a household purposely assembles for the common pursuit of any lawful object whatever. Union, and the sentiment of union, are promoted by joint participation, and the effect is appreciable where the gathering is frequent. Though it were only for exercise or recreation, for the practice of music, for an evening perusal of useful books, still there would be a contribution to mutual acquaintance and regard. But how much stronger is the operation of this principle when the avowed object of the meeting is to seek the face of God, and to invoke His blessing!

There is no way in which we can more surely increase mutual love than by *praying for one another*. If you would retain warmth of affection for an absent friend, pray for him. If you would live in the regards of another, beseech him to pray for you. If you would conquer enmity in your own soul towards one who has wronged you, pray for him. Dissension or coldness cannot abide between those who bear each other to God's throne in supplication. It is what we meet to do at family worship. Often has the tenderness of a half-dying attachment been renewed and made young again, when the parties have found themselves kneeling before the mercy seat. Every thing connected with such utterance of mutual good-will in the domestic worship tends to foster it, and thus the daily prayers are as the dews of Hermon.

The devotions of the household are commonly conducted by the parent, and parental affection often needs such an outlet. The son or the daughter might otherwise remain ignorant of the anxieties of the father. There are yearnings which the parent cannot express to man, not even to a child, but which must be poured forth to God, and which have their appropriate channel in the daily prayer. The hearing of such petitions, gushing warm from the heart, and the participation of such emotions, cannot but sometimes reach the stubborn childish mind, and tend to a strong and reigning affection. Both parent and child, if they are ever touched with genuine love, must experience it when they come together before their God and Savior.

That revelation of divine truth which is perpetually expressed or implied in family worship, in Scripture, in psalms, and in prayers, enjoins this very peace and affection. The New Testament presents it in every page. The Word of God and prayer are, from day to day, bringing the duty constantly before the conscience. The household which is subjected to this forming influence, may be expected, more than others, to be a household of peace.

Some notice must here be taken of a painful but common case. Human depravity sometimes breaks forth in friction and strife, among members of the same brotherhood, and, alas, even within the sacred limits of a Christian house. Harsh tempers, sour looks, moody silence, grudges, bitter words, and alienations, mar the beauty of the family circle. Therefore, we find slights, angry rebukes, suspicions, and recriminations entrenched in the home. Happy, indeed, is that household over which these black clouds do not sometimes hover. But what means shall we seek to dispel them? The family altar! Only an extraordinarily obstinate sinner will be able to let the sun go down upon his wrath when he is obliged to worship with the entire family. It is hard to listen long to the Word of God without hearing the rebuke of all such bitter feelings. For example, the very portion read, may say to the unrelenting one, "If thou bring thy gift to the altar, and there rememberest that thy brother hath aught against thee, leave there thy gift before the altar, and go thy way; first be reconciled to thy brother, and then come and offer thy gift." (Matthew 5:23). At any rate, the whole spirit of the exercise convicts any family member who wishes to remain hard-hearted of his sin; for it is most difficult to pray with malice on the heart. The spirit of forgiveness often comes to us while we are upon our knees.

Suppose then, what we are reluctant to suppose, that mutual reproaches, perverse separation, and open quarrel, should enter a Christian family. To offenders, in such a case, the season of prayer must be an hour of keen rebuke. Avowedly, they are bowed down to pray for one another. The hypocrisy and impiety of attempting to do so out of a mind of hatred, will stare the sinner in the face, and will often bring him to repentance. Reconciliation, begun in the heart, during moments of devotion, may lead to the restoration of peace in the home.

Sad as is the thought, even husband and wife may be at odds with each other, and may give place to the devil. Harshness, severity, distrust, and unkindness, may spring up between those who have vowed to live together as heirs of the grace of life. But it is hard to believe that such persons, if they possess a spark of grace, can come to the posture and the words of prayer, encircled by their kneeling little ones, without surrendering the selfish spite, and making a faithful effort to crush the head of the viper. Marital tenderness, forbearance and love, are guarded by the exercises of family-devotion.

Contrast all this with the condition of a domestic circle subject to the same dark influences, but without these checks and this sacred balm, and you will no longer marvel that where there is no worship, there is no place for healing. The stream of unkindly temper runs on. Brooding silence is the best that can be expected. The day closes without reference to God. The griefs of the day are carried over into the morrow and all this because of a lack of spiritual influence which would be secured by the hour of prayer.

In speaking of family worship as a means of promoting family unity, we might dwell on its influence upon absent members of the household. As children grow up, there are few families which do not send forth from their bosom some children to distant places. These children are not forgotten at the hearth which they have left. Day by day, the venerable father, joined in silent love by the more melting mother, cries to God for him who is afar upon the sea, or in foreign lands. These are moments which bring the cherished object full before the mind, and make the absent one present to the heart. Such prayers serve many useful purposes. Chiefly, they rekindle and maintain the fire of affection. Most older children who leave home will not fail to prize these parental intercessions, or disregard the supplications of the brother or the sister left at home. Often, we are sure, the recollection of the domestic worship comes up before the distant youth, on the high seas, or in remote wanderings. Often is the secret tear shed over these privileges of his childhood. In the perpetual fire of the family altar, he knows that he has a *stable* refuge in his father's house.

When, after years of absence, which may be due to some sin, the son or daughter revisits the home of his childhood, and that worship is renewed which he remembers so well-what a torrent of ancient reminiscence pours into the heart! Such associations have their influence on even hardened natures, and they go to prove the blessedness of this familiar institution.

But after all that we may urge, the great and crowning reason why domestic worship promotes harmony, is, that it promotes true religion, and religion is love. Its mission is peace on earth and good will to men. Unlike the humanistic schemes of secular philosophers and psychologists, which tear the household elements asunder, Christianity compacts the structure, and strengthens every wall. It adds a new cement, and makes the father more a father—the mother more a mother—the son more a son; so that there is not a social tie which does not become more strong and endearing by means of grace. If even enemies are reduced to toleration by the gospel, how much greater must be its influence on the ties of blood and affinity! It consecrates every natural relation, and exalts human affections by expanding them into eternity.

The daily lessons, constantly recurring in family worship, bear directly on this point. "Husbands, love your wives, even as Christ also loved the Church. Let the wife see that she reverence her husband. Fathers, provoke not your children to wrath. Children, obey your parents in all things, for this is well-pleasing unto the Lord. Servants, be obedient to them that are your masters according to the flesh, with fear and trembling, in singleness of your heart, as unto Christ. And ye masters, do the same things unto them, forbearing threatening, knowing that your Master also is in heaven. Love as brethren, be pitiful, be courteous. Honor all men. Be not forgetful to entertain strangers. Be kindly affectioned one to another, with brotherly love, in honor preferring one another. Let all bitterness, and wrath, and anger, and clamor, and evil-speaking, be put away from you, with all malice: and be ye kind one to another, tender-hearted, forgiving one another, even as God for Christ's sake hath forgiven you." Such are the touching accents of the gospel in general, and of this institution in particular, familiarized to every member of a Christian house, from their childhood. And what the Word of God enjoins, the Spirit of grace produces in the heart, where true religion finds entrance. Under the daily influence of such motives, which drop as the rain and distill as the dew, the youthful heart may be expected, in many cases, to receive the noblest charities of a renewed nature.

Amidst all the imperfections of a fallen world, there have been thousands of families, since the founding of the Church, which have realized this ideal; and what spectacle on earth is more lovely? From the very cradle, the infant lips are taught to lisp the name of God, and the soft voices of childhood join in the daily praise. Brothers and sisters, already brought by baptism within the pale of the visible church, grow up with all the additional reasons for mutual attachment, which spring from dedication to God. No day passes in which parents and children do not compass God's altars. When the father and mother begin to descend into the autumn of life, they behold their offspring prepared to walk in their steps. There is a church in the house. When death enters, it is to make but a brief separation; and eternity sees the whole family in heaven, without exception or omission.

In cases where divorce or death have prematurely fractured the husband–wife relationship, single parents have even more reason to maintain family worship. A broken family can only be fixed by the re-establishment of Christ as the covenant head of the home. And there is no better or more meaningful way to acknowledge the Lordship of Christ, the Good Shepherd, than through the instrument of the family altar. Only Christ can fill the void left by a family circle that has been broken by divorce or death.

The happiest family on earth will not always be so. The most smiling circle will be in tears some day. All that I ask is, that you would secure for yourselves and your children, a friend in that blessed Redeemer, who will wipe all tears from your faces. Your families may soon be scattered, and familiar voices may cease to echo within your walls. The children in a household do not stay children long. They quickly grow up and take off for college or careers. O see to it, that the God of Bethel goes with them, that they set up an altar even on a distant shore, and sing the Lord's song in that foreign land. They may be taken from this earth altogether, and leave you alone. O see to it, that as one after another goes, it may be to their Father's house above, and to sing with heavenly voices, the song which they first learned from you, and which you often sang together here—the song of Moses and the Lamb. And if you be taken, and some of them be left, see to it, that you leave them the thankful assurance that you are gone to their Father and your Father, their God and your God. And, in the meanwhile, let your united worship be so frequent and so fervent, that when you are taken from their head, the one whose sad responsibility it is to take your place, as priest of that household, shall not be able to select a chapter or a psalm with which your living image and voice are not associated, and in which you, though dead, are not yet speaking to them. "And thus my heart's wish for you all is,

> 'When soon or late you reach that coast,
> O'er life's rough ocean driven;
> May you rejoice, no wanderer lost,
> A family in heaven.'"

Comprehension Questions

1. Why did the author believe that family worship helped to promote close personal relationships within families?

2. Explain how family worship provides a basis for overcoming disputes among family members.

3. How can family worship benefit a household that only has one parent living in it?

4. Explain how family worship helps parents to ensure that Biblical love will continue to influence their children even after they die.

The Influence of Family Worship on Civil Government

To the earthly politician nothing can seem more absurd than to ascribe to the devotions of private Christians, any power in regard to states and empires. Religion is an element in political changes not recognized by the wisdom of this world. Yet it cannot be a matter of indifference, even in respect to civil government and national wealth, that hundreds of thousands of families, dispersed abroad in the earth, are daily addressing themselves to God in prayer. And it may turn out to be true, that a nation in which a significant number of families shall be thus employed, will derive from this very simple spiritual exercise a character conducive to public strength.

Before considering the direct influence of prayer on nations, we will turn our attention to some particulars which are too often neglected. The indispensable material of a happy State, is a body of good citizens. It is not territory, fertile soil, mines, cities, arts, navies, armies, monuments, laws, constitutions, or even liberty, which sustain and ennoble a people: but good citizens. That which makes good citizens, tends directly to the benefit and glory of a State. This will not be denied, in an age and country in which it is considered appropriate to flatter, and almost deify the people. Viewing the matter even from the low point of temporal things, virtually everyone admits that the power and stability of government resides in the virtue of its citizens.

National virtue, as we all know, does not come in a bottle; nor does it develop as a result of some clever governmental edict or legislative scheme. No general regulations, however good, can reach the hearts of a people. The seed of national virtue is the virtue of collected individuals. The power that is needed to spark virtue must be brought to people in a personal manner, especially on each family and each individual.

To make good citizens we must begin early. It is too late when the adult character is attained. Hence the acknowledged importance of academic education in a free country. But this early training may be complete in respect to intellectual discipline, and may yet be inadequate. We need moral qualities in the good citizen, in addition to, intellectual prowess. If we could, therefore, recommend to society a plan that would make every family a school of sound principles and virtuous habits, we should plainly be dealing with the very factors necessary to the development of a prosperous State; and the method which should accomplish this would be a national blessing. Such a method is domestic religion; including, as one of its principal parts, family worship. We are prepared to maintain that this institution cannot flourish in any country without directly contributing to those habits which are favorable to law, **order**, and peace.

Every Christian household is a school of good citizenship. This might be safely rested on reasons already given. But one or two particulars merit separate consideration. Family worship, as we have seen, promotes habits of order. It brings a stated regulation into the house, and gathers the inmates by a fixed law. It sets up a wholesome barrier against wanton irregularity, sloth, and night-wandering. It encourages early hours, thoughtfulness, and affection; and above all, it adds strength to the principle of subordination and obedience; a point which we dare not pass lightly.

Good citizens are such as abide by the law, and submit themselves to authority. The habit of so doing must be formed under the parental roof. All the duties of subjects and citizens range themselves under the fifth commandment; and he who is not a good son cannot be a good citizen. Here we may refer to a passage already cited, in which God says of Abraham: "I know him, that he will *command his children* and his household after him." (Genesis 43:19). Domestic discipline is an ordinance of God. As the family was the earliest community, so it was the earliest form of government; and, notwithstanding the humanistic assertions of pagan philosophers in ages past, such as Rousseau, who wrote about the basis of society in terms of a social contract, the family is the true origin of States. Observe the connection: "Abram shall surely become *a great and mighty nation:* for I know him, that he will command his children." Here is the influence of family-religion on the commonwealth. We have already said enough to show the bearing of domestic worship on family relations; our present inquiry is in regard to the tendency of this to public peace and safety.

The modern evils which threaten our country, arise in great measure from a spirit of insubordination; and this is caused by neglect of parental authority. He who has never learned to obey and honor his father and his mother, will never yield himself to magistracy and law. The spirit of rebellion is bold and increasing. Children become men without ever learning to be under authority. Travelers from abroad complain that there are no boys among us, only infants and men: the period of subordination is passed over. In our cities the streets are filled with hordes of unsupervised children, who appear to acknowledge no loyalty to any household. These young people are ripe candidates for mobs and insurrections, for gangs and prisons. It is needless to say, that the houses from which such youth proceed, enjoy no consistent worship of God; but we conceive it to be important to add, that the conscientious observance of family-devotion will go far to prevent children from embracing such destructive behavior. A nation of families worshipping God will ever be a nation of law and order.

No municipal police can make up for the absence of domestic authority. The weakening of this principle over a whole land, is nothing less than the rupture of the master link that holds the chain of society together. As the evil advances, we lose the very material of magistracy and the capacity for firm and gentle command. The scriptural maxim is that he who cannot rule at home, cannot rule abroad. The bishop, or minister, must be "one that ruleth well his own house, having his children in subjection with all gravity; for if a man know not how to rule his own house, how shall he take care of the Church of God?" (1 Tim. 3:4-5). The principle admits of an equal application to civil government. The discipline of the family cannot be invaded without a corresponding disorganization of society. And the great end is to be attained, not by adding strength to government, or stringency to laws, or terror to punishments, but by training in every house in the land, a group of Christian citizens, habituated to manly obedience.

We have still to consider the great and crowning favor which family worship confers on the commonwealth: *it brings down heavenly blessings from the prayer-hearing God.*

Take out of a nation its praying souls, and you leave it defenseless and accursed. Cities and kingdoms have been spared for the sake of Christ's people who were in them. Jehovah would have withheld his destroying vengeance from Sodom and the cities of the plain, "for ten's sake." The cries of the poor, who fear God, "enter into the ears of the Lord of Hosts." Politicians attribute no potency to the prayers of believers, but they are heard in heaven. They have, before now, averted great evils, and procured great deliverances. Israel was about to be utterly consumed at Taberah, but " when Moses prayed unto the Lord, the fire was quenched." The agonizing prayer of Daniel for his people, was mighty before God. When the Most High is about to return to a guilty people, he does it in answer to prayer, and summons those who fear him to humiliation: "Let the bridegroom go forth from his chamber, and the bride out of her closet: let the priests, the Lord's ministers, weep between the porch and the altar, and let them say, Spare thy people, 0 Lord." (Joel 2:16, 17). The angel who stands with a drawn sword over a country, is no doubt often recalled by reason of those prayers which are scorned by sinful rulers and a profane people.

True Christians believe that it is their sacred duty to pray for ministers in civil government. Though we have no prescribed liturgical form for this, in our public service, we hold it to be an important part of intercession. We have known ministers to be charmed with partisanship in politics, because they publicly prayed for the chief magistrate. No patriot and no Christian can consistently refuse to pray for the needs of all civil leaders, with fullness and earnestness. It would be dreadful, indeed, if the devotions of God's house were to take their direction from the gusts of political opinion. Real biblical intercession is not a human device to mold public opinion, but an inspired oracle, which enjoins that "supplications, prayers, intercessions, and giving of thanks be made for all men, for kings, and *for all that are in authority* that we may lead a peaceable life, in all godliness and honesty." (1 Timothy 2:1 - 2) Such prayers go up from the devout household also, and the more they are multiplied, the more reason there is to hope for national prosperity.

Men who love their country will delight to take their households with them to the throne of grace, in beseeching God's favor in any great national emergency. When questions of vast importance are in suspense, when divisions are threatened, especially when the country is at war, the prayers of Christian families in every church throughout the land, are exerting an unseen agency, outweighing, perhaps, the deliberations of senates,

THE INFLUENCE OF FAMILY WORSHIP ON CIVIL GOVERNMENT

and cabinets, and councils of war. And the youth who are trained to such prayers, are growing up in the *best* school of patriotism. No person will be more likely to love his country, than one who has been taught to pray for it every day.

    A land covered by praying families may properly be called a Christian land. That it would be consistently happy, even in civil affairs, can be denied only by those who reject righteousness and peace. Were every town in America persuaded of the profitability of family prayers and worship, our nation would, indeed, be the glory of all lands.

    It is rather ironic, that the most powerful vehicle that families can use to advance the good of their communities or nation is so easily procured. Access to family worship is neither expensive nor remote, it is not to be gained by agitation or by waiting for others to concur; it is simply for every man in his place to set up the worship of God. The true way to bring health to a diseased nation, is to carry the cure to every house. The aggregate energy of a multitude of zealous families, united in prayer for the country, is beyond all computation: it is this which "exalteth a nation." Patriotism could confer nothing better on the land she loves than to kindle this fire on every hearth. The voice of thanksgiving and joy would burst over the domestic and national walls, and reach the most distant lands. Who will not pray for such a consummation? "Let the people praise thee, 0 God; let all the people praise thee. Then shall the earth yield her increase; and God, even our own God, shall bless us. God shall bless us; and all the ends of the earth shall fear him." Psalm 67:5-7

Comprehension Questions

1. In what ways does family worship promote the success of civil government?

2. If a child never learns submission at home, how will this affect his attitude toward civil rulers or magistrates?

3. Where in the Bible does it command Christians to pray for all those who are in authority?

4. Why did the author think that faithful praying Christians should be regarded as the greatest of patriots?

5. Should civil rulers be required to "rule their households well" before they could be qualified for public office? If so, why?

The King's Quest

Part One

Once, a long time ago, there lived a king named John. He wasn't a wicked king—he just wasn't a very wise king.

For one thing, he never mingled with the commoners—the people who lived in his kingdom beyond the walls of his palace. King John surrounded himself with ministers who advised him and took care of the needs of the kingdom.

The Minister of Justice ruled over the courts.

The Minister of Finances handled income, expenses, and His Majesty's Treasure Room where the royal jewels and most of the King's wealth was stored.

The Minister of the Royal Guard saw to it that peace and order reigned throughout the land.

The Minister of Provisions kept the palace well-fed and well-stocked.

The Minister of Transportation kept the horses healthy and well-shod, and the carriages rolling.

Then, there were the Ministers of Education, Housekeeping, and the Arts.

Together, the ministers ran the palace and the countryside. King John was free to do whatever he wanted. But, since he didn't have to do anything, he did very little besides read, walk through the royal gardens, attend banquets, and ride handsome steeds.

One night, King John dreamed that a poor boy climbed up the vines that clung to the palace walls and entered his bedroom chamber.

"Pssst!" the boy hissed loudly.

"Who's there?" the king called, blinking the sleep from his eyes. His hand was poised, ready to yank the bell-rope to summon help.

"I am one of your subjects, Your Majesty," the boy replied.

"Come into the light!" the king ordered in a stern voice.

A thin, bare-foot child dressed in rags stepped closer to the royal bed.

The king studied the boy in the wavering candlelight. "Why are you so thin?" he finally asked.

"Because I'm hungry," the boy said. "Your people have little food, my lord."

"Why are you wearing ragged clothing, and where are your shoes?"

"We have no money for shoes and clothing because we are so heavily taxed, my lord."

King John thought for a moment. "If that's true, why haven't I been told?"

"Your ministers guard you very closely, Sire. They keep your people far away so you cannot see our poverty."

Before the king could ask another question, the boy disappeared. Instantly, King John awoke. He looked around the dimly lit room, his forehead wrinkling in concern. Could there be any truth to his dream, he wondered? He stroked his long, golden beard and tried to remember the last time he saw a commoner. His mind drew a blank.

Suddenly, a vague memory began to take shape. He saw himself as a child walking beside his father, the beloved King Alfred. They were surrounded by smiling villagers, and his father was dispensing alms to the adults, and candy and fruit to the children.

King John sat on the edge of his high bed and stared at the floor. How did he become so separated from his subjects, he wondered? When his father died, he was just a young boy—unprepared to rule a kingdom. Then, one by one, King Alfred's trusted aides came forward to offer advice and assistance. Somehow, over time, he had allowed them to take complete control. Was it possible that they misused the power he had given them?

As he sat thinking, the king's eyes strayed to his large washstand which held brushes, scissors, soap, a basin of water, face cloth, and towels. He glanced around the richly decorated room, observing the brocaded drapes, the man-sized fireplace, carved furniture and fur rugs. He had always thought of his kingdom as a wealthy one. Was the palace living in luxury while his people suffered?

King John stood up purposefully—an idea was beginning to form!

THE KING'S QUEST

Part Two

The Minister of Provisions, a large, portly man, swaggered into the palace kitchen. He would inspect the food and menus planned for the next day. As he approved or rejected each item—and sampled this and that—an old man in tattered clothing stepped into the circle of light.

"Can you spare a slice of bread, my lord?" the old man asked.

The minister's face turned bright red with rage. "What? How did you get in here?" the minister demanded. He raised his elegant walking cane threateningly, as if to strike the bent old man. "Get out! Leave the palace, at once! GUARDS!"

The old man slipped out of the room and was gone by the time the guards arrived.

"What's going on here?" the minister of the Royal Guard bellowed as he rushed into the huge kitchen.

The Minister of Provisions sputtered, "Quick! Find him! A beggar is loose in the palace!"

"He won't be for long," the second minister growled. "After him!" he ordered his men. "I'll see him in chains within the quarter-hour!"

But, search as they might, the guards could not find the old beggar.

A short time later, the Ministers of Justice and Finances were standing in the torch-lit courtyard near the royal stables, discussing the shocking breach of security—a commoner had actually entered the palace!

"Alms?" a weak voice called from the shadows. "Can you spare some alms for a poor man?"

"GUARDS! The wretch is here in the courtyard!" one minister cried. His companion took one step back in speechless indignation.

Once again, although the area was searched thoroughly, the old beggar could not be found. The Minister of the Royal Guard called for more soldiers and the hunting dogs. He would search all night, if necessary; the trespasser must be caught and punished for his insolence!

Around midnight, an old stable hand awakened a young page. He told him to advise the Minister of Transportation that the king's favorite stallion had reared up and badly bruised his foreleg in his stall, due to all of the excitement.

Shortly, the irate minister came storming into the stable. "Here, now," he called in an exasperated tone. "What's this about the stallion?"

A rustling to his left made him pause. "Are you there?" he demanded.

"Forgive me for disturbing you, milord." The old man hobbled into view. "I'm just a poor man seeking a bit of bread and some clean, dry hay to rest on for the night."

The Minister of Transportation stood in stunned silence for a brief moment. Then, he howled in anger and grabbed a horse whip that was leaning against a nearby stall. "AHA! So, you're the wretch who's been sneaking about the palace grounds. Well, this is what happens to those who won't stay where they belong!" Snapping the whip in the air, the minister rushed forward. But, to his confusion the old man stepped back into the shadows and disappeared from sight.

Scores of guards, stable hands, ministers, hunting dogs, and servants searched every square inch of the palace and the grounds, holding lanterns, torches, and candles high—but to no avail. The interloper had vanished and wasn't seen again.

Part Three

A cold, light rain fell as the black sky began to turn gray. Here and there, candles gleamed from the dark windows of the thatch-roofed huts. The villagers' days were long and often began before the night ended.

A door opened and a young woman stepped out of her hut carrying a large wooden bucket with both hands. This would be the first of many trips to and from the well. She was the village washerwoman.

As she walked to the well, she saw a figure huddled up against the well's jagged stone wall as if trying to seek shelter under the cone-shaped roof. "Who's there?" she asked in a fearful voice.

"A harmless vagrant ... a wanderer passing through your fair village," croaked the old man raising his wet, rag-covered head.

The young woman had never seen a more pathetic figure than the heap of rags trembling before her. "Why, you must be soaked to the bone," she cried. She dropped her wooden bucket and bent down to help the old man to his feet. "Come, warm yourself by my fire," she said. Her apprehension dissolved in the face of such misery.

With the aid of the woman's shoulder under one arm and a wooden crutch under the other, the beggar limped to her hut. Shortly, he was seated on a stool in front of a modest fireplace.

"Now," his hostess was saying, "remove those wet things and put these on." She tenderly held a pile of clothing—a workman's cap, woolen shirt, socks, and pants folded neatly on top of a heavy pair of wooden shoes. "My husband can no longer use them," she said, softly.

"Is he ill?" the old man asked glancing at the occupied cot pushed against the back wall.

The woman straightened up, blinked twice, and held out the items to him. "No," she said shaking her head slowly, "he caught pneumonia and died a year ago." Then, she added, "He would have wanted you to have these. He was a very kind and generous man."

The vagabond nodded and awkwardly took the bundle from her hands. He waited until the woman left to fetch her bucket of water before replacing his wet rags with the warm, dry clothing. A groan of gratitude filled the hut as he felt life coming back into his hands and feet.

Later, the woman chatted with her guest as she began scrubbing clothes in a vat of soapy water. A large pot of water was boiling over the open fire. The old man listened as he bent over a cup of hot porridge. He seemed to savor each spoonful, and he nibbled on a biscuit with obvious enjoyment.

"I wish I had extra cream to offer you," the woman said apologetically. "But, I must save it for my daughter." She glanced back at the cot and smiled as a small, tousled head popped out from under the covers.

"Momma?" a sweet voice said, questioningly.

"Come, child, we have a visitor," her mother responded. "Come and greet..." the woman looked at the old man expectantly.

"Alfred ... my name is Alfred." His short, scraggly gray beard parted to reveal a friendly smile. The bill of the workman's cap was pulled low over the man's forehead and shaded the rest of his face.

The small girl approached, shyly. Then, suddenly, she giggled and pointed to the cap. "Look! He's wearing Papa's hat!" As if she now felt more at ease with him, the girl walked up to the stranger and placed her hand on his arm. Her large blue eyes examined him with open curiosity.

"And, what's your name?" Alfred asked, smiling at the golden-haired child. Her curls bobbed around a heart-shaped face, and he noticed that the child looked exactly like her mother, except that the mother's hair was bound by a large white scarf.

"Forgive my lack of manners," her mother said, her cheeks flushing in a combination of embarrassment and hard work over a steaming vat. "This is my daughter, Rachel. And, my name is Mary."

Alfred raised his hand, still wearing his ragged, fingerless gloves, and touched the bill of his cap in a courtly gesture. "Delighted to meet you, milady."

Rachel giggled, again, and whispered to her mother, "He talks funny." Then, with a child's forthrightness, she asked, "Why are you wearing my papa's clothes?"

"Because mine were wet," Alfred responded with mock seriousness. "Do you think that's all right?"

Rachel studied the stranger's half-shaded face. Then, she solemnly nodded her approval. Once that was settled, she turned to her mother for her morning meal.

While Rachel ate, Mary returned to the pile of dirty clothing heaped beside her. She scrubbed as she spoke. "Perhaps the sun will come out, soon, so I can hang the clothes outside to dry. We don't care for wet clothing strung out in the hut—do we. Rachel?"

The child shook her head without responding. It was obvious that mealtime was important to her. She chewed each spoonful carefully before swallowing.

"You said you've traveled a great distance. What is your destination, Alfred?" Mary suddenly stopped and smiled at her guest. "Do you realize that you have the same name as our previous king? Are you familiar with our beloved King Alfred?"

"Yes, I've heard of him ... but, surely, you're too young to remember him well. I'm told that he died twenty years ago."

"I was Rachel's age when last I saw our good King Alfred, but I'll never forget his kindness to us. He had his workers build this hut, after my father was injured by one of the Royal Guard's horses. And, he sent servants and food until Papa was able to work, again."

Alfred leaned forward in interest. "And, what do you think of King John?" he asked.

Mary's smile disappeared, and she bent over her washboard, once more. "It's not my place to say. I've never seen him ... nor have I met anyone who has seen or spoken to him since he was a boy."

Alfred sat back in the shadows and rubbed his beard. "Since I come from a distant province, I know nothing about King John, although, I have heard his name. How does he rule his kingdom?"

Mary scrubbed harder. "He doesn't," she said, shortly. "He has given his ministers dominion over his realm."

"And, do they rule wisely?"

Mary stared at her guest in dismay. "You have, indeed, come from a distant province!" Then, she said with a sigh, "When Rachel has eaten, I'll take you to see Brother Roland. He can tell you all about the king's officials." Her lips tightened grimly as she added, "If it wasn't for Brother Roland and his wife, Rachel and I would be homeless."

"But, who could take away the home that was given to you by King Alfred?" the old man asked in confusion.

"The Minister of Finance," Mary replied, bitterly. "After my husband died, I had no money to pay taxes. Abigail, Brother Roland's wife, convinced some of the villagers to bring clothes to me for laundering and sewing. What I earn pays our taxes, but there's little left over for food. So, although he can barely feed his own family, Brother Roland sends us home with a small basket after service on Sundays."

Mary sighed, again, and returned to her washboard. "I shouldn't speak ill of the king," she said. "Brother Roland tells us to pray for King John. He said the Lord will take care of us."

"Brother Roland is a pastor?"

"Yes. And, he's the village carpenter, as well. You see, with the taxes being so high, neither the farmers nor the villagers have money to support a minister and his family. So, Brother Roland became a carpenter." Mary smiled fondly as she added, "He says, our Lord was a carpenter when He walked upon the earth. So, he feels it's only fitting."

"I look forward to meeting Brother Roland," Alfred said with a thoughtful nod.

Part Four

"Why, it's Mary and our little poppet, Rachel! Come in! Come in!"

Mary and Rachel entered a hut located at the entrance of the village. Then, Mary turned and motioned for Alfred to enter, as well.

"Abigail, this is a visitor from a far land. His name is Alfred, and he would like to speak to Brother Roland." Mary stepped aside so Alfred could meet the small, gray-haired woman she had spoken so highly of.

Alfred limped forward on his crutch, touched the bill of his cap, and bowed as low as his crutch allowed. "How do you do?" he croaked in his odd voice.

Abigail acknowledged his greeting with a nod and responded, "I'm pleased to meet you. Come, let's all sit in the kitchen. I've just baked some biscuits. And, Daisy gave Tom two gallons of milk, this morning! Imagine that! Do you think that old cow knew we were going to have company?" Abigail's eyebrows lifted, her eyes grew large, and she laughed in a most delightful way.

Alfred instantly felt welcome. He looked around the hut with interest as he followed the small group into the kitchen. Where Mary's hut was one large room, Abigail's hut seemed to be made up of three large rooms—as if Brother Roland had added each room, as needed.

The kitchen was as big as Mary's dwelling and consisted of a long wooden table, two long benches, a worktable, miscellaneous wooden pantries, two straightback chairs, a stool, a rocking chair, and a huge fireplace with multiple openings on either side. The delicious aromas emanating from the fireplace made Alfred's mouth water.

Abigail motioned for the three of them to be seated at the long table. Then, she smiled at Alfred and said, "It's handy to have a carpenter for a husband!" Once again, she laughed her musical laugh, and her eyes twinkled with merriment as she set about arranging biscuits on tins and pouring small cups of milk.

"Thank you, but I've already eaten," Alfred told Abigail.

"Nonsense!" she replied. "You never know when your next meal will be... that's an old saying, and in these days it's a true one. Besides, it's our custom to feed visitors and strangers. You wouldn't want to break one of our customs, would you?"

She stood next to Alfred and watched him expectantly. So, Alfred relented and bit into the warm biscuit. It was so light and fluffy, it seemed to melt on his tongue. He'd never tasted anything like it! "It's ... wonderful!"

With an abrupt nod of satisfaction, Abigail served Mary and Rachel, smiling at their obvious pleasure. Then, she went to fetch Brother Roland who was working under a lean-to behind their home.

She returned immediately, followed by a tall, thin man with a curly white beard embedded with wood chips. When he took off his hat, chips flew in all directions, and Abigail's eyebrows raised in mock despair.

Introductions were rapidly made, and Brother Roland shook hands with the stranger. Then, he and his wife took their customary seats at either end of the table. "So, you're a traveler from a distant land, Alfred?" he asked when his guest had eaten the last crumb.

"Yes," Alfred said in a low voice. "I have no family, and the village where I lived was very poor—work and food was scarce. So, I decided to settle in another province. I'd heard that this territory was blessed with abundance and ruled wisely."

Brother Roland exchanged sad glances with Mary and Abigail. "At one time, that was true. When the king whose name you bear still lived, this was a rich kingdom—not so much in material wealth, although food and employment was plentiful, but in peace, joy, and fellowship." Brother Roland looked down at his rough hands folded on the table.

"And, now?" Alfred prompted.

With a deep sigh, Brother Roland looked up at his guest. "And now, we have an invisible king who has given his ministers free reign over his kingdom. And, they have chosen to enrich their own lives at the expense of the king's subjects." Brother Roland glanced at the crutch leaning on the table beside Alfred. "Although this may not be your final destination," he continued, "you're welcome to stay in our village for as long as you wish—or, at least, until you're able to travel more comfortably."

Alfred looked down at the long table and back at his host. "You're very kind," he said, "but, I can't impose. You, obviously, have a large family to care for. If I could work for food and shelter … is there a stable, nearby? I'm very good with horses."

Abigail's face brightened, and she turned to her husband. "Perhaps he can help Big George!"

Mary smiled and nodded in agreement, "Yes, he's been in need of help ever since Jacob was conscripted into the Royal Guard!"

"Conscripted?" Alfred asked in confusion.

"The Minister of the Royal Guard regularly scours the countryside seeking new recruits," Brother Roland explained. "Big George's son, Jacob, was recently taken—as well as our two oldest sons, Bartholomew and Joshua."

Abigail turned her head to hide her tears, and Brother Roland continued, "Now, we have only our three daughters and young Tom, left. They work for farmers at harvest time to help feed the family—and assist needy villagers." He patted Mary's hand, and Alfred remembered her weekly food baskets.

"But, why would conscription be necessary? The country is not at war."

Brother Roland looked at Alfred and shook his head. "Some things are better left unsaid." Suddenly, he stood up. "But, come! Let's visit our good friend and neighbor, Big George the blacksmith. His stable and hut are located down the road, a short distance."

Mary helped Alfred to his feet, and Rachel held out his crutch. "Thank you for sheltering, feeding, and clothing an old man," he said, his voice thick with emotion.

Mary blushed and lowered her eyes.

Rachel yanked on Alfred's shirt, and he bent over the crutch and patted her blond curls. "Won't you come to visit us, again?" she asked.

"Of course, I will," Alfred replied. "After all, I'll be your neighbor, now." Then, he added in a whisper, "And, I'll take good care of your Papa's clothes."

Part Five

While Alfred, Mary, and Rachel visited with Brother Roland and Abigail, the rain had stopped. The sun now filtered through the dripping trees, sparkling on the surface of the puddles that Alfred carefully avoided as he limped along the muddy road on his crutch. He was on his way to meet Big George.

Brother Roland walked slowly beside him. "I've been known to treat various ailments in the area. Do you want me to take a look at your foot?" he asked solicitously.

"No need," Alfred replied, "it's only a sprain—I slipped on a rock a couple of days ago. A few days' rest is all I need."

The sudden sound of horns blaring in the distance made them both stop in their tracks.

"I wonder what's happening at the palace?" Brother Roland said, looking back the way they had come.

"Oh, is that where the king lives—back there?"

Brother Roland glanced at Alfred, then continued walking along the road. "I suppose he does—although, I haven't seen him for many years."

"So, he truly is invisible, as you said earlier." They walked in silence for a moment. Then, Alfred asked, "If you could speak to the king, what would you say?"

Brother Roland looked at the thatch-roofed huts and waved at the curious villagers who peered through their open doorways. "I would remind him of his sacred duty to his people. I would ask him to follow in his father's footsteps and turn to the Lord for guidance. I would advise him to reject his evil ministers..." He stopped in mid-sentence and glanced at Alfred. "But, then, who am I to advise the king?"

"You're a very wise man, from what I hear."

Brother Roland smiled and said, "Of course, you've only spoken to Mary, Rachel, and my wife, so far. They're not exactly unbiased." He touched Alfred's arm, then pointed to a barn-like structure. "There's the stable."

Alfred followed Brother Roland through the large doorway. The interior reeked of burning coal, leather, horses, and hay. They passed empty stalls and followed the sound of a hammer clanging on metal. In an open area behind the stable, a huge, dark-haired man was trying to shoe a horse. The horse kept prancing nervously away.

As quickly as his crutch allowed, Alfred hurried to the horse's side and grabbed a handful of mane. Then, dropping the crutch, Alfred stroked the horse's nose with his other hand and whispered to the animal.

Big George glared at the stranger, at first. But, when the horse stood completely still, he grabbed the hoof and hammered the shoe on without further trouble.

Brother Roland grinned at the large, muscular blacksmith. "I'd like you to meet a visitor to our village—this is Alfred."

Big George picked up Alfred's fallen crutch and handed it to him. Then, with a gruff, "Thank you," he shook the stranger's hand.

"Alfred is in need of shelter for a while," Brother Roland continued, "and I thought you might be willing to let him sleep in the stable, and, perhaps, have a meal or two—in exchange for work. As you saw, he's good with animals. And, now that Jacob is gone…"

Big George frowned down at Alfred from his great height, taking in his gray beard, bent back, and the crutch.

"I can clean the barn, brush down the horses, feed them … whatever you need," Alfred said in a low voice.

Big George turned to Brother Roland in exasperation but dropped his eyes when he saw the look of hope on his Brother's face. "We'll give it a try," he finally grumbled.

"Splendid! Now, then, I'll leave the two of you alone to get acquainted." Brother Roland smiled at Alfred and said, "I'll drop by to see how you're getting along. If you need anything, just let me know. Oh, and I hope to see you on Sunday morning—we have a small service at my home. You can come along with Big George and his daughter, Bess."

Alfred limped over to Brother Roland and shook his hand solemnly. "I'll be there," he agreed. Then, he stood watching the Brother's vanishing back as he retraced his steps.

"Hmm… well, I guess we can fix up a stall for you to sleep in while you're here," Big George mumbled, grabbing the reins of the newly shod horse.

Alfred followed his new employer into the stable.

The big man removed the horse's bridle and bit and spoke to the mare tenderly as he filled her feed sack. Then, he closed the stall door and looked at Alfred. "Well, take your choice!" He gestured in both directions. "Which stall do you prefer? They're all empty, except for this one."

"Have you no other horses to shoe, or carriages and wagon wheels to mend?" Alfred asked, looking around the empty stable.

"Just this mare—and she belongs to a farmer up the road. I'll take her home, tomorrow, and ask if he has any farm tools in need of repair. If not, I'll go on to the next farm ... and to the next ... until I find more work." Big George scratched his short black beard in vexation, and Alfred noticed for the first time spots of singed hair. His worn clothing displayed patched burn holes, here and there, as well ... the hazards of a blacksmith's trade.

"Perhaps you could ask for work at the palace," Alfred suggested.

A brooding scowl darkened the big man's eyes. "The palace has taken my son, my horses, and my wagon. I'll not go begging to them for work!"

"Yes, I heard about your son's ... conscription. But, surely, you were paid a fair price for your property?"

A look of disbelief crossed the blacksmith's face. Then, he shook his head. "You're a stranger in these parts. The Royal Guardsmen take what they want. They don't ask, and they don't pay!"

Alfred's head dropped to his chest. "How could this happen?"

"A good king dies and a bad king inherits the kingdom," Big George said in a weary voice.

"So, King John is an evil king?" Alfred raised his head to watch the other man's reaction.

Big George appeared to think the question over. Then, he said, "Can a good king place his subjects in the hands of wicked men?" He shook his head. "Well, my friend, there's not much people like us can do, is there? Except pray, as Brother Roland says. Ah, but, it's hard ... "

"So," Big George folded his arms in resignation, "which stall would you like to occupy? We'll heap up fresh hay, and you can use the horse blanket as a cover. Not quite a king's bed, but it's better than sleeping on the ground."

STUDYING CHRISTIAN LITERATURE

Part Six

Early the next morning, Big George left to return the farmer's mare. Alfred stayed behind to clean out the stable.

At noon, young Bess, the blacksmith's daughter, brought him a small bowl of thin soup and a biscuit. As the old man settled down to eat his lunch, the girl lingered. She was very curious about him—it was not every day that a stranger passed through the village. But, she was shy, and didn't know how to start a conversation with the old man.

Alfred saw that she wanted to talk, so he said, "How old are you?"

"Thirteen," Bess replied with a blush.

"Shouldn't you be attending school?"

"Oh, no!" she said, her eyes round with surprise. "There are no schools for commoners. The few church schools we did have were closed by the king's men."

"No schools?" Alfred stared at the girl. "But, how will the children learn to read and write?"

"My mother taught Jacob and me to read the Bible and write, a little, before she died. Then, Father taught us. I read to him every evening before going to bed. My favorite story is about Queen Esther. That's my best friend's name, too. Esther is Brother Roland's youngest daughter." Bess paused to make sure Alfred was listening. When he nodded, she asked, "Which is your favorite Bible story?"

The question caught Alfred off-guard. He lowered his spoon and looked out the open stable door where dust motes floated in the bright sunshine. "I haven't read the Bible since I was a boy," he finally admitted.

"Oh!" Bess looked perplexed. "But, Brother Roland teaches that the Bible should guide our lives, day by day. He said, if we read and study God's laws, we'll know how to live." She looked at Alfred questioningly.

Alfred handed his empty bowl to Bess and struggled to his feet. "Brother Roland is right," he agreed. "In fact, I would like to study the Bible, again. I don't know why I stopped reading it, years ago. But, as you see, I don't have one with me." Alfred looked down at his hands as if a Bible might miraculously appear.

"You can use ours!" Bess cried happily. "Father and I don't need it until after our evening meal. You can begin reading it, now!"

Alfred smiled at the girl's enthusiasm. "Well," he said, "if you think your father wouldn't mind..."

Bess' brown eyes sparkled. She hugged the bowl tightly and replied, "Father wouldn't mind, at all. I'll just go get it for you. Don't go away!"

The young girl ran from the stable, and Alfred smiled at her youthful zest. He limped over to a low wooden stool sitting inside the doorway. His ankle was feeling somewhat better, so he left his crutch leaning against a stall and pushed the stool into the sunshine. He was just sitting down when Bess came running back carrying a large book.

"Here it is!" she said unnecessarily.

Alfred took the heavy book from her hands and set it on his lap. Then, he opened it and carefully turned the thin pages. "What would you recommend I read, first?" he asked.

Bess studied Alfred for a moment. "Well, if you had your own Bible, you could start at the beginning and read straight through. But, Father said you're just visiting..." She paused, then leaned over to find the appropriate page, pushing her heavy dark hair aside. "There!" she said, pointing to the Book of Psalms.

Alfred adjusted his cap to keep the sun out of his eyes. Then, he began to read aloud, "Blessed is the man that walketh not in the counsel of the ungodly, nor standeth in the way of sinners, nor sitteth in the seat of the scornful. But his delight is in the law of the Lord; and in his law doth he meditate day and night (Psalm 1:1-2)."

Bess sighed. "Isn't that beautiful?"

"Yes," Alfred said slowly. "It's beautiful, and it's true. Shall I continue to read out loud?"

"Please do," Bess urged. She spread her patched skirt wide and sat down on the grass. "You sound just like Brother Roland. I love to listen to him on Sunday mornings."

Alfred began to read, again. His voice was measured and low, and the longer he read, the more pleasant it sounded. Time seemed suspended as the words flowed from Alfred's mouth. When he finished reading the twenty-third Psalm, he looked up and was surprised to see that he had a small audience.

Mary and Rachel were sitting next to Bess. An elderly couple sat in the shade a short distance away, and a young boy was standing nearby. His bare feet were spread apart and his thin arms were folded across his chest. A large bundle of twigs sat on the ground next to him.

The boy looked familiar to Alfred. "What's his name?" he asked Bess.

She glanced back and said, "That's Tom, Brother Roland's youngest son." Suddenly, Bess jumped up. "Look! Father's coming!"

Bess and Rachel both ran to meet Big George who was pushing a large wooden cart. They walked on either side of him chatting and laughing all the way back to the stable.

As Alfred watched them approach, it occurred to him that, although the villagers were poor, deprived, undernourished, and ill-treated—they were happy. He closed the Bible on his lap and touched the cover reverently. I have a great deal to learn, he thought.

Slowly rising to his feet, Alfred moved the stool back into the stable. "So, you found more work," he said to Big George.

"Yes, praise God!" the blacksmith said with a broad smile. "The farmer whose mare I returned, this morning, gave me this fine cart when he heard that mine had been seized by the Royal Guard. Then, he asked me to repair these wheels and straighten this saw. Before I left, I helped him remove a tree stump from his field, and—bless him!—he sent home some potatoes, three ears of corn, and a small slab of bacon! We'll eat well, tonight, my friend!"

Alfred handed Bess the Bible, waved good-bye to Mary and Rachel, and followed Big George into the stable. He helped lift the wheels out of the cart, and admired the bacon, corn, and potatoes that Bess was transferring into a woven basket. The blacksmith's stomach growled, hungrily, as she hurried into the hut to begin preparing the evening meal.

While Alfred examined the cart and farm implements, Big George casually commented, "Bess tells me you sound like Brother Roland when your read the Bible. Were you a Brother in your village?"

Alfred's head jerked up in surprise. "Why, no—although, that's a fine thing to be. I—uh—worked with horses...and, did some gardening." Alfred frowned down at his hands which held the farmer's saw. "Frankly, I wasn't very good at anything," he admitted. Then, he added, "But, I intend to change my ways!"

THE KING'S QUEST

The sound of a galloping horse interrupted them and drew their attention outside. Alfred followed the blacksmith to the road.

Near Brother Roland's hut, they saw a small group of villagers talking excitedly to one of the king's messengers. The messenger spoke abruptly, then wheeled his horse around and galloped past the stable and around the bend, out of sight.

Big George frowned. He turned to Alfred and said, "Wait here. I'll find out what's happened."

Alfred leaned against the stable and watched the blacksmith hurry toward the cluster of villagers. They surrounded Brother Roland, talking excitedly and waving their hands about. Big George waded through the group and bent over to talk to the Brother. Just then, Mary and little Rachel broke away from the crowd and ran toward him.

"What is it?" Alfred called as they came closer.

"Oh, a most dreadful thing has happened," Mary cried. "The king has been kidnapped! And, his officials think one of the villagers kidnapped him!"

Part Seven

Mary ran to Alfred's side, and Rachel clung to her mother's skirts, her eyes wide with fear.

"Surely, the king has not been kidnapped!" Alfred said in a reassuring voice.

"Then, where could he be? The messenger said they searched the palace for two days, and he's not there!" Mary tried to catch her breath, and then she added, ominously, "A villager was found inside the palace, the night before last."

"Is that so strange?"

"Oh, yes! It's a crime punishable by imprisonment!"

"Imprisonment!" Alfred's mouth fell open in shock. "Never have I heard of such a thing! A king's subjects forbidden to approach the king? Impossible!"

"Perhaps it's allowed in your province—but, it was outlawed in this kingdom many years ago." Mary hugged her daughter, protectively. "The king's soldiers are scouring the countryside, trying to find King John and the fugitive. The messenger said our village will be searched, next. If they don't find the king by tonight, the Minister of the Royal Guard has ordered all of the men to be taken to the palace and brought before the

Minister of Justice."

Mary gripped Alfred's arm. Her eyes filled with tears. "What will happen to them?"

Alfred patted Mary's hand, reassuringly. "I promise you, they will be all right," he said. His eyes narrowed thoughtfully as he watched the blacksmith and Brother Roland walking toward him.

"You heard the news?" Brother Roland asked. His face was drawn with concern.

"Yes, Mary just told me," Alfred replied.

"I wonder what happened to King John?" Big George said. His dark eyebrows came together as he puzzled over this latest incident. "And, why would a commoner enter the palace ... unless...." The blacksmith turned to Alfred and his eyes lit up with instant understanding. "It was you!"

Alfred nodded slowly.

Brother Roland stared at Alfred in dismay.

"You were the intruder?" Mary asked in a frightened whisper.

"Lord, help us!" Brother Roland prayed.

"Look! Here come the king's soldier's, now!" Big George ran his hands through his hair in an unusual display of anxiety. Scores of horsemen could be seen less than a mile away, galloping toward the village.

"Quick, you must hide!" Mary cried to their ill-fated visitor. She picked Rachel up in her arms and told Alfred, "Follow me! You can lie down on Rachel's cot and pretend to be my sick father! Hurry!"

"You would place yourself in danger to protect me?" Alfred asked in a tone of wonder. "But, there's no need. I'll just explain to the king's officials that I'm a stranger to this province and was unaware of the law prohibiting commoners from entering the palace grounds."

"You don't understand," Brother Roland said, "there is no justice for commoners in this kingdom. The fact that you're a stranger will not save you from imprisonment!"

The Brother tugged on his curly white beard pensively. Then, he straightened up to his full height and said, "There is only one thing to do. I will turn myself in and say I was trying to find my two sons—that I missed them and wanted to see them, again."

"No, Brother Roland, you can't do that! What will your family do without you?" Big George folded his arms across his chest and stubbornly raised his chin. "I'll turn myself in and tell them I was looking for Jacob—to see if he was all right!"

"But, what about Bess? What will she do?" Mary cried. "Neither one of you can go to prison!"

The soldiers had almost reached Brother Roland's hut.

Rachel reached out to touch Alfred's arm. "Are you going to prison?" she asked. Her chin trembled and tears rolled down her cheeks.

"No, my dear, I'm not," Alfred said, squeezing her small hand. "And, my friends, you will not take my place," he said to Brother Roland and Big George.

"Mary, will you fetch my crutch for me?" Alfred asked with a strange calmness. The two men looked at him, curiously. The old man appeared to be taller and his voice had lost its raspiness.

Mary set Rachel down and ran to retrieve Alfred's crutch from inside the stable. Bess came running from the hut to see what was happening, and Mary told her about Alfred's unfortunate situation. Together, they rejoined the group.

Once his crutch was firmly tucked under his arm, Alfred limped down the road to meet the newly arrived legion of soldiers.

Exchanging worried glances, Brother Roland and Big George fell into step on either side of Alfred.

Mary took hold of Rachel's and Bess' hands, and they followed the three men. Whatever happened, Alfred would not face his fate alone.

As they approached the soldiers, the rest of the villagers quietly joined the small group. By the time they reached Brother Roland's hut, the entire village surrounded Alfred.

The Captain was talking to Abigail who stood in her open doorway with her arms wrapped around her youngest son, Tom. "Stand aside!" the Captain ordered in a sharp voice. He turned to order his soldiers into the hut to begin their search, when he saw the villagers. Immediately, his hand went to the hilt of his sword.

"Stop!" Alfred commanded in a powerful voice. "Stand back and instruct your men to remain on their horses!"

A look of uncertainty passed over the Captain's face. Then, he scowled at Alfred and snapped, "We're here to find the king and his kidnapper..."

"And, you have found both!" Alfred exclaimed.

The villagers gasped and backed away from Alfred.

The soldiers tightened their grip on their reins and looked at each other in stunned confusion.

Suddenly, the Captain bellowed, "SEIZE HIM!"

"HALT!" Alfred countermanded. He whipped the workman's cap off of his head, and his hair shone golden in the sunshine, contrasting sharply with his dingy gray beard.

A cry arose from the villagers and the soldiers, alike.

Then, Alfred stepped toward Abigail and smiled. "May I have a small bowl of water and some soap?" he asked in a kind voice.

Abigail closed her mouth and blinked in astonishment. Then, she nodded and gently pushed Tom into the hut. A moment later, he was back with a basin, a towel, and a sliver of soap.

"Now, see here..." the Captain sputtered, trying to regain control. He stepped forward, unsure of what to do next.

Ignoring the Captain, Alfred splashed water in his face. Then, he vigorously soaped and scrubbed his face, chin, and neck, splashed more water, and dried himself with the towel. When he removed the towel, his face glowed and his beard was as golden as the hair on his head. "Ashes," he stated, briefly, to explain his formerly gray beard and face. Then, he turned to the Brother and said, "And, I really did sprain my ankle, the other night."

Brother Roland quoted. "Be not forgetful to entertain strangers: for thereby some have entertained angels unawares (Hebrews 13:2)."

The golden-haired stranger walked over to Brother Roland, tall, handsome, standing straight, and barely limping. "Oh, no, my friend ... I'm not an angel. I'm King John."

"But ... why?" Brother Roland asked.

"Yes, why this charade?" Big George growled, his powerful arms crossing his wide chest. His dark eyebrows met, once again— this time, in puzzled indignation.

"I will explain everything, shortly," the king assured them.

"Where's Alfred?" little Rachel asked her mother.

"I'm here, my child," the king said, stooping down to speak to her, face-to-face. "You see, my real name is John Alfred." He stood and smiled down at her. "Will you hold your papa's cap for me?" he asked.

Rachel studied him as she had done when they first met. Then, she smiled with total acceptance and took the workman's cap from the king's hand.

King John turned to Mary who regarded him with bewilderment. When he smiled at her, she, too, responded with a smile of acceptance.

Finally, the king turned to the Captain and his men and said with authority, "Return to my stables and bring three coaches back to the village. Inform the Ministers that I want everyone, from stable hands to the officials, themselves, assembled in the throne room by four o'clock, this afternoon."

Red-faced and chagrined, the Captain bowed to the king, mounted his horse, and led his men back to the palace.

When the soldiers were gone, King John turned back to the villagers. They stood in silence, and several wore hostile expressions on formerly friendly faces.

"I have a great deal of explaining to do," he confessed.

Part Eight

By four o'clock, the great hall known as the Throne Room was filled with people. The eight ministers and their families stood close to the steps leading to the empty throne. They glared at the small group of villagers who had accompanied the king to the palace in his three carriages. The villagers were standing to one side of the room, gazing with awe at the ornate chandeliers and rich tapestry that decorated the great hall. Even the marble floor fascinated them.

Behind the ministers and the villagers, the palace workers were assembled. The maids, butlers, pages, messengers, cooks, servers, barbers, stable hands, carpenters, prison guards, and gardeners...everyone who worked and lived in the palace was there, wearing the uniform of his trade.

The rest of the hall was packed with the king's men. Cavaliers, captains, cavalry, and foot soldiers all stood side-by-side.

With so many people crowded together, the noise level was high. Everyone was speculating on where the king had been for the past two days, why the villagers were allowed inside the palace walls, and why they had all been summoned.

Suddenly, a trumpet sounded over the buzzing of the crowd.

There was an instant hush, and the assembly seemed to hold its breath as the court crier struck the floor three times with his staff. Then, in a loud voice, he announced, "All hail King John!" And, as custom demanded, everyone bowed or curtsied as the king entered the room.

The small group of villagers stared in wonder at the man they had called Alfred. He wore the royal cape and crown, and carried the scepter that had been handed down from king to king for generations. He bore no resemblance to the beggar they had aided. With regal dignity, he walked to the throne and sat down, facing his subjects.

"My people," he began, "I have gathered you together to tell you a story."

Movement rippled through the audience as they turned to look at each other in amazement.

"Two nights ago, I had a dream," King John continued. "I dreamed that a young boy... in fact, that young boy...," he pointed to Tom with his scepter, "came to advise me of the suffering of our citizens who live and work outside of these palace walls."

The Minister of Justice stepped forward and said, "But, Your Highness..."

King John silenced him with a wave of his hand. Then, the official stepped back and exchanged anxious glances with his fellow ministers.

The king looked around the room. "When I awoke from my dream, I began to wonder if the boy's charges were true. I realized that I had no way of knowing because I had not seen or spoken to anyone outside of the palace since King Alfred's death. I asked myself, how could I determine the truth? The answer was simple. I would disguise myself as a poor, elderly beggar seeking food and shelter. Then, I could experience, firsthand, how my loyal subjects are treated by my wise and trusted officials."

The ministers began to fidget and nervously pluck at their clothes.

"I cut short my hair and my beard and burned the clippings in the fireplace," King John continued. "Then, I found my oldest riding costume and used the scissors to 'age' it a bit. However, I was still too young and far too clean to pass as an old beggar. So, I smeared ashes from the fireplace on my beard, face, and clothing, wrapped a dirty cloth around my head, covered my hands with

THE KING'S QUEST

some old gloves, and hunched over like a man bent from a lifetime of hard labor."

The king paused in his recital to glance at the villagers. They were spellbound by his tale, as were the rest of his subjects. "When I looked in the mirror, I didn't recognize myself. So, wearing my disguise, I slipped down the back stairs and entered the kitchen."

At this time, the king rose to his full height. Then, he pointed to the Minister of Provisions. "You were the first official I approached!"

The portly minister stepped forward on trembling legs and whispered, "But, Sire, I didn't know..."

"Exactly!" snapped King John. "You thought a starving old man was begging for a slice of bread—and, rather than feed him from our bountiful supply, you signaled for the guards!"

Next, the king pointed to the Minister of the Royal Guard. Haughtily, the minister stepped forward. "You sent dogs, soldiers, and servants to find one starving, old man!" the king said. "You would have placed him in chains for being hungry!"

The Minister of the Royal Guard shrugged and replied, "He might have been a thief or a murderer."

King John's face grew rigid with anger. "And, who gave you the right to seize my subjects' property—and to induct their sons into my army against their will?"

The minister raised one eyebrow but didn't answer.

The king took a deep, calming breath. Then, he pointed to the Ministers of Justice and Finances. Quaking with fear, the two men joined their colleagues.

"Is it moral to arrest a man because he asks for bread?" the king questioned the Minister of Justice. "And, for what purpose did you create a law forbidding subjects to approach their monarch? Was it because you were afraid I might discover these wrong-doings?" The red-faced official seemed incapable of responding. So, King John turned to the Minister of Finances.

"You keep a purse filled with gold coins from my Treasure Room tied to your waist, isn't that true?"

The man nodded.

"Then, why couldn't you spare a single coin for a poor man?"

The Minister of Finances cleared his throat and said, "If I

were to give coins to one, I'd soon be overrun with beggars!"

"But, you could have had this poor man, and others like him, do some task to earn their gift. But you didn't, did you? And, perhaps you can explain why you tried to seize the home of a villager for taxes when it was a gift from my father?"

The man dropped his eyes and said nothing.

"And, you!" King John summoned the Minister of Transportation. "You were prepared to whip me, rather than give me shelter in the barn!"

The king motioned for the three remaining ministers to step forward. Then, he told the assembly, "The Minister of Housekeeping had no desire to help an honest citizen find temporary shelter—he was too busy seeing to his own comfort! And, the learned Ministers of Education and the Arts secretly closed the church schools for commoners, following King Alfred's death. At the same time, they sent away my father's religious advisors. They couldn't take a chance on my learning about the laws of God which would have helped me rule my kingdom!"

King John studied his eight ministers and gripped his scepter with both hands. Then, he sat down, once more. "To continue my story," he said, "I escaped from the palace and ran toward the nearest village. It was raining, by then, and I slipped on some rocks, twisting my ankle. So, I fashioned a crutch from a forked tree limb and, somehow, made it to the village before dawn."

The king's eyes softened as he pointed to Mary, Rachel, and the rest of the villagers. "The first person who saw me cold, wet, and hungry, took me into her home, gave me dry clothes to wear, and shared the little food she had. Thereafter, each person I encountered opened their homes and hearts to me, as well.

"What I found in the village had been denied me within these walls! Truth, acceptance, generosity, and the love of God still lives within my people. But, what Tom had told me in my dream was, also, true."

King John turned back to the ministers. He stood up, pointed his scepter at the eight men, and pronounced in a stern, formidable voice, "You have violated the trust I placed in you! Therefore, you are banished from my kingdom forever!"

The audience gasped, and the ministers staggered under the weight of the unexpected sentence.

The king continued, "You will each be given a horse and wagon, one month's supply of food, and two silver coins—which is more generous than you deserve. The guards will accompany you to the outskirts of my territory before sundown—and, may God have mercy on you!" With a signal from the king, the Royal Guard surrounded the ministers and their families and escorted them out of the Throne Room.

Those remaining in the great hall whispered among themselves until the crier struck the floor with his staff, once more, calling for silence.

King John sat upon his throne and glanced sadly around the room. "I am as guilty, in my own way, as the ministers are, because I allowed those men to take over my kingdom. For this, I ask your forgiveness."

Once more, murmurs swept through the room.

"However," the king said, holding up a large Bible with both hands, "I promise that—from this day forth—God's laws will be my laws." He opened the Bible to a certain page and said, "Brother Roland thought this passage would be appropriate." In a clear, deep voice, the king read aloud.

At Gibeon the Lord appeared to Solomon during the night in a dream, and God said, "Ask for whatever you want me to give you."

Solomon answered, "You have shown great kindness to your servant, my father ...because he was faithful to you and righteous and upright in heart. You have continued this great kindness to him and have given him a son to sit on his throne....

"Now, O Lord my God, you have made your servant king in place of my father ... But, I am only a little child and do not know how to carry out my duties ... So, give your servant a discerning heart to govern your people and to distinguish between right and wrong..."

The Lord was pleased that Solomon had asked for this. So God said to him... "I will do what you have asked..." (1 Kings 3:5-12).

Closing the Bible, King John kneeled in front of the throne, bowed his head and prayed, "Lord, please guide me in the direction You want me to go, and may Your words come true. Amen."

Then, rising once more to his feet, he said, "Will the villagers approach the throne?"

Eyes wide with apprehension, the small group walked to the steps leading up to the throne and stopped. King John descended to one step above them and asked them to turn and face the crowd. Once they had done so, King John placed his hand on Brother Roland's head. "From this day forth, he will be called Lord Roland. He will teach me the words and the ways of the Lord our God and help me administer justice and mercy. Chapels and churches will abound and Brothers will comfort and instruct my people."

The king moved to stand behind Big George and touched his head. "This is Lord George. Because of his wisdom and courage, he will help me direct the Royal Guard and maintain peace in my kingdom."

Next, King John stood behind Mary and Abigail and placed one hand on each of their heads. "Ladies Mary and Abigail will assist me with the operation of the palace so we can stop wasting the peoples hard-earned money on needless luxuries. In addition, with their help and that of Bess and Tom," the king moved to touch their heads, "schools will be reopened throughout the land, and parents will be free to educate their children in the schools they choose to develop."

Rachel turned around to look at him, and he winked at her.

Then, he returned to the throne and held his scepter high. "Taxes will be reduced to match those of my father's days. Conscription is abolished, and those men who were unlawfully drafted may return home. The soldiers who wish to join or remain in my army will receive monthly wages. All seized properties will be returned to their rightful owners. The crimes of all prisoners will be reviewed, and those unfairly imprisoned will be set free with compensation. The palace gates will be left open and my subjects are invited to observe and approach their king and his new officials as desired.

"These laws are in effect, immediately; notices are to be sent, this very day, throughout the land. May peace and happiness reign, and may God bless our kingdom!"

In the silence that followed, the people could hear the scratching of the quills as the recorders rapidly wrote down the king's words.

THE KING'S QUEST

Suddenly, Brother Roland, now known as Lord Roland, raised his tear-streaked face and cried out, "Praise God! And, long live the King!"

The crowd repeated, "Praise God! And, long live the King!" Then, they cheered, and cried, and whistled, and shouted in a celebration that would last for a long, long time.

Comprehension Questions

1. Why did King John fail to do a good job during the early years of his reign?

2. Why did King John decide to take a trip outside of his palace?

3. Do you think that King John inherited his problems from his father? Explain your answer.

4. Why do you think that the wicked ministers from the palace decided to close down the church-run schools shortly after King John came to the throne?

5. When do you think it is proper for a government leader to give help or charity to needy people?

6. What suggestion did Bess give to the beggar named Alfred regarding spiritual things?

7. Do you think that the ungodly ministers of King John's court were punished properly or sufficiently for their crimes?

8. Why do you think that the simple or common people, whom King John visited, were able to find happiness in the midst of their worldly poverty?

A Story Of An Eccentric Woman

From Matthew 26:1-16 and Mark 14:1-11

The Apostles and Disciples were, of course, the historians of the time of Christ; but what strange historians they were! They omitted many things which secular historians would have written, and they recorded just that which the worldly would have passed over. What secular historian would have thought of recording the story of a widow and her two mites? Would a modern journalist or sociologist have spared half a page for such an incident? Do you think that even an ancient historian could have found it in his pen to write down a story of an eccentric woman, who broke an alabaster box of precious ointment above the head of Jesus? Nevertheless, the record of the New Testament Scriptures stands for all to see.

Jesus values things, not by their glare and glitter, but by their intrinsic value. For example, Christ was sitting, or reclining, at the table of Simon the leper in the village of Bethany, when a sudden thought strikes this eccentric woman. She obtains an alabaster box of ointment which she brings to Simon's house in haste. Without asking anyone's permission, or communicating her intention, she breaks the alabaster vase, which was itself of great value, and down flowed a stream of the most precious ointment, with a very refreshing fragrance. This she poured on His head, and doubtless the whole house was filled with the odor of the ointment. The disciples murmured against this woman, but the Savior commended her. Now, what was there in the action of this woman worthy of such praise—indeed, of such high commendation—that her memory must be preserved and transmitted with the gospel itself throughout all ages?

I think, in the first place, this act was done from the impulse of a loving heart, and this is what made it so remarkable. A loving heart, after all, is better than human logic and a renewed heart is infinitely superior to the mind. Nevertheless, grace will no doubt renew the understanding; and yet the heart is what must first be touched before the mind can perceive what is right.

In our day, we fall into the habit of calculating whether a

thing is our duty or not; but have we ever had an impulse of the heart more impressive, and more expressive, than the mere arithmetic of moral obligations? For instance, our heart may say to us, "Arise, go and visit so and so who is sick." But our mind immediately asks, "Is it my duty? If I do not go, will not somebody else go? Is this service absolutely necessary?" Or, perhaps, your heart may have said at one time, "Devote of your substance largely to the cause of Christ." If we obey our heart we should do it at once; but instead of that, we stop and shake our head, and we begin to coldly calculate the question whether it is precisely our duty.

This woman did no such thing. It was not her duty; speaking broadly, it was not her explicit duty to take the costly ointment and pour it on the head of Christ. In other words, she did not do it from a mere sense of obedience; she did it from a loftier motive. There was an impulse in her heart, which gushed forth like a pure stream overflowing every quibble and questioning—saying, "Duty or no duty, go and do it." She takes the most precious thing she can find, and out of simple love—guided by her renewed heart—she goes at once and breaks the alabaster box, pouring the ointment on His head. If she had paused but a minute to consider, she would not have done it at all; if she had pondered, and reckoned, and reasoned, she never would have accomplished it. However, this was the heart acting—the invincible heart, the force of a spontaneous impulse, if not of actual inspiration. It was the heart's dictate fully and entirely carried out.

Now, in these times, we lace ourselves so tight that we do not give our hearts room to act; we just calculate whether we should do it—whether it is precisely our duty. Oh, that our hearts would grow bigger towards God! Let our minds be as they are, or let them be improved; but let the heart have full play, and how much more would be done for Christ than ever has been done as of yet! But I would have you understand that this woman, acting from her heart, did not act as a matter of form or duty. She did not play the Pharisee by drawing close to God in lip service and sacrifice while her heart was far from the Lord.

Will you give to Christ no more than His due, just as you give to Caesar when you pay your tax? What! if the custom be but a shekel, is the shekel all he is to have? Is such a Master as this to be served by calculations? Is He to have His everyday penny, just as the common laborer? God forbid we should indulge such a spirit! Alas! for the mass of Christians, they do not even rise so high as that; and—if they once get there—they fold their arms and are quite content. "I do as much as anybody else; in fact, a little more; I am sure I do my duty; nobody can find any fault; if people were to expect me to do more, they would be really unreasonable." Ah! then, you have not yet learned this woman's love, in all its heights and depths. You know not how to do an unreasonable thing—a thing that is not expected of you—out of the Divine impulse of a heart fully consecrated to Jesus.

The first era of the Christian Church was an era of wonders, because then, Christian men obeyed the prompting of the Holy Spirit upon their hearts. What wonders they used to do! A still small voice within the heart said to an apostle, "Go to a heathen country and preach." He never counted the cost—whether his life would be safe, or whether he would be successful; he went and did whatever the Holy Spirit told him. To another, the Spirit spake, "Go thou, and distribute all that thou hast." And the Christian went and did it, casting his all into the common store. He never asked whether it was his duty, because his sanctified heart bid him do it, and he obeyed at once. However, in our day, we have become stereotyped; we run in the ancient cart-rut of doing exactly what other people do. We are only content with performing the routine, and accomplishing the formalism of religious duties. How unlike this woman, who went out of all order, because her heart told her to do so, and she obeyed from her heart. This, I think, is the first part of the woman's act that won a deserved commendation.

The second commendation is due to the fact that what this woman did was done purely to Christ, and for Christ. Why did she not take this spikenard, and sell it, and give the money to the poor? "No," she might have thought, "I love the poor, I would relieve them at any time; to the utmost of my ability I would clothe the naked, and feed the hungry; but I want to do something for Him." Well, why did she not get up, and take the place that Martha did, and begin to wait at the table? "Ah!" she thought, "Martha is at the table, dividing her services; Simon the leper, and Lazarus, and all the rest of the guests, have a share in her attention. I want to do something directly for Him, something that He will have all to Himself, something that He cannot give away, but which He must have and which must belong to Him." Now, I do not think that any other disciple, in all Christ's experience, ever had that thought. I do not find, in all the Evangelists, another instance like this. He had disciples whom He sent out two by two to preach, however, they right valiantly did it because they desired to benefit their fellowmen in the service of their Lord. He also had disciples, no doubt, who were exceedingly happy when they distributed the bread and fishes to the hungry multitudes, because they felt they were doing an act of humanity in supplying the needs of the hungry. But I do not think He had one disciple who thought about doing something exactly and directly for Him—something of which no one else could partake, something that should be Christ's, and Christ's alone.

The very beauty of this woman's act lay in this, that she did it all for the Lord Jesus Christ. She felt she owed Him all because it was He who had forgiven her sins; it was He who had opened her eyes, and given her to see the light of heavenly day; it was He who was her hope, her joy, her all. Of course, her love went out in its common actings to her fellowmen—towards the poor, the sick, and the needy; but, oh! it went in all its ardor to Him. That Man, that blessed Man, the God-Man, she must give something to Him. She could not be content to put it in a bag; she must go and put it right on His head. She could not be content with the thought that Peter, or James, or John, should have a part of it—the whole pound must go upon His head; and though others might say it was waste, she felt it was not—whatever she could give unto Him was well bestowed, because it went to Him to whom she owed her all. The scene is a very simple one, but it is extremely captivating. You will do your service for God far better, if you can cultivate always the desire to do them all for Christ.

This woman did an extraordinary thing for Christ. Not content with doing what other people had done, not wishful to find a precedent, she ventured to expose her ardent attachment—even though she might have known that some would call her mad, and all would think her foolish and wasteful. Yet she did it—an extraordinary thing—for the love she bore for her Lord. It seems to me that Jesus praised this woman, and handed down this memorial because her act was so beautifully expressive. There was more virtue in it than you could see. The manner, as well as the matter, of her special sacrifice, might well excite the rebuke of men, whose practical religion is mercenary and economical. It is enough that she pours out the ointment with such reckless profusion, but she is so rash and extravagant that she felt led to break the box as well. Marvel not, but admire the rapt enthusiasm of her godly soul. Why? love is a passion! If you did but know and feel its ardor, you would never marvel at an act so expressive. Her love could no more tarry to conform to the rubrics of service, than it could count the cost of her offering. A mighty impulse of devotion carried her soul far above all ordinary routine. Her conduct did but symbolize the inspiration of a grateful homage. A sanctified heart, more beautiful than the transparent vase of alabaster, was broken that hour. Only from a broken heart can the sweet spices of grace give forth their rich perfume. "Love and grief, our heart dividing," we sometimes sing—but, oh! let me say it—love, grief, and gratitude—the spikenard, myrrh, and frankincense of the gospel—blend together here. Hence, the heart must expand and break, or the odors can never fill the house. Every muscle of her face, every involuntary motion of her frame—frenzied as it might appear to the unsympathizing onlooker—was in harmony with her heart's emotion. Her every feature gave evidence of her sincerity. And what these spectators would coldly criticize, Jesus delivers to them for study. Here is one on whom the Savior's love has produced its appropriate effects. Here is a heart that has brought forth the most precious fruits. Not only admiration for her, but kindness to us, moved our Lord when He resolved henceforth to illustrate the gospel—wherever it is published—with this portrait of saintly love. Why, that woman meant to say to Christ, "Dear Lord, I give myself away." She brought out the most precious thing she had; if she had anything worth ten thousand times as much, she would have brought that—in fact, she did really bring Him all.

Christ said, "She hath wrought a good work upon Me." Note these two last words, "Upon Me!" "Why," say they, "it is not a good work to go and spill all that ointment, and perpetrate so much waste." "No," says Jesus, "it is not a good work in relation to you, but it is a good work upon Me." And, after all, this is the best sort of good work—a good work that is wrought upon Christ—an act of homage, such as faith in His name and love to His person, would dictate. A good work upon the poor is commendable; a good work upon the Church is excellent; but a good work upon Christ, surely this is one of the very highest and noblest kinds of good works. But

I will be bound to say that neither Judas nor the disciples could comprehend this. There is a mystic virtue in the acts of some Christians that common believers do not and cannot comprehend. That mystic virtue consists in this, that they do it "as unto the Lord, and not unto men," and in their service they serve the Lord Jesus Christ.

Moreover, our Lord protects the woman with another defense. "Do not trouble her; do not reflect upon what might have been done for the poor, 'for ye have the poor always with you, but Me ye have not always.' (Matthew 26:11) The Lord proceeds to turn the argument back upon her accusers. "If there are any poor about, give to them yourselves; empty that bag of Mine out, Judas; don't be hiding that away in your girdle. 'Whensoever ye will, ye may do them good.' (Mark 14:7) Don't begin talking about the poor, and about what might have been done; you go, and do what might have been done yourselves; this poor woman hath done a good thing for Me; I shall not be here long; don't trouble her."

And so, if you murmur at people because they do not go in your ordinary ways—because they venture a little out of the regular line—you may well be wasting words. Your calling, perhaps, is not identical to other people, but there is plenty for you to do; go and do it, and do not blame those who do extraordinary things. There are multitudes of ordinary people to attend to ordinary things. If you want to secure the help of those who want to do the minimum for Christ, you can have them; however, it is those who give all they have, that are unusual. They will not trouble you. There are not many of them; so you will have to travel from here to China before you run into many dozen. They are rare creatures not often discovered. Do not trouble them. They may be fanatical, and they may be excessive; but if you should build an asylum to put them all in, it would require only a very small building. Let them alone. There are not many who do much for their Master—not many who are irrational enough to think that there is nothing worth living for but to glorify Christ and magnify His holy name.

This woman thought she was just anointing Christ. "Nay," says Christ, "she is anointing Me for my burial." There was more in her act than she knew of. And there is more in the spiritual promptings of our heart than we shall ever understand this side of glory. When, first of all, the Lord said to the famous English evangelist, George Whitefield, "Go and preach out on Kennington Common," did Whitefield know what was to be the result? No; he thought, doubtless, that he should just stand for once on the top of a table, and address some five thousand people. But there was a greater intent in the womb of Providence. The Lord meant that to set the whole country in a blaze, and to bring forth a glorious renewal of Pentecostal times, the like of which had not been seen before. Only seek to have your heart filled with love, and then obey its first spiritual dictate. Stop not, unless the order violates the truth of Scripture. No matter how extraordinary may be the mandate, go and do it. Have your wings outstretched like the angels before the throne, and the very moment that the echo vibrates in your heart—fly, fly, and you shall be flying, to an area of service yet unknown. You shall be upon an errand higher and nobler than your imagination has ever dreamed. You shall mount up with wings, as eagles.

The eccentric woman depicted in Matthew chapter twenty-six and Mark chapter fourteen may have had an unusual personality, but she never permitted the man-made rules of religious expression to pull her away from her first love. She kept her heart focused on pleasing Christ. If we wish to give our Lord Christ the pre-eminence in all things, then we must go and do likewise.

Comprehension Questions

1. In what respect did the author believe that the historical record left by the writers of the New Testament was unique?
2. Briefly explain two reasons why Jesus Christ chose to commend the eccentric woman.
3. In what manner do many Christians treat Jesus like a common laborer or a tax man?
4. What type of good work did the author state was better than helping the poor or assisting the church?
5. Did the act of the eccentric woman truly hinder the Disciples from helping the poor?
6. Why did the author believe that it was unnecessary to be concerned about Christians who do extraordinary things?
7. Did the author believe that we should follow our heart if it leads us away from the truth of Scripture?

The Word and the Image

The Importance of Reading

Will reading become obsolete? Some people think that with the explosion of video technology, the age of the book is almost over. Television monitors, fed by cable networks and video recorders, dominate our culture today. Our fads and fashions, politics and morals, entertainment and leisure time are all shaped and controlled by whatever is transmitted on the diode screen. As electronic communication develops at an astonishing rate, who is to say that such arcane skills as reading and writing can or even need to survive?

One thing, however, is certain: Reading can never die out among Christians. This is because the whole Christian revelation centers on a Book. God chose to reveal Himself to us in the most personal way through His Word—the Bible. The word *Bible* is simply the Greek word for "the Book." Indeed the Bible is the primal Book, the most ancient of all literary texts and the source of all literacy. Reading the Bible tends to lead to reading other books, and thus to some important habits of mind.

PEOPLE OF THE BOOK

The centrality of the Bible means that the very act of reading can have spiritual significance. Whereas other religions may stress visions, experiences, or even the silence of meditation as the way to achieve contact with the divine, Christianity insists on the role of language.

Language is the basis for all communication and so lies at the heart of any personal relationship. We can never know anyone intimately by simply being in that person's presence. We need to have a conversation in order to share our thoughts and our personalities. By the same token, we need a conversation with God—two-way communication through language—in order to know Him on a personal basis. Just as human beings address God by means of language through prayer, God addresses human beings by means of language in the pages of Scripture. Prayer and Bible reading are central to a personal relationship with God. Christians have to be, in some sense, readers.

Creation itself was accomplished by God's Word (Hebrews 11:3), and Jesus Christ Himself is none other than the living Word of God (John 1: 1). The Word of the gospel, the good news that Jesus died for sinners and offers them eternal life, is a message in human language that calls people to salvation. "Faith comes from hearing the message, and the message is heard through the word of Christ" (Romans 10:17). God's Word is written down in the pages of the Bible. Human beings, inspired by the Holy Spirit, have recorded what God has revealed about Himself and His acts in history. In the Bible, God reveals His relationship to us, setting forth the law by which we should live and the gospel of forgiveness through Christ. As we read the Bible, God addresses us in the most intimate way, as one Person speaking to another.

When we read the Bible, we are not simply learning doctrines or studying history—although we *are* doing those things. "The word of God is living and active. Sharper than any double-edged sword, it penetrates even to dividing soul and spirit, joints and marrow; it judges the thoughts and attitudes of the heart" (Hebrews 4:12). As we read the Bible, all of the senses of "The Word of God" come together—God's creative power, His judgment, Jesus Christ, and proclamation of the gospel—and are imprinted in our minds and souls. In the Word, the Holy Spirit is at work.

Certainly the Word of the gospel can be proclaimed orally and not in writing alone. In church we hear the Word of God preached, and even in casual witnessing, the Word of God is being shared. In cultures that lack Bibles or people who know how to read them, the church has managed to survive through the oral proclamation of the Word, although often with many errors and difficulties. Still, the priority that God places on language and the idea that God's Word is personally accessible to us in a book has meant that Christians have always valued reading and writing.

Even when books were rare and expensive, having to be copied out by hand, so that common people remained uneducated, at least the priests had to know how to read. The Reformation was providentially accompanied by the invention of the printing press, enabling books to be cheaply mass-produced. This meant that the Bible could be put into the hands of every Christian. Every Christian, therefore, needed to learn how to read. Universal literacy, taken for granted today, was a direct result of the Reformation's reemphasis upon the centrality of Bible reading, not only for theologians but also for the spiritual life of every Christian.

Missionaries to nonliterate cultures often begin by mastering the people's language and giving them a system of writing. They then translate the Bible and teach the people how to read it in their own language. The Word of God begins to transform its readers. Once people know how to read the Bible, of course, they can read anything. Tribes go on to discover modern health care and the need for social change, just as the Reformation Christians, empowered by Bible reading, went on to develop scientific technology, economic growth, and democratic institutions.

When ideas and experiences can be written down, they are, in effect, stored permanently. People are no longer bound by their own limited insights and experiences, but they can draw on those of other people as well. Instead of continually starting over again, people can build upon what others have discovered and have written down. Technological, economic, and social progress becomes possible. The impact of writing can be seen plainly by comparing nonliterate cultures, many of which still exist on the Stone Age level, with those that have had the gift of writing. Nonliterate peoples tend to exist in static, unchanging societies, whereas literate societies tend toward rapid change and technological growth.

Christians, along with Jews and Muslims, are considered "people of the Book." Such reverence for reading and writing has profoundly shaped even our secular society. Certainly, non-Biblical cultures have made great use of writing, but this was almost always reserved for the elite. The religious idea that everyone should learn how to read in order to study the Bible (a view implicit in the Hebrew *bar mitzvah* and carried out in the Reformation school systems) would have radical consequences in the West. Universal education has led to the breaking of class systems, the ability of individual citizens to exercise political power, and a great pooling of minds that would result in the technological achievements of the last four hundred years. It is no exaggeration to say that reading has shaped our civilization more than almost any other factor and that a major impetus to reading has been the Bible.

ELECTRONICALLY GRAVEN IMAGES

Reading has been essential to our civilization, yet today its centrality is under attack by the new electronic media. If reading has had vast social and intellectual repercussions, we should wonder about the repercussions of the new media. Can democratic institutions survive without a literate—that is, a reading—populace, or will the new modes of thinking lend themselves to new forms of totalitarianism? Can educational and intellectual progress continue if visual imagery supplants reading, or will the new information technologies, ironically, subvert the scientific thinking that created them, resulting in anti-intellectualism and mass ignorance?

Such issues are critical for the culture as a whole, but they are especially urgent for the church. Is it possible for Biblical faith to flourish in a society that no longer values reading, or will the newly dominant images lead to new manifestations of the most primitive paganism? Ever since the Old Testament, graven images have tempted God's people to abandon the true God and His Word. Today the images are graven by electrons on cathode ray tubes.

Nell Postman is a media scholar and one of the most astute social critics of our time. His writings focus, with great sophistication, on how different forms of communication shape people's thinking and culture. Postman says that he first discovered the connection between media and culture in the Bible: "In studying the Bible as a young man, I found intimations of the idea that forms of media favor particular kinds of content and therefore are capable of taking command of a culture." He found this concept in the Ten Commandments: "You shall not make for yourself a graven image, or any likeness of anything that is in heaven above, or that is in the earth beneath, or that is in the water under the earth" (Exodus 20:4 RSV).

> I wondered then, as so many others have, as to why the God of these people would have included instructions on how they were to symbolize, or not symbolize, their experience. It is a strange injunction to include as part of an ethical system *unless its author assumed a connection between forms of human communication and the quality of a culture.* We may hazard a guess that a people who are being asked to embrace an abstract, universal deity would be rendered unfit to do so by the habit of drawing pictures or making statues or depicting their ideas in any concrete, iconographic forms. The God of the Jews was to exist in the Word and through the Word, an unprecedented conception requiring the highest order of abstract thinking. Iconography thus became blasphemy so that a new kind of God could enter a culture. People like ourselves who

are in the process of converting their culture from word-centered to image-centered might profit by reflecting on this Mosaic injunction.

According to Postman, "word-centered" people think in a completely different mode from "image-centered" people. His distinction is especially important for Christians, for whom the "Mosaic injunction" is eternally valid.

In an important book on education, Postman explores the differences between the mental processes involved in reading and those involved in television watching. Reading demands sustained concentration, whereas television promotes a very short attention span. Reading involves (and teaches) logical reasoning, whereas television involves (and teaches) purely emotional responses. Reading promotes continuity, the gradual accumulation of knowledge, and sustained exploration of ideas. Television, on the other hand, fosters fragmentation, anti-intellectualism, and immediate gratification.

Postman does not criticize the content of television—the typical worries about "sex and violence" or the need for quality programming. Rather, the problem is in the properties of the form itself. Language is cognitive, appealing to the mind; images are affective, appealing to the emotions.

> This difference between symbols that demand conceptualization and reflection and symbols that evoke feeling has many implications, one of the most important being that the content of the TV curriculum is irrefutable. You can dislike it, but you cannot disagree with it.... There is no way to show that the feelings evoked by the imagery of a McDonald's commercial are false, or indeed, true. Such words as *true* and *false* come out of a different universe of symbolism altogether. Propositions are true or false. Pictures are not.

Postman goes on to connect the newly emerging dominance of electronic images over words to habits of mind that are having monumental social consequences: to the undermining of authority, the loss of a sense of history, hostility to science, pleasure-centeredness, and the emergence of new values based on instant gratification and the need to be continually entertained. The new media direct us "to search for time-compressed experience, short-term relationships, present-oriented accomplishment, simple and immediate solutions. Thus, the teaching of the media curriculum must lead inevitably to a disbelief in long-term planning, in deferred gratification, in the relevance of tradition, and in the need for confronting complexity." The social acceptance of sexual immorality, the soaring divorce rates, and the pathology of drug abuse may well be related to this pursuit of instant pleasure at all costs.

And yet, human beings—made as we are for higher purposes—can scarcely live this way. The untrammeled emotionalism, the isolation, and the fragmentation of mind encouraged by the new information environment lead to mental illness, suicide, and emotional collapse. "Articulate language," on the other hand, according to Postman, "is our chief weapon against mental disturbance." If the trends he sees continue to develop, Postman foresees a future in which we have "people who are 'in touch with their feelings,' who are spontaneous and musical, and who live in an existential world of immediate experience but who, at the same time, cannot 'think' in the way we customarily use that word. In other words, people whose state of mind is somewhat analogous to that of a modern-day baboon."

The impact of the TV mentality on politics is already clearly evident. Rational, sustained debate of issues has been replaced by "sound bites"—brief "media events" that can play on the evening news. Political campaigns are managed by "image consultants," and candidates are chosen for their charisma and the way they appear on TV rather than for their ideas and policies. American democracy was the creation of a word-centered culture and a literate populace. Whether the traditions of freedom and democracy can be sustained without that basis is questionable. An easily manipulated population that cares mostly for its own amusement may be more ready for tyranny (which can keep the masses happy with "bread and circuses") than for the arduous responsibilities of self-government.

The impact of the new mentality upon religion is even more significant. The appeal of the New Age movement with its almost comical irrationalism is evidence that categories such as true or false, revelation or superstition, have become irrelevant for many people. The sophisticated and affluent pay large sums of money to hear the wisdom of ancient Egyptian warriors or extra-terrestrial aliens purportedly taking over the bodies of the "channelers." Well-educated socialites plan their lives by horoscopes. Trendy movie stars solve their problems by means of magical crystals. How can anyone believe such things? If people stop thinking about religion in propositional terms (part of the heritage of "the Word"), abandoning truth or falsehood as religious categories, then belief hardly enters into it. Even among Christians today, religious discussions often focus upon "what I like" rather than "what is true." Those whose main concern is self-gratification search in exactly the same way for religious gratification.

Of course, Christians know that there is nothing "new" in the New Age movement, which the Bible terms demon possession, divination, and idolatry. The New Age movement is simply the paganism of the Old Age. Such primitive and oppressive superstitions squelched human progress for millennia. Ironically, our advanced technology is resulting in a new primitivism, in which the gains of thousands of years of civilization are glibly rejected by a post-literate culture that closely resembles preliterate ones. Even infanticide, a commonplace practice of pagan societies, has become socially acceptable in the form of abortion on demand. As Scripture warns, graven images can lead to paganism of the most horrific kind.

And yet, evangelicals too have been seduced by the electrical graven images of television and the kind of spirituality that it encourages. In his study of contemporary "TV ministries," Postman is remarkably charitable towards television evangelists, but he shows how the medium itself inevitably distorts the Christian message:

> On television, religion, like everything else, is presented, quite simply and without apology, as an entertainment. Everything that makes religion an historic, profound, and sacred human activity is stripped away; there is no ritual, no dogma, no tradition, no theology, and above all, no sense of spiritual transcendence. On these shows, the preacher is tops. God comes out as second banana.

Postman quotes a religious broadcaster who admits that in order to attract an audience, TV ministries must offer people something they want.

> You will note, I am sure, that this is an unusual religious credo. There is no great religious leader—from the Buddha to Moses to Jesus to Muhammed to Luther—who offered people what they want. Only what they need. But television is not well suited to offering people what they need. It is "user friendly." It is too easy to turn off. It is at its most alluring when it speaks the

language of dynamic visual imagery. It does not accommodate complex language or stringent demands. As a consequence, what is preached on television is not anything like the Sermon on the Mount. Religious programs are filled with good cheer. They celebrate affluence. Their featured players become celebrities.... I believe I am not mistaken in saying that Christianity is a demanding and serious religion. When it is delivered as easy and amusing, it is another kind of religion altogether.

Since Postman wrote these words, we have seen the collapse of various television ministries. The moral and spiritual failures of the TV preachers may well be a symptom of the shallowness of the TV theology, which lured them away from the spirituality of the Word.

The problem, however, is not only for TV ministries. As evangelicals, we too are tempted to conform to the world rather than to the Word, just as the children of Israel were tempted by their neighbors' graven images and the thought-forms these embodied. We too often stress feeling rather than truth. We tend to seek emotional religious experiences rather than the cross of Jesus Christ. Because we expect worldly "blessings," we do not know how to endure suffering. We want to "name it and claim it"—instantly—rather than submit ourselves without reservation to the will of God. We are impatient with theology, and we dismiss history, thus disdaining the faith of our brothers and sisters who have gone before us and neglecting what they could teach us. We want entertaining worship services—on the order of a good TV show—rather than worship that focuses on the holiness of God and His Word. We want God to speak to us in visions and inner voices rather than in the pages of His Word. We believe in the Bible, but we do not read it very much.

Like the ancient Israelites, we live in "the land of graven images," amidst people who are "mad upon their idols" (Jeremiah 50:38). Also like them, we subtly drift into the ways of "the people of the land" unless we are rescued by the Word of God.

THE IMPORTANCE OF READING

Postman may well be exaggerating the dangers of television and its impact on our lives. He himself does not advocate the elimination of television, as if that were possible or desirable. Instead, he argues that its worst effects can be countered by a reemphasis upon language in our schools and culture, providing a stabilizing balance to the role of the media.

The electronic media still employ language. The gospel can be effectually proclaimed in a television or radio broadcast. For that reason, Christians can and should become involved with the new electronic media. The radio is intrinsically an oral medium, and so is quite appropriate for the oral proclamation of the Word. Straightforward Biblical exposition and preaching can be effectually broadcast on television, although presentations that feature people speaking instead of images are often derided as "talking heads" by media experts. Billy Graham does not stage "media-events"; rather, he broadcasts actual revival services in front of real people in real cities. Christian journalists should by all means produce Christian news and documentary programs. Religious drama, a time-honored contribution of Christian literature, especially deserves expression on television and film.

The Word of God proclaimed orally has always been central in evangelism and in the life of the church, and the electronic media can transmit that Word to the ears of millions of listeners. Nor are all "images" necessarily in opposition to God's Word. I have elsewhere written about what the Bible says about the arts, and I have found that sheer iconoclasm—the rejection of all artistic images as idolatrous—is not Biblical.

However, God's people have always had to be very cautious lest, without thinking, they slip into the ways of their pagan neighbors. The forms can distort the message—an evangelist broadcasting over the airwaves is not exactly the same as a pastor addressing his congregation or a Christian personally witnessing to a friend. The intimacy, the person-to-person presence is lost in an electronic broadcast, and the temptation may be to manipulate the unseen audience or to entertain them by sub-Biblical teachings. This need not happen, but religious broadcasters will have to struggle against the demands of the electronic media. Christians must become conscious of how the image-centered culture is pulling them in non-Christian directions. The priority of language for Christians must be absolute. As the rest of society abandons language-centeredness for image-centeredness, we can expect to feel the pressures and temptations to conform, but we must resist.

One way to do this is simply to read. A growing problem is illiteracy—many people do not know how to read. A more severe problem, though, is "aliteracy"—a vast number of people know how to read but never do it. If we cultivate reading—if we read habitually and for pleasure, reading the Bible, newspapers, the great works of the past and the present, the wide-ranging "promiscuous reading" advocated by the Christian poet Milton—we will reinforce the patterns of the mind that support Christian faith and lead to a healthy and free society.

Even if the masses sink into illiteracy and drug themselves by "amusement," the influential and the powerful will still be readers, as they are today. In the ancient pagan world, reading was a zealously guarded secret for the priests and the ruling elite, who, because they had access to knowledge, had access to power. Postman explores the paradox of a society increasingly dependent upon its scientists but undermining the literate thought-forms science demands. "It is improbable that scientists will disappear," he concludes, "but we shall quite likely have fewer of them, and they are likely to form, even in the short run, an elite class who, like priests of the pictographic age, will be believed to possess mystical powers."

Thinking, planning, imagining, creating—processes encouraged by reading—remain essential to society. Even television shows must have writers. Without people oriented toward language, very little would be accomplished. The point is the wielders of influence will always be those who read and write, who still work within the framework of language. If Christians remain true to their heritage, if they train themselves to be people of the Word and pursue the disciplines of reading and writing, their influence will be felt once again as it was in the formative moments of our civilization.

George Washington Carver

by James Saxon Childers

A stooped old black man, carrying an armful of wild flowers, shuffled along through the dust of an Alabama clay road toward one of the buildings of Tuskegee Institute. His thin body bent by years, his hair white beneath a ragged cap, he seemed pathetic to me.

At the door of one of the buildings, I heard the bent old man's secretary say, "That delegation from Washington is waiting for you, Doctor Carver."

Fantastic as it seemed, this shabbily clad old man was none other than the distinguished black scientist of Tuskegee Institute, Dr. George Washington Carver, renowned for his many discoveries about plants that grow in the South.

Born a slave, he began life without even a name. He never knew his father or mother. To the day of his death in 1943, he did not know when he was born, though he believed that he was over eighty years old that year. All his life he worked joyously with everyday things, making something out of nothing or next to nothing. Out of his labors at Tuskegee came such marvels as these:

From the peanut he made nearly three hundred useful products, including cheese, candies, linoleum, instant coffee, pickles, oils, shaving lotions, dyes, lard, flour, breakfast foods, soap, face powder, shampoo, printer's ink, and even axle grease!

From the lowly sweet potato he made more than a hundred products, among them starch, library paste, vinegar, shoe polish, ink, dyes, and molasses.

From wood shavings he made synthetic marble. From the muck of swamps and the leaves of the forest floor he made valuable fertilizers.

And more still, Doctor Carver was an artist, especially skilled in painting flowers. He made all his own paints, using Alabama clays. He painted on paper made from peanut shells, and the frames for his pictures he made out of cornhusks. He wove gorgeous rugs with fibers made from cotton stalks. He was a skilled musician, too.

"When you do the common things of life in an uncommon way," Doctor Carver once said to his students, "you will command the attention of the world." There lies the secret of his own achievement.

He was born in a rude slave cabin on the farm of a white planter, Moses Carver, near Diamond Grove, Missouri. When he was six months old, night raiders carried away his mother.

The Carvers reared the sickly child, bestowing his given name, "George Washington." Frail and undersized, he was nevertheless able to perform household chores, and he became an excellent cook and learned to mend clothes. The Carvers wanted him to have an education but could furnish no money. Without a cent he set out for a school eight miles away. Alone among strangers, he slept at first in an old horse barn. Soon he picked up odd jobs and entered the school.

In his early twenties, having completed a high school course, he mailed an entrance application to a college in Iowa, and by mail was accepted. But when he arrived, they refused to admit him because he was an African American. Undismayed, again he worked at odd jobs. Before long he had accumulated enough money to open a small laundry.

The next year he entered Simpson College at Indianola, Iowa. When he had paid his entrance fee, he had ten cents left; and he had to live nearly a week on corn meal and suet. For three years he worked his way; then in 1890 he enrolled in Iowa State College. Four years later he took his degree in agriculture, having earned every penny of his expenses. His work so impressed the authorities that they appointed him to the college faculty.

It was while Carver was at Iowa State that Booker T. Washington invited him to Tuskegee. In accepting, Carver saw a great opportunity to serve his own people in the South. He saw that the cotton lands were wearing out through failure to rotate crops. He saw debt-burdened farmers facing poverty. He set himself to preach a gospel of native money-crops other than cotton. After study and experiment, he decided that the Southern farmer could get his money with more certainty and with less damage to his soil by growing peanuts and sweet potatoes. Doctor Carver began to write bulletins and make speeches to prove his beliefs. After a time he had persuaded Southern farmers to increase their peanut and sweet potato acreage. And then, suddenly and sadly, Doctor Carver awoke to what he had done. He had increased the supply of these foods without increasing the demand for them. People were eating no more sweet potatoes and peanuts than before, and the huge new crops were rotting. The farmers who had planted them were losing money.

Almost fiercely the scientist went to work, spending days and nights in his laboratory, which he called "God's Little Workshop." He determined to find new uses for the peanut and the sweet potato. His success in doing so has already been mentioned; he discovered more than four hundred different useful products hidden in the sweet potato and peanut. In addition, Dr. Carver worked out tempting recipes and issued pamphlets for farm women; one of them is entitled "105 Different Ways to Prepare the Peanut for the Table."

One of Dr. Carver's first big jobs at Tuskegee was to take over and work nineteen acres of the worst land in Alabama. The best methods of farming had previously netted a loss of $16.25 an acre on this land. Within a year, Carver showed a net gain of four

dollars an acre. Later he produced two crops of sweet potatoes in one year, with a profit of seventy-five dollars an acre. These experiments proved that the world allows to go to waste an almost unlimited supply of fertilizer that most soils need—the muck from swamps and the leaves from forests.

As each new product of the potato and peanut was perfected, Doctor Carver gave it freely to the world, asking only that it be used for the benefit of mankind.

A friend told me this story that illustrates the point: Some wealthy peanut growers in Florida were suffering from a diseased crop. They sent Doctor Carver some specimens. He told them what was wrong and how to cure it. After his treatment had been proved correct, they sent him a check for $100, promising the same amount monthly as a retainer. He sent back the check, telling them that God didn't charge anything for growing the peanut, and that he shouldn't charge anything for curing it."

Some years ago when I visited his laboratory and saw rope made from okra fiber, insulating board from peanut shells, and dyes from dandelions, I asked Doctor Carver how he found time for all his accomplishments.

"Chiefly because I've made it a rule to get up every morning at four o'clock," he said. "I go out into the woods. Alone there with the things I love most, I gather specimens and study the great lessons that Nature is so eager to teach me. In the woods each morning, while most other persons are sleeping, I best hear and understand God's plan for me."

Inevitably his work brought offers to leave Tuskegee. In Doctor Carver's office I once saw two autographed pictures of Thomas Edison. "He sent me one of them when he asked me to come to his laboratory and work with him," Doctor Carver explained. "He sent me the other, the larger one, when I told him that my work was here in the South, and that I didn't think God wanted me to leave it."

Another offer tempted the elderly Carver with a salary of $100,000. But he stayed on at Tuskegee, where his meager salary was quickly consumed in anonymously paying the bills of worthy boys trying to get an education. To the day of his death he continued to wear the old alpaca coat and black trousers, which he had so often mended, and neckties, which he knit of fibers produced by his own labors.

But if Doctor Carver refused every tempting offer to move from Tuskegee and accept a large income, he could not ignore the many honors that were showered on him. Humbly he accepted the award made in June 1941, by the Southern farm magazine, *The Progressive Farmer*, for his "outstanding service to Southern agriculture." Two years earlier the world's opinion of Doctor Carver had been summed up when he was awarded the Theodore Roosevelt Medal as "a liberator to men of the white race as well as the black."